The Farm Girl's Guide to
PRESERVING THE HARVEST

Also from Lyons Press:

Welcome to the Farm

Family Table

Seasons at the Farm

The Backyard Gardener

Backyard Treehouses

The Homesteader's Herbal Companion

Living with Chickens

Living with Goats

Living with Sheep

Living with Pigs

The Farm Girl's Guide to
PRESERVING
THE
HARVEST

HOW TO CAN, FREEZE, DEHYDRATE, AND FERMENT YOUR GARDEN'S GOODNESS

ANN ACCETTA-SCOTT

FOREWORD BY JOEL SALATIN

LYONS
PRESS

Guilford, Connecticut

An imprint of The Rowman & Littlefield Publishing Group, Inc.
4501 Forbes Blvd., Ste. 200
Lanham, MD 20706
www.rowman.com

Distributed by NATIONAL BOOK NETWORK

British Library Cataloguing in Publication Information Available

Library of Congress Cataloging-in-Publication Data

Names: Accetta-Scott, Ann, author.
Title: The farm girl's guide to preserving the harvest : how to can, freeze, dehydrate, and ferment your garden's goodness / Ann Accetta-Scott ; foreword by Joel Salatin.
Description: Guilford, Connecticut : Lyons Press, [2019] | Includes bibliographical references and index.
Identifiers: LCCN 2018053933 (print) | LCCN 2019000642 (ebook) | ISBN 9781493036653 (ebook) | ISBN 9781493036646 (pbk.)
Subjects: LCSH: Canning and preserving.
Classification: LCC TX601 (ebook) | LCC TX601 .A33 2019 (print) | DDC 641.4/2—dc23
LC record available at https://lccn.loc.gov/2018053933

♾™ The paper used in this publication meets the minimum requirements of American National Standard for Information Sciences—Permanence of Paper for Printed Library Materials, ANSI/NISO Z39.48-1992.

Printed in the United States of America

CONTENTS

FOREWORD

When I tell people that Teresa, my bride of 38 years, cans 600 to 800 quarts of food a year, most gasp. Rare is the person who thinks that's normal or doable. And yet for us, this is such a natural normal routine that it flows from our lives nearly effortlessly. It's just what we do because it's what we've always done. Kind of like brushing your teeth.

By effortlessly I don't mean without work. Effort speaks to our investment, to what we value in life. The cheater puts effort into circumventing ethics. The soccer mom puts effort into bundling the kids into the car, fighting traffic, filling the gas tank, dealing with emotional highs and lows that naturally flow from wins and losses in highly competitive environments, washing the athletic uniforms, sitting in the take-out line because no time exists for making supper. To me, that's real work.

I'd much rather turn the food mill to squeeze applesauce or press homemade butter into a mold. When I see the frenetic effort put into modern society's celebrity-based and non-home-centric lifestyle, I feel sorry for all these folks who have not enjoyed the delicious pleasure of homemade summer sausage or barbecue sauce. Many folks call our family members workaholics. I call those folks frenetic unsatisfieds.

I don't feel like our family puts any more effort into gardening, butchering, and preserving than anyone else puts into whatever their lifestyle demands. The question is what are we getting for our effort? Most of us aren't lazy; we're busy. But where does our busyness land us? Is it worth the effort?

In case you've been away and missed it, a self-reliance tsunami is springing up in the hearts and minds of sophisticated Americans, both urban and rural. Everywhere people seek life anchors, roots, and connections to an ecological umbilical cord. Burgeoning mistrust toward corporate and industrial food systems, toward compromised regulatory agencies, and toward conventional farming drives more people every day into this integrity-living movement.

The hippie back-to-the-land movement of the 1970s, the birthing and breast-feeding revolution of the 1980s, the interest in organics in the 1990s, mad cow disease and genetically modified organisms in the 2000s, and tainted food imports have all provided impetus for renewed do-it-yourselfism. Personal autonomy screams for atomization in an increasingly networked, bar-coded, and invasive global technocracy.

Coming home never looked so good. Coming home never felt so refreshing. Opting out of industrial helter-skelter looks better by the day. The problem is that when people try to re-establish home-centricity and autonomous living, they're struck by the profound information implosion of basic life skills that impoverishes our culture. How to cut up a chicken? How to make a hamburger? How to cook a poached egg?

A mere half century ago, these were ubiquitous life skills. Recently I asked a graduate-level class of college students if they knew what a pullet was. Nobody knew. Digging deeper, I asked them if they knew what a heifer was. Nobody knew. Could anyone tell me what blanching was? Nobody knew. We do a lot of farm tours for school groups here at Polyface Farm. When a middle schooler sees a chicken lay an egg, she's yucked out. "Oh, you mean *that's* where they come from?"

As our culture's pendulum swings further to the *Star Wars* apogee of techno-nirvana sustained by artificial everything, a yearning to return to sanity awakens in many. Not all but many. But finding the old paths, recovering Great Grandma's skills is intimidatingly difficult. Find them we must, though, before we reach the tipping points of energy consumption, soil erosion, desertification, pharmaceuticals, and health crises. Already we're seeing, for the first time in modern history, reduced life expectancy for children born today.

From opioids to Alzheimer's, autism to obesity, we're seeing health and behavioral issues unprecedented in human history. Talk to any school teacher today, and you'll hear heartbreaking stories of mental, emotional, and familial dysfunction. What's the antidote? Many of us believe that returning to clean food, clean living, family meals, slower-paced lives, and visceral participation in foundational life skills will yield sweet benefits.

That Ann Accetta-Scott has made the journey herself, with her beloved husband, Justin, and kids, and found a soul-satisfying and health-nurturing destination is testament to the wisdom of the way back. And we can all be thankful that in *The Farm Girl's Guide to Preserving the Harvest*, she takes wandering, yearning, seeking pilgrims with her.

Our family is blessed to enjoy an unbroken chain of farmsteading, food preserving, and domestic culinary arts. I grew up this way. Teresa grew up this way. We still don't have a TV. This growing, putting by, communal dining on scratch-fare is in our DNA. But most folks just waking up to the validity and profound cultural impact of home-centric living don't have that kind of experience or that legacy. The chain broke somewhere between Enfamil, TV dinners, and high school vending machines.

For all of you who are wandering, this book is a wonderful part of the road map back. From canned bone broth, to drying milk, to seasonings, sauces, jerky, curing, smoking, kombucha, cold storage, and even freeze-drying, Ann takes us by the hand—all of us—and with dirt-under-the-fingernails know-how, leads us home. It's a safe place. A warm place. A haven in a hurried and harried world. Perhaps never before has home been this important.

I deeply appreciate that Ann doesn't sledgehammer her lifestyle on anyone. She even applauds and recognizes the validity and importance of convenience foods and fast foods—made in our own kitchens and grabbed when we're on the go. Of course, we need snacks

and ready-to-eat foods. But they need not come from the grocery store. They can come from our local farmers to be processed in our own kitchens to be preserved in our own larders and then deliciously enjoyed when we're in a hurry. I've often said that if our family could grow toilet paper and facial tissues, we could almost pull the plug on groceries. You can do that too, and it's an incredibly awesome place to be.

Effort? Yes. We're all putting effort into something. Goodness, in my opinion it takes a lot of effort to read labels and try to suss out what's edible in the grocery store. Fixing our health when we've eaten junk from the industrial orthodoxy takes effort. Knowing which drugs to use takes effort. Why not just invest effort in a good place from the start? Instead of cheating, why don't we just learn the material?

I guarantee that anyone taking Ann's hand to follow her through this harvest preservation journey will agree that this effort offers the greatest return on investment. Food security, safety, and satiation all begin with personal responsibility and kitchen accountability. Whether you grow it or purchase it from someone who grows it, you can join this healing team. Thank you, Ann, for guiding us home. Your readers will love where this book takes them. Welcome home.

Joel Salatin
Polyface Farm
Editor, *The Stockman Grass Farmer*

INTRODUCTION

It's hard to believe there was a time in my life when I wasn't homesteading. Though the transition wasn't that long ago, it seems like a lifetime. I went from being a suburban housewife to a self-sustaining mother and wife, all in the blink of an eye. I can barely remember the woman I was, and I'm in awe of the woman I have become. The strength and knowledge I have now has led my family to living a healthier, happier life and has taught us the values of living simply. The woman I am now has inner strength and drive, an individual who seeks to encourage others to bring back and live through small family farming. I am a self-taught homesteader, and with my husband by my side, we are returning to a world that

many do not know or have no desire to know. Our ability to live by example allows us to impact the lives of those around us, and in truth, that is how change begins.

When I think back to our time in the suburbs, the quality of the foods we consumed was not something I spent much time thinking about. How it was grown, where it was grown, or what it took to reach our table were afterthoughts. Snacks for the kids were rarely healthy, processed foods filled the pantry, and a meal generally contained at least one box item or frozen food. Fresh vegetables came from the market, with the only concern being that they looked fresh. More times than not, fruit went to waste once the kids were bored of it because there was no garden in which to compost and no chickens or pigs to consume it. I didn't have the knowledge or the energy to take unwanted fruit and transform it into jam or jelly. I was wasteful. That, my friends, was once how we lived our lives. I wasn't a bad mother or wife; I had other priorities more important than our food source.

I often wonder if this was due to not being born into the homesteading or farming life, and in truth I had no idea what it meant to homestead. I grew up as a military brat and, as an adult, assumed the role of suburban housewife. Never once did I think I would spend my days mucking out a goat pen or maintaining a large garden, and nothing I ever imagined involved cleaning poop from the coop or barn daily. And I can promise you, life certainly did not include raising our own meat. During that season of life, the concept of preserving foods meant placing it into plastic containers and consuming it within a few days. I can honestly say I was oblivious of the ability that one could live off the land and what it meant to live simply.

Growing up on military bases left little room to maintain a garden when I was a child, yet I watched as my mother tried. She managed a small mint garden while living in Massachusetts and a container garden while stationed in Hawaii. Generally, our food came from the commissary or the open markets when they were available, and there was never a dinner that wasn't homemade. I remember the time she spent sprouting bean sprouts, and there was often a jar of homemade pickled mangos in the fridge, but I think my most favorite memory was watching her forage. Being Thai, she taught us how to collect a spice that grew in the grass while living in Panama, and we'd often find wild mango and guava trees, which we happily gleaned from. Harvesting fiddlehead ferns in Massachusetts after the rain is still fresh in my mind, but it wasn't until we lived in Hawaii that I learned about foods that even the islanders never would have thought to harvest. My mother did not realize then that the simple things she did would prove to be such important examples in how my husband, Justin, and I would end up living our lives.

The world I grew up in was completely opposite of Justin's. From the moment I met him, he made it clear he had no desire to live in town; it was a stepping stone until he found a piece of land that he could call home. His heart desired space away from prying neighbors, the constant traffic, and restrictions of city living. You see, unlike me, Justin grew up with the memories of large gardens, canning, and meat provided through hunting and fishing. His family processed the game, and the meat was then preserved, often being divided among family members. He remembers trips to the cellar to gather canned goods or vegetables,

which would be used to make their daily meals. This is what he sought to return to. All it was going to take was convincing me that his dream was also mine. Convince me he did, and everything the kids and I knew was left behind. He took us to a single-family home on two acres in the mountains, and our lives changed forever.

To this day I can remember the season when I felt empowered to live a more sustainable life. It began with a few tomato, cilantro, jalapeño, and zucchini plants that grew inside a little greenhouse in the pasture. Then there were fifteen chicks that would grow to free range and live as they should. The next shift occurred the moment we collected our first warm eggs from those little feathered dinosaurs.

The final shift occurred on the hottest day of the month when a canning jar pinged, then another, and another, until every jar of freshly canned raspberry jam was removed from the canner and vacuum-sealed itself. I was able to take freshly harvested raspberries that I grew and cared for and turn them into a shelf-stable item. *In that instant, I became my own grocery store*. Not really, but it felt that way. Can you even begin to realize how empowering that feels?

You see, it took a growing season of 3 short months for me to comprehend that the small amount of produce we grew, the farm-fresh eggs we collected, and the first jars of food we preserved had the power to free me. Those accomplishments led us to dream of living a truly self-sustaining life. They freed us to learn what real food was about and to realize

how important food preservation would be to live sustainably. But more importantly, our food sources became free of the use of chemicals, preservatives, and hormones.

And so the journey began.

We have been able to expand the garden and fruit trees yearly, taking us one step closer to growing food year-round. Much of what is harvested between spring and fall is consumed fresh. Any excess is preserved for later use by being canned, frozen, fermented, dehydrated, and even freeze-dried. Though the garden is bountiful, there are often times when it doesn't provide the quantity needed to be preserved for the year. For this reason, we're extremely thankful for the relationships we have formed with local farms in the area. These farms compensate for what we can't grow or for what did not grow well. Maybe a section of the garden failed due to a certain blue-eyed Nigerian goat who decided it would make a delicious snack. Whatever the reason, a good relationship with local farmers is necessary and one you will come to value.

Aside from the garden, having livestock was always in the plans. And to the person who said that chickens are the gateway to keeping livestock, well, they were right. Onto our homestead came chickens, ducks, goats, guineas, rabbits, turkeys, and quail. Soon pigs and Boer goats will be added for meat, giving us the ability to truly own our food source.

We believe in homesteading as our forefathers did, meaning that each livestock animal that joins the property is loved, respected, well cared for, and treated humanely. Our journey to keeping livestock began with fifteen chickens for egg laying. When molting caused their egg production to dry up, we knew we needed a plan to continue receiving eggs. We smartened up and began freezing eggs in preparation for molting season. Eggs that are frozen are excellent for baking and cooking foods such as scrambled eggs, frittatas, and quiche. The frustration of not having eggs on hand was no longer an issue, and we could continue to enjoy farm eggs while our flock was on a break. Looking back, I realize that a simple step such as freezing eggs when they are bountiful set us up to begin our life as sustainable homesteaders. Bread and pasta making couldn't happen without eggs, making me aware that we needed to plan ahead.

It wasn't until we began raising our own meat that we finally understood the phrase "know where your food comes from." This was the last step for us to be considered a self-sustaining homestead, and man, were we ever thankful to finally make it to this point. We went from butchering a rooster here and there to raising enough meat to be consumed throughout the year. By the end of fall, the freezer is filled with chicken, turkey, duck, quail, guinea, and rabbit, which are all raised and butchered on our homestead. Livestock which we did not raise, such as beef and pork, was purchased from a friend's farm, allowing us to once again know where our food came from. We gained confidence in learning how to preserve various types and cuts of meat through curing, canning, and freezing. If you've never cured your own bacon, you're truly missing out; and I hope you'll use this book to help you learn how.

So, exactly what does all this mean? It means we have successfully reclaimed our source of food. We own it, and it no longer owns us. This one-time suburban housewife now knows where her food comes from, how it was grown, whether it was raised humanely, when it was harvested, and, most importantly, how to preserve it.

The fruits of our hard labor are put up to be consumed during a time when we allow our bodies to rest. Winter becomes the season in which we can appreciate the bounty of the harvest. It is also the time when we begin canning much of the meat and vegetables that were frozen after they were processed as soups or stews, or cut into pieces to be preserved as canned meat.

The ability to put food in jars, cure meat, dry food, and freeze-dry just about anything under the sun allows us the freedom to do so without the use of chemicals or preservatives. Not to mention, foods that we preserve ourselves are done in a manner in which we like to consume them. If you have children, I know you understand how important that is. We can control the type of sugars used (and how much) as well as the amount of herbs and spices we add to canned or cured foods. This is empowerment—even something as simple as this.

Society has taught us to be afraid of handling meat—heck, panfrying a steak comes with a list of safety instructions nowadays. But once you know the process for curing your own meat and fish, you will wonder why you ever hesitated. Something as simple as smoking garlic allows you the opportunity to increase how foods can be flavored as well as how they are preserved.

There is legitimate fear for those who are new to preserving foods. Maybe it's because there is no mentor available to walk them through the steps, or maybe they are afraid they will do it incorrectly. Many who are new to the world of canning are terrified that they are going to make someone extremely ill, so they hesitate to begin. More individuals are comfortable

with the process of hot water bath canning, but the moment a pressure canner is mentioned, they tend to freeze up. I was once terrified of using a pressure canner, but I ended up putting my fear aside and taught myself how to get it done. My family was depending on me being able to preserve food.

Preserving foods in no way should be intimidating, and that's exactly why I needed to write this book. You're on your way to becoming your own grocery store. Get ready to be freed, to be empowered, and to enjoy the process along the way.

Together, we will get you to where you need to be. Our family has been able to achieve so much, and because of this we are now living as self-sustaining homesteaders. I am here to help and cheer you on along your journey, regardless of what phase of home preservation you are currently in. Be prepared. We are going to talk about the basics of how to begin, the dos and don'ts, along with the hows and whys. I have included our favorite recipes for each method of food preservation that our family and friends have come to love, allowing you to give them a try as well.

Of course, being the farm girl that I am, one who loves farm-fresh eggs, I include tips on preserving and cooking with fresh eggs in every chapter. Consider this an ode to the little feathered dinosaurs that bring us joy each day.

My goal is to guide you on the journey—consider it a foundation of knowledge. Build on the information you find here to be confident in how you preserve the harvest.

Alright y'all, grab a cup of coffee and let's get started! From one farm girl in the making to another, *you've got this.*

One WHERE TO START?

Goodness, where do you start when you're looking to preserve foods? Besides the obvious method of canning, you need to know about the plethora of other options available to you. Many begin with freezing as it's truly the easiest method, although even then they might wonder if there are specific things they need to do before putting food in the freezer. From there, they tend to move on to canning and dehydrating and then maybe, just maybe, curing and smoking meat and fish. More advanced home preservers might progress to utilizing a freeze-dryer and learning the importance of fermented foods to build good gut flora for optimal health. Whatever phase you're in, take a bow. You are now entering a league where millions of others will never go.

However, learning each phase of food preservation requires one to know the lingo as well as the how, why, and what. Some people were taught from family members or friends with traditions being passed down. You are simply taking a different route by learning with me, one that is just as comfortable as if we had known each other for years.

With that said, let's start at the beginning.

THE GARDEN

In true farming fashion, we spend months planning the gardens (and by gardens I mean the growing cycle of spring, summer, and fall). Many of us have our seeds ordered by January, and I would be a liar if I said we *never* order too many seed packs. I may learn one year, but until then I will continue to hoard seeds.

The seed company you select will depend on the type of seeds you wish to plant. Seed selection will vary based on your growing zone, whether you wish to grow heirloom, non-GMO, organic, or just the average seed, and for this very reason, you will see variations in pricing with heritage seeds generally higher in cost. Due to our growing zone and mountainside living, we tend to go with a seed company that is specific to our area. We sometimes select specialty seeds from other companies, but that can be a gamble for our wet, unpredictable, cooler temperature here in the Puget Sound area of Washington State.

SOME OF MY FAVORITE SEED COMPANIES

Territorial Seed
Sow True Seeds
Pinetree Garden Seeds
Baker's Creek Seeds
Botanical Interest
Seed Savers Exchange
Irish Eyes Garden Seeds

Our main goal as homesteaders is to maximize the garden's yield throughout each growing season and the only way to accomplish this is by relying heavily on succession planting and successfully planting cool weather crops twice a year. Once the season ends, we are mindful to pull vegetables to make room for another season of planting. Trust me when I say it's not always an easy decision to pull a plant that is still producing, but to grow in a small garden space, it needs to be done.

How much of something to plant is always the question most asked. If I had a dime for every time, I'd be rich. Really, there is no right or wrong answer to this question. How much space you have in the garden and what you intend to grow will determine this for you, not to mention a garden map will help you to properly plan and lay out the space to help maximize the yield. But again, it is all about trial and error and no two growing seasons will ever be the same.

The second most frequently asked question from those who are new to this world of growing foods and preserving is: does your garden produce enough to sustainably feed you throughout the year? The answer could very well be yes, but at some point, you are going to want to consume the foods which you cared for and labored over for months on end, as it should be! Until the growing season has ended you will never know how much

food you will be able to preserve, causing many to rely on small batch canning or freezing until the very last items have been harvested from the garden.

And let's not forget Mother Nature. She can be a wicked beast and destroy almost everything you have worked so hard to achieve, or maybe unwanted visitors like slugs, squirrels or deer have obliterated everything growing. And then there is the obvious: the size of your garden based on the size of your property. We will never be able to produce as much food as the 10-acre farm down the road is capable of, but guess what? That is okay! We have the ability to work with local farmers, as well as glean or forage items to help compensate what we fall short on or cannot grow.

A garden space changes every year, at least ours does. Each year new beds are added, or existing beds are reworked, additional containers are added to expand the concept of container gardening, and trellises are added where they can allow us to grow plants vertically. We have learned to maximize the space we have in order to live as sustainably as possible.

Our garden space expands each year to make room for new produce or create more space for items we consume the most. I will never be able to grow everything that is needed, so I try to grow produce that is specific to my zone. This does not stop me from trying to

PRODUCE POUND EQUAL TO JAR QUANTITY

For planning purposes, especially if you are purchasing in bulk from local farms or the farmers' market, here is a rough estimate of how many pounds of food are needed to produce a desired jar amount. Keep in mind, this is a rough guide that can be used when you're planning the garden or making a purchase.

	produce	pounds	jar amount
fruit	APPLES	48 pounds	16-20 quarts
	APPLESAUCE	48 pounds	15-18 quarts
	BERRIES	24 pounds	12-18 quarts
	CHERRIES	22 pounds	9-11 quarts
	PEACHES	48 pounds	18-24 quarts
	PEARS	50 pounds	20-25 quarts
	PLUMS	56 pounds	24-30 quarts
	TOMATOES*	50 pounds	15-20 quarts
	TOMATOES, WHOLE	20 pounds	7 quarts
	TOMATOES, SAUCE	14 pounds	9 pints
vegetables	BEANS (GREEN/WAX)	30 pounds	12-20 quarts
	BEETS	52 pounds	15-25 quarts
	CARROTS	50 pounds	16-25 quarts
	CORN	35 pounds	6-10 pounds
	PEAS, SHELLING	30 pound	5-10 quarts
	PICKLES	48 pounds	16-24 quarts

*Roughly, it takes 3 pounds of tomatoes to fill a quart-size jar

grow items out of my zone such as peppers, which do not do well at our elevation outside of a greenhouse. But here I am still trying year after year, just to be disappointed each and every year. Let's just say I am a stubborn farm girl.

So many factors come into play when planning a garden to be used for food preservation, as well as what is to be consumed throughout the growing season. Just remember, whatever shortcomings your garden may have, it can always be supplemented by purchasing items through your local farmers' market or from local farms.

YOUR LOCAL FARMERS' MARKET

There are very few of us who can grow it all. I know I can't. Though I will say, many home preservers will only put up foods which they themselves have grown, gleaned, or foraged, and I applaud them for this.

Like I mentioned, there are many variables as to why a garden is not producing well, or maybe you would simply like to preserve an item that you just cannot grow based on your location. Whatever the reason, I am going to highly suggest you utilize local farmers' markets and even your local market.

These two locations will help to fill the shortcomings of the garden. Because of space restrictions, we are limited to how much we can grow on our homestead. A great example is tomatoes. Though we have an entire raised bed and numerous pots dedicated to growing several varieties of tomatoes, the garden does not yield what we need in order to preserve for the year. At this point, we have two options—preserve only what the garden produces, which then forces us to purchase from the market when we run out, or reach out to the farmers in our area, which will allow us to put up the quantity our family consumes without having to buy from the market.

This is where the relationship between farmer and consumer becomes important. Many farmers are willing to provide a discount when vegetables and fruit are purchased in bulk, often between 10 to 20 percent off the suggested price. And more times than not, once a relationship has been established, you will find that they often gift items as a sign of appreciation for your business.

Local markets also offer a discount for items purchased in bulk. For example, I prefer home canned mushrooms to purchasing them from the market. The produce department provides me a large discount when I purchase a box of mushrooms at a time, allowing me to preserve a better tasting product than the item in a metal canned jar.

Visiting your local farmers market towards the end of the day allows you the opportunity to purchase many items and even seconds at a greater discount. These farmers tend to not want to bring back items which have not been sold due to the inability to keep these food items looking fresh by the next day.

PURCHASING SECONDS

Nothing makes me happier than the opportunity to purchase seconds from local farms or vendors at the farmers' market. This may not seem like much, but it is vital to our way of living. The term "seconds" refers to fruits and vegetables that do not make the cut to be sold, but there is absolutely nothing wrong with them other than not being cosmetically appealing. Seconds also consist of food items which took a bit longer to ripen, missing the prime market for sale, and will cost a fraction of what they normally would.

Fruit seconds can be purchased at your local orchard, through vendors at the farmers market, or farm stands within your area. Your local supermarket should also have a seconds' area, often selling bags of fruit for a dollar or two. When dealing with seconds you must be quick when it comes to preserving. The longer you delay the less likely you can preserve the vegetables or fruit due to spoilage. The best tip I can provide when dealing with seconds is to make sure your calendar is cleared in order to can, freeze, or dry them.

On the surface, seconds do not look appealing, though once the bruised or wilted sections of the fruit or vegetable have been removed you are left with an item that is perfectly good to use. Apple seconds can be used to make applesauce, apple juice concentrate, apple butter, dehydrated apple rings, or even freeze-dried apples for snacks. Of course, you should always strive to use the freshest, minimally bruised produce and fruit when preserving as the National Center for Home Food Preservation states. But remember, if the goal is to live sustainably "waste not, want not" should always be the focus. At our homestead, what can't be used is either composted or fed

to our livestock. Apple cores and peels, for example, can be transformed into making apple scrap jelly, dehydrated into powder for cooking, or for making raw apple cider vinegar. Purchasing seconds will save you a substantial amount of money in the long run and will allow you to preserve food items which the garden or orchard may fall short on.

HOME-GROWN MEAT

The switch from backyard hobbyist to self-sustainable homesteader occurs the moment you begin raising and harvesting your own meat (unless you're a vegetarian). Because the goal is to raise and grow food which will provide for my family, I am very strategic about the livestock we raise, and more importantly on how it will be preserved. With that in mind, we raise

and breed only what we will be consuming throughout the calendar year. Our freezer space is limited, so canning becomes a secondary option for us, which works very well on the nights the kids cook dinner or during the winter months when we lose power due to weather conditions. The canned meat is easy to reheat and serve with either a fresh item or another jar of canned food from the pantry. When my children cook, this empowers them and teaches them the value of being sustainable.

For a family of four, based on our property size, we can raise fifty-six broiler chickens, four litters of rabbits (averaging eight per litter), seven turkeys, and twenty-four

ducks for meat purposes. We also raise guinea and quail, with an average of eighteen guineas and a hundred and twenty five quail, which are harvested from early spring through late fall. We also purchase a pasture-raised pig from a local farmer twice a year, and half a cow once a year.

What's in store for our small acre homestead? The incorporation of a pig and the addition of Boer goats as a source of red meat. The meat harvested from these sources will be frozen, cured, and canned allowing us to be even less dependent on others.

If you're unable to raise your own small livestock for food consumption, look for local farmers to purchase from throughout the year. Keep in mind that most of us who raise livestock for meat tend to have everything butchered and processed by October, before winter sets in, so make sure to plan accordingly.

> If purchasing a whole cow or pig is not within your means, or you lack the freezer space, find friends who would be willing to go in on purchasing with you.

WORDS OF WISDOM, GUIDELINES, AND TOOLS TO GET YOU STARTED

Your journey to preserving the harvest is about to begin, yet you may still be nervous. That's okay! I am sure your main concern is whether you are going to make someone sick by the foods you are putting up. Let me assure you, we all felt this way when we began. Heck, this exact thought went through my head over and over. You are venturing into a new life. Find value and comfort in this. Preserving foods at home not only allows you to own your food source, but it allows you to also own your healthcare.

Let me say this again. Consuming foods which contain no unnatural preservatives and have been grown or raised by you or a trusted party is one of the steps towards owning your healthcare. Feel empowered by this. It is vital to the life we live.

Does the nervousness ever go away? To a degree. With each passing year we tend to become more comfortable working with our canners, dehydrators, and vacuum sealers. It is always important to stay current with new techniques, studies, tools, and even recipes. Times change, studies are updated, new resources are provided, and adapting to these changes will make you more comfortable with the foods you wish to preserve for the years to come. Understanding the science behind home food preservation is vital to being able to make smart decisions.

On the flip side—yes, there is a flip side—the old ways and methods, which people like the Amish still practice, are homesteading survival skill we should all know. Does that mean we should practice them? Not at all. But there may come a time when these skills are needed.

As your need to learn various methods of preserving increases, your skills will expand. Freezing foods like leafy greens, for example, may be more ideal than canning. Whereas green beans can be either canned or frozen. This allows us to not only enjoy them as convenience foods but also in soups, casseroles, or stir-fries. A freeze dryer is an amazing appliance to have on hand for long-term storage or for preserving items such as milk and eggs, and even leftover meals. Curing meat, making sausage, even salting egg yolks are excellent examples of preserving at a moderate or advanced level.

There is really no method of home food preservation that you should not know. They are all vital to owning your food source. Take your time with each phase, and do not rush mastering it. I have yet to stop educating myself on various methods of home food preservation and am now learning how the rest of the world preserves food. A good mentor is one who does not stop learning.

TOOLS YOU'LL NEED

Over the years, many tools used to preserve foods have entered and exited my kitchen. Small home living forces me to be particular about what is most beneficial. I have tested both inexpensive and high-end gadgets, tools, and appliances, allowing me to narrow down what is necessary for working smart rather than hard. The tools listed in this section will help you optimize different methods of preserving the harvest, but in no way do you need to purchase every one for your home, and remember, use what you can in order to make the job easier. You will thank me in the end!

Aside from a few major preserving tools, you will find gadgets and common kitchen items that will help minimize your workload. Here are the tools and appliances I use regularly on our homestead:

- Pressure Canner
- Immersion Blender
- Dehydrator
- Steam Juicer
- Canning Tools (jar lifter, lid lifter, timer, air bubble remover)
- Mini Slow Cooker
- Stainless Steel Stockpot
- Stainless Steel Food Tray (for meat curing)
- Vacuum Sealer with Jar Sealer Attachment
- Camp Chef Propane Stove
- Glass and Ceramic Vessels for Fermenting
- Fermenting Lids and Weights
- Electric Roaster Oven
- Slow Cooker
- Freeze Dryer

Keep in mind, this list works for us and the size of our home. By all means, if you would like to try other items than what's listed here, go for it! You may enjoy the use of a food mill over an immersion blender, and that is okay. Utilize what works best for you.

WATER CANNING TOOLS (HOT WATER BATH, STEAM AND PRESSURE CANNING)

Hot Water Bath Canner

This tool is used for preserving foods high in acidity or that have properly met the acidic levels allowed for water bath canning. Food items such as jams, jellies, marmalades, fruit butters, pickled items, infused vinegar, whole fruit, chutney, and tomatoes (with assistance of an acidic lifter) fall into this category.

The typical hot water bath canner is made of a durable steel core that has a porcelain overlay and is available in various sizes. The most commonly sold hot water bath canner is the 33-quart size, which is capable of holding as many as nine quart-size jars, fourteen pint jars, or seventeen half-pint jars. If you are canning for a smaller family, a 21-quart canner may be a bit more ideal, holding seven quart jars, nine pint jars, or twelve half-pint jars.

Ideally, a water canner should be used on a gas and electric stove but is not recommended for glass top stoves. The concern is that the weight of the water bath canner may cause the glass top to shatter, or that the canner will vacuum seal itself to the glass.

However, with the increasing interest in preserving foods at home, many newer glass stove tops are being constructed with sturdier pieces of glass. Make sure to consult the manual of your stove prior to using it for canning purposes. In addition to this, newer models of hot water bath canners are flat on the bottom rather than concave, preventing them from vacuum sealing themselves to the glass stove tops.

If you are *still* hesitant to use a water bath canner on a glass stove top, Ball has created two versions of an electric canner. The price for the electric canners range between $100 to $300 depending on the model, with the higher priced model equipped with what Ball calls "smart preserve technology." What does this mean? It is an automatic canner which controls the exact time and temperature needed to can most recipes. Ball's electric canners are designed to can high acidic items only and are *not* considered to be pressure canners.

The University of Wisconsin Extension Service (along with many others) does not recommend that hot water bath canners be double stacked. The concern is that jars will tip over when they're jostled by boiling water. This can affect them sealing correctly. However, if the canner is filled, preventing any jars from tipping, this is not an issue.

Steam Canner (aka, Atmospheric Steam Canner)

A steam canner is, hands down, by far the best tool on the market to be used when preserving high acid food items. In 2015 the steam canner was approved as a safe canning tool to use on high acidic items, changing the world of canning for many individuals, myself included.

This water canner uses only two inches of water, prevents wear and tear on the stove burner, and is also safe to use on glass top stoves. Much like a hot water bath canner, the steam reaches 212°F allowing for proper penetration through the jar to kill any possible bacteria while allowing for foods to become shelf stable.

The processing time is the same as a hot water bath canner, though food which requires a processing time over 45 minutes should not be canned using a steam canner. In this case, a traditional boiling water canner is required.

Pressure Canner

A pressure canner allows low-acid foods to become shelf stable. Foods such as meat, seafood, vegetables that are not pickled, soups, stocks, stews, and dried beans are ideal items

to be pressure canned. Pressure canners kill and prevent bacteria from within the jars by reaching 240°F. In addition to providing the appropriate temperature needed and the proper pounds per square inch (psi) reduce the risk of spoilage caused by *Clostridium botulinum* and its toxin-producing spores.

Pressure canners are available through various brands and will range in price between $60 to over $300. There are three models of canners available for purchase: dial, weight-gauge, or dual-purpose. Keep in mind that a pressure cooker and an Instant Pot are not the same as a pressure canner and should not be used as one.

- A dial gauge lists various levels of pressure, which makes matching the correct psi needed for food preservation easier.
- A weight gauge measures three different pounds per pressure (5, 10, and 15). The weight gauge is designed to "jiggle" several times a minute, rocking gently when it can maintain the correct pressure. The manufacturer's manual will provide information on how the weight should rock or jiggle, indicating the proper pressure is being met.
- The dual-purpose pressure canner contains both a weighted *and* dial gauge.

In truth, what you choose will depend on preference, how much you'd like to spend, and the possible wear and tear on your stove.

Steam Juicer

A steam juicer should not be confused with a fruit and vegetable juicer, which should not be used for longer-term storage of juices. What is extracted from a regular juicer contains food particles, making it unstable to be canned. A steam juicer extracts the liquid from items such as fruit and vegetables and creates a concentrate that is safe to be canned. The fruit is added whole, including stem, peel, and seed, into the colander, and the steam extracts the fluid. In addition to fruit and vegetables, bones can be steamed to create bone broth.

Water Canning Tools

There are many tools that will make working with a water canner easier. Many can be purchased as either a kit or individually, if an item needs to be replaced. Most tools can be used interchangeably with the various types of water canners, excluding jar racks. Jar racks are specific to fit each type of canner.

Canner Rack. Canner racks are available for both pressure and hot water bath canners. A pressure canning rack sits at the bottom of the canner, allowing for heat to flow under the jars and to prevent jars from rocking and hitting the bottom of the canner, which could cause the jars to crack or fall over. The canner rack for a hot water bath canner is much different. It contains handles that allow for easier placement of jars into and removal from the boiling water bath. Again, the rack prevents the jar from touching the bottom of the canner, allowing for heat to penetrate every aspect of the jar and to prevent the jars from falling over or from banging the bottom of the canner.

When putting rings into hot water, place them so that the wax sides are facing each other. This will prevent the lids from being stacked too tightly together and will allow you to easily grab them.

Jar Lifter. I would advise you to always have a jar lifter. Jars and rings are extremely hot once they have completed the processing cycle, making the jar lifter an ideal tool in removing jars from the canner. A jar lifter, also known as jar tongs, removes jars easily without burning your fingers. Note: Make sure you know which end actually grips the jar. During my first three years of canning, I was actually using the wrong end of the jar lifter to remove the jars from the canner. Rookie mistake that lasted longer than it should have!

Magnetic Lid Lifter. This wand has a magnetic end that allows it to adhere to a lid so that the lid can be removed easily from hot water.

Air Bubble Remover. Though not always visible, air bubbles can hide between food items in the jar. Avoid using metal utensils to remove air bubbles from jars, because the metal may scratch the insides of the jars, possibly causing the jars to crack while in the canner. A plastic air bubble remover is excellent for removing all air bubbles from jars prior to water canning.

Jar Funnel. Filling jars is not a neat task, and spills are bound to happen. Jar funnels are designed to help you fill jars faster and more efficiently while keeping the jar rims clean and preventing waste. Jar funnels are available in plastic as well as stainless steel. Some are made to fit specific jar sizes, but you are better off getting a universal one that fits both wide- and regular-mouth jars.

Jar Wrench. A jar wrench is used to help loosen the rings from jars. This canning tool is not a necessary item to purchase; however, it is generally included when you purchase a kit.

Digital Food Timer. I added this tool to the list simply because it is often overlooked and thought to not be necessary. As a matter of fact, I went years without one. Not any longer! A small magnetic timer is an excellent item to ensure that goods are processed within the allocated time.

Nonreactive Pots. High-acidic foods are best if prepared in nonreactive pots. Pots made from metals such as aluminum or uncoated cast iron can react with the acid in the foods being preserved and can alter the flavor of the items. Stainless steel and enamel-coated cast iron are great options to use in preparing foods to be canned.

Dish Drying Mat. Normally, dish towels or large towels work well under jars that are cooling, although they tend to be too thin. Thick drying mats create a barrier between the hot jars and delicate surfaces such as wood, which helps to prevent water rings from forming on wood surfaces.

Tattler Lids. These are reusable canning lids for hot water bath, steam, and pressure canning. This is an American-made product that is capable of lasting for many years (some people have told us they've used the same lids for more than 15 years). The rubber ring can be replaced as needed, and the plastic lid is BPA-free. Getting the lids to seal can be difficult, and I suggest tightening them more than finger tight to help them seal properly. Tattler lids are excellent for reducing waste, unlike traditional canning lids and rings.

Immersion Blender. An immersion blender is a stick blender which works well for making sauces, fruit butters, and jams. This is very convenient for those who do a lot of preserving and has replaced the food mill here on our homestead.

Food Mill. Food mills help to process foods that will be preserved without seeds or peels, such as spaghetti sauce, tomato paste, and ketchup. A stainless steel model is nonreactive and will help preserve the taste in foods which are high in acidity.

Jelly Strainer Bag. Jelly is a clear product that contains no pulp, skin, and seeds. A fine mesh bag assists in achieving this by straining the liquid mixture from the solids, creating a clear liquid that is ideal when preserving jelly or juice.

Slow Cooker. A slow cooker is a great tool for those who have limited time and seek convenience when cooking down items such as tomato sauce, fruit butters, applesauce, and salsa.

Mini Slow Cooker. This mini version of the slow cooker is used for keep the canning lids warm by submerging them in water prior to use. Canning lids should not be boiled but rather kept warm to allow the plastisol (the wax found on the lid) to soften before use. In 2014 Ball announced that canning lids purchased from them no longer needed to be warmed in warm water prior to use; they can simply be used straight out of the box. With that said, I still warm my lids since I also use other brands.

Camp Stove. Though a camp stove is not necessary for canning, it is one of the most valued items for those who

SELECTING THE RIGHT MASON JAR FOR THE JOB

There is a price difference between regular-mouth and wide-mouth Mason jars. To save a few dollars, be sure to select the right jars for the job. With that said, this does not mean that you have to use one type of jar over another. If you have a plethora of wide-mouth jars on hand, use them before spending the money on regular-mouth jars.

- **Regular-Mouth Jars.** This style costs less than the wide-mouth version and is generally used to help prevent food items from floating. The shape of the jar helps to keep most foods in place, maximizing the amount of food being canned. Canned vegetables, fruit, meat, and soups are excellent candidates for using regular-mouth jars.
- **Wide-Mouth Jars.** Generally, this type of jar will cost a few dollars more than regular-mouth jars and works well for preserving juice, sauces, jams, jellies, chutneys, and items not in a whole form.

Both types of jars can be used for fermenting, although which mouth size to use depends on the fermenting lid you have.

Though it is not recommended to use half-gallon jars for canning, the Clemson Extension Cooperative Office has stated that apple and grape juice can be canned in half-gallon Mason jars. The processing time begins at 10 minutes at the elevation of 0-1,000 feet. For processing times higher than 1,001 feet above sea level refer to page 65.

> To maximize my time, and to prevent myself from standing over the stove in order to keep food from scorching, I will often use a slow cooker to cook items being canned overnight. Then, first thing in the morning I will process this food, freeing me up to move on to other tasks. Remember, work smart, not hard. We are modern homesteaders for a reason!

are canning during the summer months. The opportunity to can outdoors during the peak of summer will not only keep your house cooler, but it will keep you cooler as well. Because of their durability, they are an excellent tool for those concerned about using a canner on a glass-top stove. The National Center for Home Food Preservation suggests using camp stoves no higher than 12,000 BTUs.

Canning Jars. Mason jars are used for canning, as well as for short- and long-term storage of dried goods. There are many brands available, with size selection including half pint, pint, quart, and half gallon. When used for water canning, half-pint, pint, and quart jars are used, while half-gallon jars are used for fermenting or storing dry goods.

TOOLS FOR DRYING AND FREEZING

Dehydrator. Drying foods such as herbs, flowers, jerky, fruit, vegetables, fruit leather, eggs, and milk work well in a dehydrator. This drying tool ranges in price from forty dollars to well over two hundred dollars depending on the brand you select. Industrial large-scale dehydrators can cost more than five hundred dollars. Fan placement (top, back, or bottom) and the amount of stackable trays being used will determine how quickly and efficiently items will dry.

Herb and Flower Drying Rack. A drying rack is ideal for hanging outside or inside and is another form of drying if you do not wish to utilize a dehydrator for the job. Drying racks work well for individuals who plan to dry herbs and flowers throughout the season. Nothing smells quite as amazing as fresh herbs drying in the kitchen or over the wood burning stove during the summer months.

Jerky Gun. This tool is used to make homemade jerky strips for smoking or dehydrating. It's a small hand-held gadget that transforms raw ground meat into thin strips or round sticks.

Vacuum Sealer. A vacuum sealer extends the life of the preserved foods and is excellent to use for items stored in the freezer, refrigerator, or as dry goods, once the oxygen has been extracted from the vacuum-sealed plastic bags. Dry goods can be stored long term in Mason jars, freezer foods tend not to become freezer burnt, and refrigerated foods will also keep longer. Certain vacuum sealers also come with a jar sealer attachment.

Jar Sealer. Dry goods store well in jars if they will be consumed quickly, although if storing items for long-term storage it is best to vacuum seal the jars. A jar sealer attachment for a food saver works to remove the oxygen and moisture from the jar, allowing the dried goods to stay preserved for their maximum allotted time.

Freeze-Dryer. For individuals seeking to preserve raw or cooked foods for easy reconstitution, this is the tool for you. Not only does it preserve many food items for up to 25 years, it maintains 97 percent of the nutrients in the foods and herbs being freeze dried. Items such as whole meals, vegetables, fruit, milk, yogurt, and even ice cream can become shelf stable with the use of a freeze-dryer. If you are looking for healthy snacks for your next camping, hunting, or hiking trip, this tool will easily provide them.

Oxygen Absorbers. To maintain freshness for long-term, shelf-stable items, oxygen absorbers are needed. Oxygen absorbers contain iron powder, and the packets are made of material which allows oxygen and moisture to enter while preventing the iron powder to not leak out. The packets can be used in Mason jars, vacuum-sealed bags, food-grade buckets, and mylar bags.

Shrink Bags for Poultry and Small Game. Home-processed poultry and small game keep longer when stored in shrink-wrap bags. The meat is placed into BPA-free bags, then dipped into boiling water between 180 and 195°F. The heat of the water allows the poultry bags to shrink around the meat, removing any air and moisture, so that the meat can be frozen with little concern of freezer burn.

FERMENTING TOOLS

Fermenting Lids. Fermenting foods through small-batch fermentation with the use of Mason jars has revolutionized how to ferment foods. Fermenting lids are designed to fit onto wide- and regular-mouth Mason jars, allowing for those who ferment regularly to do so without the use of a large ceramic crock or gallon-size glass vessels. Fermenting lids are available in various materials (stainless steel, food-grade silicone and plastic), shapes and sizes, and price ranges. When selecting a fermenting lid, keep in mind the size jar you wish to use, and what you seek to ferment.

Fermenting Weight. Weights are used to keep the foods being fermented submerged in the brine. They are available in glass and stone and can be purchased to fit wide- or regular-mouth Mason jars.

Kraut Pounder. Kraut pounders are used to pound vegetables to help release the natural liquid found in the produce. A pounder can also be used to help submerge fruits

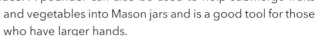

and vegetables into Mason jars and is a good tool for those who have larger hands.

Fermenting Crock (stone and glass). Crock selection will depend on what you are fermenting, whether foods items, kombucha, or kefir. Stone crocks are excellent when fermenting in batches larger than half-gallon Mason jars, whereas glass crocks are great for brewing kombucha and kefir. Both ceramic and glass crocks can be used for fermenting foods and drinks.

Swing-Top Bottles. Airtight swing-top bottles work well to store fermented drinks, especially ones you wish to become carbonated.

Bottle Funnel. Bottle funnels are available in stainless steel or plastic and in two sizes to fit Mason jars as well as swing-top bottles.

Plastic Mason Jar Lids. Plastic Mason jar lids are used to cap the jars once the goods have completed fermenting. Unlike metal lids, plastic lids will not corrode during storage.

MISCELLANEOUS TOOLS

Spice Bags. These are little fabric bags made from finely woven muslin and are used to extract the flavor of spices and are often used in pickling brines and for ferment.

Food-Grade Storage Buckets. Dry goods purchased in bulk will keep longer when stored in food-grade storage buckets, which will keep foods dry, fresh, and bug-free. Items such as legumes, flour, sugar, and grains are ideal for long-term food storage in food-grade buckets. Look for #2 buckets made out of HDPE (food-grade) plastic.

Free or very inexpensive food-grade buckets can be gathered from local bakeries in 2-, 3-, and 5-pound sizes. New lids can be ordered to ensure a proper seal is achieved. Food-grade buckets are ideal for foods being stored for 10-plus years. I use food-grade buckets to store bulk dried goods such as flour, sugar, and rice.

Sausage Maker. A sausage maker is an ideal tool for those who are looking to preserve meat. If you raise your own meat, I would strongly suggest a standalone sausage maker versus one which attaches to a popular kitchen appliance.

Smoker. Some foods, such as meat and fish, preserve well when smoked. The size and type of smoker can vary, as well as the types of wood chips used. This tool is excellent when you begin harvesting your own meat and fish.

Food Thermometer. A food thermometer is great to have on hand whether it is for canning, testing water temperature for processing meat, making cheese, or for curing and smoking meats and fish. There are two choices available: (1) a traditional one, which is inserted directly into the food being prepared, or (2) a battery-operated laser scanner, which works well for liquids.

Mandoline. Every kitchen needs a mandoline. The convenience, speed, and accuracy of a cut cannot be achieved when slicing fruits and vegetables by hand. There are various types of mandolines available on the market, ranging from tabletop versions to handheld ones. What you select will depend on what you are comfortable using. Just keep in mind, the blade on a mandoline is extremely sharp. Make sure you use the correct tools to ensure you do not cut your fingers.

TERMS YOU SHOULD KNOW

As you begin the journey of preserving foods, you will come across acronyms and terms that you may need help deciphering in order to make the experience easier. This cheat sheet of mine will help, and you will have it down in no time!

Altitude. The vertical elevation of a location above sea level. The altitude level will determine the amount of time needed to process foods in a water canner, hot water bath, steam, or pressure canner.

Anaerobic environment. The absence of oxygen in the fermenting process.

Approved/tested recipes. Recipes that have been scientifically tested for adequate pH balance for home-canned goods. These recipes can be found on sites such as the National Center for Home Food Preservation, state extension sites, and the Ball website and books, as well as extension offices located at university websites. The University of Minnesota, South Dakota State University, and Iowa State University are excellent resources.

Blanching. Blanching is a method used to remove skin easily from fruits and vegetables, as well as for removing air from fruits and vegetables to prevent floating (see floating on pages 28-29). This method is also used to soften foods prior to being dehydrated or prepared for the freezer.

HOW TO BLANCH FRUITS AND VEGETABLES

- Using a stockpot or deep pot, bring water to a boil.
- How long to blanch an item depends on what is being blanched. Fruits and select vegetables are blanched between 30 and 60 seconds, whereas root vegetables can take up to 2 to 3 minutes.
- Foods should be immediately submerged in ice water once removed from the boiling water. This stops the cooking process and makes working with the food items easier.
- Fruit skins should slip off easily, and vegetables will still have a firm texture.
- Items being blanched or steamed to be pressure canned do not require an ice water bath to cool the item, but instead can be added to sterilized canning jars to be processed. This method is known as hot packing. See pages 29 and 222 to learn more of this method.

Botulism. Although rare, toxins produced by spores of the bacterium *Clostridium botulinum* are found in foods that have been preserved using improper methods, or equipment and tools that were not properly sterilized. The spores thrive in items which are low in acidity and in an environment which is low in oxygen. In addition to improper canning, foods which are improperly frozen and dehydrated can also host the spores. Since botulism does not contain a smell and is flavorless, an individual may not know the preserved foods have gone bad until it is too late. Signs of botulism poisoning can be found on page 41.

Brine. Generally, a saltwater solution, which may also consist of sugar, spices, and herbs used for pickling, canning, fermenting, and curing. A dry brine is a blend of herbs and spices without the use of liquid.

Browning. Color change in fruits and vegetables caused when the cut end is exposed to oxygen. The term is also used in reference to canned foods that have turned brown due to exposure to air. The best way to avoid browning is to process cut fruits and vegetables immediately and ensure water levels are met when processing canning goods.

Cold pack. See Raw pack.

Culturing. Another term for fermenting when a microbial starter is used to initiate fermentation.

Curing. The process of preserving meat, fish, garlic, and even eggs through salting, water brining, sugaring, dry hanging, and smoking.

Dirty water. This is not a term you will hear often, but it is used in reference to the liquid in which a vegetable or fruit was blanched or cooked prior to canning. Some recipes will say to use this water; however, it is best to use freshly boiled water instead.

Extension Office. Also known as the Cooperative Extension System. An educational program implemented through each state to help people use research-based knowledge to improve their lives. These sites offer information not only for home food preservation but also for livestock, agricultural zoning, 4H, gardening, and informative classes on all topics listed above.

False seal. This term is used when, during canning, the lid is no longer vacuum-sealed to the Mason jar, yet it remains attached, giving the appearance that the lid has not broken its seal. When this occurs, the food within the jar will spoil and mold will begin to grow.

FDA. Abbreviation for the government agency known as the Food and Drug Administration.

Fermentation. The process of preserving foods by creating the intentional growth of yeast. Fermentation can occur in alcohol, water, vinegar, kombucha, food products, and some dairy products.

Finger tight. This describes how the ring should be tightened while preparing jars for canning. No force or utensils should be used to overtighten the rings.

Floating. Floating occurs when the item being canned shrinks during the canning process, causing the food to rise in the jars leaving a gap of liquid between the bottom of the jar to where the produce begins.

Foam. This term applies when making jam and is caused when air bubbles become trapped in the jam as it reaches its boiling point. Foam contains air, which will need to be skimmed prior to filling jars. Often the foam can be minimized by adding 1 teaspoon of butter during the cooking down of the fruit, but I find that even with the added butter, foaming still occurs.

HOW TO PREVENT FLOATING

Food naturally contains air, and in order to help eliminate the issue of floating in canned fruit, vegetables, and even mushrooms, these items will need to be blanched prior to being canned. Take a look at the steps on how to blanch foods on pages 27 and 222. Blanching not only removes the air found in foods but also preshrinks it, allowing for more foods to fit into a jar than if they were to be raw packed. Here are the steps:

- Blanch items for roughly 30 to 60 seconds, depending on the items being preserved. Soft fruit can be blanched for roughly 30 seconds, whereas root vegetables should be blanched up to 60 seconds.
- Utilize the hot pack method to fill jars.
- Make sure to fill jars tightly.
- Fill jars with boiling water or simple syrup.
- Remove all air bubbles using an air bubble remover.
- The tighter food is packed into jars the less likely these items will float. Not to mention, a minimum number of jars will be required if this method is used.

Headspace. The unfilled space from the top of the food or liquid to the underside of the lid. The space allows for food expansion as the food is heated and a strong seal once the jar has cooled. Improper headspace can prevent a proper vacuum seal, so make sure to follow the suggested head space in all recipes to prevent this issue.

Heat penetration. Heat should be allowed to penetrate through the jars of food to properly destroy bacteria and the spores of *c. Botulinum*. Thickeners such as cornstarch and flour, along with pureed foods and other items often prevent proper heat penetration and should not be used for home preservation.

High-acidic foods. These are food items that are capable of being hot water or steam canned and meet a pH balance less than 4.6. Such foods consist of jams, jellies, fruit butters, relishes, vinegars, pickles, salsas, chutneys, and some tomato items with the addition of vinegar or citric acid. Foods high in acid can be processed at 212°F.

Hot pack. Packing jars with food that has been preheated. Hot packing allows for a tighter pack in jars and reduces floating.

HWB. Abbreviation for hot water bath, a method of canning high-acid foods.

Inversion. A method of preserving by filling hot jars with hot foods, applying lids and rings, then placing the jars upside down (top down) for a period of time. Though sugar is a natural preserving agent, the National Center for Home Food Preservation suggests against this method in order to prevent the possibility of food spoilage.

Lacto-fermentation. Also known as lactic acid fermentation. *Lacto* refers to the specific bacteria, *Lactobacillus,* a bacteria present on anything grown in the earth.

Low-acidic foods. These are foods low in acid and containing a pH of 4.6 and higher. These items will need to be pressure canned to prevent spoiling, bacteria growth, and *c. Botulinum* and its spores from growing. Vegetables, meat, seafood, and poultry are low acid and should be heated to 240°F for a specific period of time in order for them to become shelf stable, which can be achieved with the use of a pressure canner.

Mold (visible). Microscopic fungi that are visible and may contain a foul smell found on food, including those high in acid. The color of mold can be red, black, white, or even pink.

NCHFP. Abbreviation for National Center for Home Food Preservation.

Nitrates. A preserving agent used to keep bacteria down in cured foods. Nitrates can be found in natural food items such as celery, making celery powder a natural preservative in meat curing.

Nitrites. A preserving salt used when curing foods such as bacon, pepperoni, and sausage, just to name a few. Nitrites are not necessary for meat curing, and this preserving agent should be used with great care.

PC. Abbreviation for pressure canner. This canner is used to process foods low in acidity, meat, vegetables, seafood, and poultry.

Ping/pop. The sound made during canning when the lid has been sucked down in a vacuum after processing.

Do not be surprised to hear multiple pinging as new jars sit in their original packaging or as you are preparing the jars to be water canned. This is caused by an external fluctuation in temperature or if gases in the jar escape. This does *not* mean the jars have vacuum-sealed themselves.

psi. This is the abbreviation for pounds per square inch, which is applicable to the use of a pressure canner. The psi (pressure) and length of time needed for canning is determined based on the foods being preserved, and often the jar size. Most low-acid foods will need to be pressure canned between 20 to 100 minutes in order to prevent bacteria and toxic spores from forming within the jars.

Raw pack. Filling jars with raw, uncooked, or unheated food prior to hot water, steam, or pressure canning.

Rebel canning. A term used for practicing traditional canning and preserving methods aside from what is approved by the USDA and the National Center for Home Food Preservation.

SC. Abbreviation for steam canner.

Self-sealing. The concept that a jar filled with boiled food or liquid will seal itself due to the heat content in the jar forming a vacuum seal. This is a traditional method of canning, which many people no longer practice. Although the lid may have sealed, this does not guarantee that all bacteria have been eliminated. The only methods that can ensure this are the hot water bath or steam canning for the required period.

Siphoning. The loss of liquid from jars during processing, especially during pressure canning.

Starter. Starters can consist of whey, pickling starter, sauerkraut starter, kefir grains, SCOBY, or the "mother" (beneficial bacteria) found in raw apple cider vinegar.

USDA. Abbreviation for United States Department of Agriculture.

Water canning. I use the term *water canning* to refer to all tools used for water canning, hot water bath, steam and pressure canning.

Wild fermentation. Occurs when microbes naturally found on foods or in the air are used to initiate the fermentation process. Think of this as planned spontaneous fermentation.

WHAT CAUSES THE LOSS OF LIQUID DURING PROCESSING

- Siphoning
- Improper cooldown
- Air bubbles that rise to the top of the jar during processing
- Lid-related issues (reusing lids, not wiping jar rims, rings placed on too loosely, inappropriate venting time during pressure canning)
- Jars are not covered with sufficient water during hot water bath canning

HOW TO DETERMINE THE CORRECT HEADSPACE

The correct amount of headspace is based on what you're canning (see table below). Air bubbles can affect proper headspace and should be removed prior to adding lids and rings. Additional food or liquid should be added if the required headspace decreases when air bubbles have been removed.

Improper headspace will affect whether the lids seal properly. Too little headspace can force the food to push the lid up and can even cause the liquid to leak out of the jar. If a jar has too much headspace, any remaining air could prevent a proper vacuum seal. Proper headspace is also needed for foods to expand. Beans and apple pie filling are great examples of foods that will expand.

canned item	proper headspace
JAM, JELLIES, MARMALADE, CHUTNEY, SPREADS, BUTTERS	¼ inch headspace
PICKLES, TOMATOES, FRUIT	½ inch headspace
NON-PICKLED VEGETABLES (PRESSURE CANNED)	1 inch headspace
MEAT, POULTRY, FISH (PRESSURE CANNED)	1 inch headspace

A FEW SIMPLE LESSONS

There are a few lessons I've learned throughout the years of canning and preserving. Many are simple tricks, while others I've stumbled upon. As the years go by, I continue to learn new ways to better my skills. For this very reason, I am going to save you some time and give you a jump start to a better experience! Please note that this section will speak specifically to canning. Tips for fermenting, dehydrating, freezing, curing, and smoking can be found in the following chapters.

GLASS-TOP CANNING

Many glass-top stove companies will warn against canning on their stoves. Like anything in life, the decision is yours whether you want to move forward or heed their warnings, but this is what you should know:

Older canners have concave bottoms. Concave bottoms can cause a seal between the canner and the stove top. The suction that occurs when this happens can result in a cracked or shattered glass top. Many newer canners have flat bottoms. Make sure to check this before purchasing.

Canners are heavy. Once filled with water and full jars, the canner becomes extremely heavy and *could* cause the stove top to buckle under the weight. I would highly advise that a canner be emptied prior to moving it.

The heat cycles on and off. Many glass tops tend to cycle the heat on and off, which means the temperature of the water will fluctuate and therefore cannot guarantee a constant boil. The inability to hold the water temperature at the correct boiling point will result in goods not being processed correctly.

ALTERNATIVE HEAT SOURCES

If you choose not to utilize your glass top for hot water and pressure canning, there are alternatives. Keep in mind you will have to get acquainted with the following tools. The electrical current will run differently between propane and electricity, so I would suggest running a test batch in your hot water bath canner (see page 44) to ensure that the water reaches 212°F and holds that temperature for a minimum of 20 minutes.

Propane camp stove. We love our Camp Chef propane stove, and it has come in handy for various reasons. You can select from a single burner or multiple burner models. Just make sure you have a full propane tank and a spare tank handy before starting the canning process. This camp stove is excellent for canning outdoors during the summer months or in the garage during the winter months. Keep in mind, the garage door must be opened slightly to prevent CO_2 emissions from being a danger.

Tabletop burner. This is a perfect tool for those not interested in processing foods in an outdoor environment. For those with small homes or those who are looking for something compact, the tabletop burner is ideal. You have the option of butane or electrical, depending on whether you want to keep butane on hand or if you want the convenience of an electric plug-in. If selecting a butane burner, make sure the area is properly ventilated when in use.

CANNING METHODS NO LONGER PRACTICED AND WHY

Here is a list of preserving methods that the NCHFP states should no longer be practiced due to the inability to keep bacteria and botulism spores in check. There are individuals who still practice many of these traditional methods and as homesteaders we should know why they are no longer advised.

Self-sealing (also known as open kettle). This method relies on jars sealing themselves when they are filled with boiled food or liquid. The lid and ring are then wrenched on tightly. It's a method still commonly practiced, mainly when pickled items are being preserved. Though this method works to create a vacuum seal, the food within the jars has not been heated with the use of hot water or steam canner, ensuring the correct temperature for the allocated amount of time to be met to prevent bacteria growth within the jars.

Solar canning. This method uses the sun to heat a box, or solar oven, to process foods. The temperature and weather can be inconsistent, and dry heat is not a method that allows for proper heat penetration to kill any bacteria spores found in foods.

Compost canning. Jars of canned foods are placed into a compost bin with an internal temperature of more than 140°F for an extended period of time. Though the compost pile can maintain high temperatures to "cook," the compost is not capable of reaching a high enough temperature to penetrate the canned goods for a consistent period of time in order for the goods to be shelf stable.

Inversion canning. Jars that have been filled with boiled food or liquid are turned upside down with the band and lid on a flat surface. The goal is that the air will be forced out due to the jar being inverted, causing the lid to vacuum seal.

The NCHFP *does* list inversion canning as an option for processing jams and jellies. They do warn that the vacuum seal *may* not be as strong as one processed through a hot water bath or steam canner. The NCHFP also states that much oxygen is left in the jars which *may* cause mold issues. With that said, they are *not* stating this method is unsafe, just an unstable one.

Slow-cooker canning. Originally, many felt canning foods through a slow process such as using a slow cooker would retain most of its nutrient. Canning foods for a long, slow time allows bad bacteria to breed and grow rapidly.

Microwave canning. This method does not heat evenly, and the metal lids and rings cannot be microwaved.

Oven canning. The jars do not get hot enough and cannot maintain heat consistently. The dry heat found in the oven cannot provide the type of heat necessary such as a pressure, steam, or boiling water canner can.

Dishwasher canning. The theory is to utilize the steam during the sterilization time to process foods. This method does not work simply because the heat does not reach high enough temperatures to properly penetrate through the jar.

Hot water canning. This method refers to processing *all* foods, high and low in acidity, in a boiling water bath canner.

STORING HOME-CANNED GOODS

Finding storage for your canned goods can be a struggle for many, especially when root cellars are not available and you live in a small home with minimal space. Temperature also plays a role in proper storage. Then there is the ongoing debate on whether to store jars with the rings on or off.

How and where to store jars. The NCHFP states home-canned goods can be stacked, but I advise you to stack no more than two layers high, and put material, like cardboard, between the jars. If you need additional storage space, consider storing the jars under the bed, in other closets, on a baker's rack in the kitchen, or even in the garage.

The right temperature. Canned goods store best between 50 and 70°F. Storing them above 95°F can cause the goods to degrade in quality within a few weeks or months and spoil. If you're storing cans in a cold environment (like an unheated garage) which drops below 50°F, it is best to wrap them in newspaper, store them in heavy cardboard boxes, and cover them with blankets to prevent them from freezing. If the food should freeze in the jars, it won't spoil unless the lids become unsealed.

Should rings remain on the jars? This is a pretty hot topic for canners. Some will argue that the lids need to be removed to prevent a false seal (see page 28). Others, like myself, will sometimes keep the rings on the jars once they have been washed and dried. The National Center for Home Food Preservation states, "It is recommended that jars be stored without ring bands to keep them dry as well as to allow for easier detection of any broken vacuum seals. However, if you choose to reapply the ring bands, make sure all surfaces are clean and thoroughly dry first." The decision is yours to make.

WHY CANNING LIDS MAY NOT SEAL PROPERLY

As frustrating as it is, when a lid does not vacuum seal to the jar it helps to understand why. Since there are many variables, finding out why is done through the process of elimination. Here are a few tips to help you figure it out:

Headspace is incorrect. Make sure to allow for the correct headspace based on the recipe and item being canned. Too little headspace or too much headspace may leave either too little or too much room for a proper vacuum seal.

Air bubbles. During the canning process, food often settles. When the process of removing air bubbles is skipped, the air moves to the top of the jar, creating more space than what was initially intended.

HOW TO TELL IF A JAR HAS SEALED

Upon the completion of the cooldown process, which can take up to 24 hours, press the middle of the canning lid with a finger. If the lid springs up when you release your finger, the lid is not sealed. If the lid remains down, the lid has properly sealed. Do not attempt to touch the seal until after the jar has completely cooled or after the 24-hour mark.

Rim not cleaned. Cleaning the rim of the jars is an important step in ensuring that canning lids seal properly. Though wiping the rims with water and a clean towel is often enough, I suggest using distilled vinegar or even vodka to clean the rims to remove any food particles. When canning meat or foods high in fat, I tend to wipe the rims down with vodka to help remove the natural oils or grease, helping to ensure a proper seal.

Bad canning lids. If you have followed the steps necessary to ensure a proper seal, sometimes the issue is simply a bad batch of canning lids. Though this does not happen often, it does happen. The lids should be tossed, and the food items can either be canned again or stored in the refrigerator and eaten as soon as possible.

Overheating canning lids. The wax found on the bottoms of the lids only needs to be heated slightly to allow a proper seal and should never be placed into boiling water. Water that's too hot can remove the wax thereby preventing a seal. Simply placing lids into a mini slow cooker or warm water will soften the wax enough to create a good seal.

CAN JARS BE REPROCESSED IF THEY DID NOT SEAL?

You can try reprocessing unsealed jars as long as you do so within 12 hours from originally being processed. Check the jar for any breaks in the rim. If none are found, wipe the rim very well, and add a new warm lid and ring. Reprocess using the correct processing time as indicated in the original recipe. A bit of advice: Stick to reprocessing highly acidic items, *not* items that were pressure canned. Due to the length of time it takes to pressure can many goods, canning the jars again will result in produce becoming extremely soft. Meat and fish tend to become extremely dry.

If you are not interested in reprocessing unsealed jars, store them in the refrigerator and use them as quickly as possible.

USING RECYCLED JARS FOR CANNING

With careful use and storage, Mason jars can be reused for many years, requiring only new lids with each use. All jars should be checked for chips on the rim and cracks prior to use. Jars purchased from thrift stores or those that have been regifted should also be checked closely prior to use, as even the slightest chip on the rim will cause a lid to not seal properly. Keep in mind, used jars tend to weaken with continual use over the years and can crack easily while being processed.

Recycling and reusing are key factors in homesteading. The National Center for Home Food Preservation has stated that commercial glass pint- and quart-size mayonnaise or salad dressing jars can be used with new two-piece lids for canning in a hot water bath or steam canner but *not* in a pressure canner. They also warn to expect more seal failures and jar breakage if you choose to go this route.

If you are hesitant to give recycled glass jars a try, remember you can use them to store dehydrated and freeze-dried goods, though goods stored this way cannot be properly vacuum-sealed and will generally last only a year.

REUSING CANNING LIDS

Reusing canning lids is a bit more difficult to do, so I don't suggest it. If a lid is bent, it runs the risk of not creating a vacuum seal. Also, the sealing compound, once warmed, is designed to melt around the rim of the jar to create a tight fit.

Lids can be reused for storing dried goods, but I don't think I'd risk using them a second time for canning purposes. Well, unless there was a zombie apocalypse, then yes, I'd use them over again.

If you are looking to minimize waste when it comes to canning lids, I would suggest Tattler lids, which can be reused often.

DEEP-CLEANING MASON JARS

When using recycled jars, whether they are from a thrift store or from your own storage, make sure to sterilize them prior to use. Submerge the jars in boiling water with 1 cup distilled white vinegar (5 percent acidity) for 10 minutes. Pre-soaking the canning jars in distilled white vinegar and water for several hours will help to remove film caused by hard water left on jars.

THE USE OF DAIRY AND OIL IN HOME-CANNED GOODS

The one thing I have learned living a self-sustaining life is to not be wasteful. And in truth, preserving foods that contain milk, buttermilk, eggs, cheese, butter, and oil *can* cause an item to go rancid, which in turn causes waste. Keep in mind, dairy items are low-acidic food items and cannot be water canned in order to make them shelf stable.

SMALL-BATCH CANNING

Small-batch canning generally occurs when there is a minimal amount of goods that need to be preserved or when canning for small households.

Many recipes, though they may not state it, cater to small-batch canning, which generally means seven jars of goods at a time. Items such as pickled goods or chutney fall into this category. When preserving jams or jellies, follow the recipe based on the amount of pectin needed to allow the fruit to set. If you're interested in small-batch canning, I refer to a book on page 239 that is my go-to guide for this method.

Foods that are pressure canned can easily be done in a 10-quart pressure canner, which holds four pint-size jars. Simply adjust the portions into the appropriate number of jars needed.

RECIPES THAT MAKE YOU GO "HUH?"

Every once in a while, I come across a recipe that makes me scratch my head. Trust me, it's going to happen to you too. I'm a firm believer that what you do in your home is your business, but when you go out and share it, it becomes everyone's business.

So, what do you do when you come across a delicious, yet questionable, recipe? You have two options—move on and forget you saw it or educate yourself about the recipe. Personally, I advise newcomers to the world of canning to take said recipe and find one similar on the National Center for Home Food Preservation website. In truth, this is how I have learned so much about the world of canning. It is all about educating yourself and then deciding what you will do with all that knowledge.

If you are new to the canning world, I advise you to stick to what we call "tested recipes." These recipes have been tested by official government agencies to ensure that the proper pH balance is met, minimizing the risk of food-borne botulism being present in your home-canned goods. Once you are seasoned—and by seasoned I mean knowing which foods are naturally high in acid, knowing which foods cannot be water canned, and having a clear understanding of how spices, herbs, vinegars, and acid work to create and maintain a high pH balance—then and only then should you consider creating pickling brine, salsa, or canning homemade recipes. Jams, jellies, marmalades, infused vinegars, chutney, juice concentrates, and whole fruit are the easiest things to preserve.

With home recipes you will never get an accurate reading for the pH level. Home testing kits can present a close reading, but they're not 100 percent accurate. The choice is yours and only yours to make. My job is to give you knowledge on how to find this information.

THE SCIENCE OF PH BALANCE

If you are one of the privileged few who was given stories and recipes from family members who canned foods, feel honored. Store the recipes in a keepsake box and write down each story. Never forget that each item represents a survival skill from a world long gone.

Over time, we have learned that each food item being water canned must meet the required pH balance to prevent bacteria from forming. We've also learned that vegetables and all meat and fish are low in acidity and should not be water canned. You'll hear the term

acidity level mentioned quite a bit in the world of canning, especially when hot water bath canning is being used. Anything with a pH balance of 4.6 or below is considered safe to be water canned. Although vegetables are considered to be low in acid, many can safely be water canned *if* the acidity level can be increased. This is generally met by adding vinegar, which is 5 percent acid or higher creating a pickled item.

THE NASTY B WORD: BOTULISM

Any individual who preserves food through canning or who is wishing to learn will know this word. Be afraid of it, but do not let this nasty little word chase you away from canning.

Botulism is caused by a nerve toxin released by the bacterium, *Clostridium botulinum*, and is commonly known as food-borne botulism. Once the toxins have been consumed, symptoms of the poison can take anywhere from 6 hours to 10 days to present themselves, resembling flu-like symptoms. If these symptoms occur after consuming home preserved foods immediately consult a doctor.

Is there a way to guarantee that food-borne botulism will not occur in home-canned goods? Absolutely not. If it helps, botulism has virtually been eliminated in the United States, with fewer than one hundred fifty cases reported yearly. Out of the reported cases, only 15 percent (or twenty-two people per year) were food-borne.

There is a science to canning, yet much of it is common sense. Take your time to ask questions and do research. If something doesn't sound right, find out why. And always, *always,* follow this rule: when in doubt, throw it out. It is always better to be safe than sorry.

Now it's time to move on to what we set out to do: preserve some food!

HOW TO KEEP BOTULISM AWAY

By following a few simple guidelines, you will find that it is quite easy to keep botulism spores at bay. It's as simple as developing good habits and routines and keeping yourself educated with updates provided by such sites as the National Center for Home Food Preservation, Ball, and extension offices. Canning foods that meet proper pH levels is just one step in helping to manage and control botulism spores from forming. However, there are a few other steps such as:

Properly sanitize canning jars. Prior to filling your canning jars with bits of delicious goodness, make sure to take the time to sanitize them. The easiest way to sanitize jars is to run them through the dishwasher on the hot wash cycle and then allow them to dry on high heat. If you do not own a dishwasher, hand wash the jars with dish soap and hot water. The jars will then need to be boiled in hot water for a minimum of 10 minutes to ensure that any remaining bacteria are killed. The jars are kept in hot water and removed as needed. I find that working with no more than two or three jars at a time keeps the jars warm and perfect for hot packing.

The Jarden Company has recently stated that new jars do not need to be sterilized prior to use if food is processed at 212°F or higher for a minimum of 10 minutes. Processing time less than 10 minutes requires new jars to be sanitized prior to adding food.

Process foods properly. Foods which are not processed properly are at risk for carrying spores of the bacterium, *Clostidium botulium*. This bacterium grows quickly and excretes toxins in the absence of oxygen, making it vital to process foods properly.

Two LET'S TALK WATER CANNING

You know, to this day I can remember the first thing I ever canned and how awesome it was. I mean, pat-myself-on-the-back awesome. I felt invincible. Heck, I just made shelf-stable food in jars! I knew where this food was grown, how it was grown, and every ingredient that went into the jars! I was addicted immediately. Who would have thought that putting up raspberry jam could do that to a person?

There's no denying that my greatest reward was having my youngest child at my side helping me along the way. Isn't the intention to preserve food not only to reclaim our food source but also to teach our children how to do it as well? Over the years I've watched jams and jellies lathered onto peanut butter or added to freshly baked bread. Man, my children's messy faces filled my heart more than you could ever imagine.

Nothing beats opening the very first jar of Honey Crisp apple juice for the season. Over the years we have put up a lot of juice concentrate, but this juice is truly a favorite on our homestead. As a momma, I know that it contains no sugar other than the natural sugars found in the apples themselves. Can it *really* get any better than this? I think not.

Water bath canning is where it all starts, and in this chapter, I will tell you everything you need to know. Let me give you one tip right off the bat: put up foods that your family will consume. There are hundreds of recipes for preserves, pickles, and chutneys, and although they may all sound delicious, there is nothing more frustrating than seeing your hard work go uneaten.

WHAT CAN BE WATER CANNED

When I first started hot water bath canning, I was overwhelmed. Here is a list of the items that can be produced through water or steam canning:

- Jams
- Jellies
- Salsa
- Chutney
- Juice concentrate
- Whole fruit
- Marmalades
- Fruit butters
- Pickled items
- Infused vinegars

THE BASICS OF WATER CANNING

There is really nothing to hot water bath canning other than a pot, water, heat, and allowing the goods to process for the correct amount of time. That's all there is to the method, folks. It's easy peasy! Just in case you missed that, let me break it down a bit better.

TOOLS YOU'LL NEED

There are a few tools that will help make your hot water canning adventures a lot easier. Are they required? No, but trust me when I say convenience and preparation are everything. Here's what I use:

- Hot water bath or steam canner
- Mason jars of various sizes (half pints or pints preferred)
- Extra lids (you'll always have a stash of jar rings laying around)
- Jar lifter (tongs)
- Canning rack
- Heavy towel
- Permanent marker or fancy jar labels
- Digital timer

HOW TO USE A HOT WATER BATH CANNER

Each time I bring out the canner, I get giddy with excitement. It may be because I'm making food for my family, but I honestly think it is because I've removed myself a bit more from having to buy at the market. You gotta love that feeling of independence. Hot water bath canning is so easy that it becomes second nature by the second time you put up something. You'll feel like a pro!

The key is to be prepared and have all the items ready before you start. Steps can easily be missed if the tools are not visible when you begin, so take a minute to gather everything

needed. This will ensure that your time is used appropriately and the foods are preserved in a proper timeframe. Ready? Here we go. Trust me, you've got this.

1. Before you start preparing your food or brine, fill the water canner roughly three-quarters of the way with clean water. The amount of water may need to be adjusted to ensure that jars are appropriately covered by 1 to 2 inches of water.

2. As your water is preheating, begin food preparation.

3. Load the filled jars, with lid and ring attached, onto the canner rack. Using the handles, lower the rack into the water. Make sure to keep the jars upright. Fallen or tilted jars can cause food to spill into the sealing area of the lid, which can prevent a jar from sealing.

4. Make sure the water level covers the jars by at least 1 inch. For items that need to be processed longer than 30 minutes (tomatoes, for example), the jars must be covered by a minimum of 2 inches of water.

5. Set the heat to the highest position, cover the canner with its lid, and allow for the water to reach a hard boil, also known as a rolling boil.

6. Once the water has reached a hard boil, processing time may begin. Make sure the lid of the canner is on properly throughout the processing time.

7. If, by some freak of nature, the water stops boiling, you will have to start the process from the beginning. Reset your timer once a full boil has been reached.

8. For items being processed for more than 30 minutes, I would suggest checking the water level around the 20-minute mark and adding more boiling water. Keep a hot kettle on reserve if the water should need to be freshened; this will ensure the water reservoir will not run dry.

9. When the jars have processed for their appropriate time, turn off the heat and remove the canner lid. Allow the temperature to cool for roughly 5 minutes before removing jars.

10. Using a handy dandy jar lifter, remove the jars, place them onto a thick towel, and listen for the magical ping.

11. Allow the jars to cool at room temperature for 12 to 24 hours before removing the rings, and gently wash any residue from the jars.

12. Make sure to label the jars with the food content and the year. Fancy labels are great if you plan to give the preserves as gifts, but if using at home, tagging the lid with a permanent marker works just as well.

TIPS

- Remember, rings should be only finger tight and should not be tightened. The rings are there to hold the lids in place and prevent them from floating away in the canner. Rings which are wrenched on tightly can prevent the air from exiting the jars, hindering the sealing process.
- Adding a splash of distilled vinegar to the water within the canner will keep the jars sparkling clean and free of residue during the processing time.
- Do not boil canning lids. Simply warm them in hot water or in a mini slow cooker to soften the paraffin wax on the ring.

STORING RINGS

Once you have been canning for a while, you will build up a nice collection of jar rings. Realistically, you do not need to keep every ring, just enough to cover what you plan to open.

How many to keep can range from ten to twenty rings, which can easily be stored in a container, kitchen drawer, or tied together with a string and hung in the pantry.

Some people store their jars with the rings on while others do not, thinking it can cause a false seal, allowing oxygen to enter the jars, creating an environment for bacteria growth and spoilage.

The National Center for Home Food Preservation advises that jars can be stored with the rings on as long as you confirm the lids have maintained a vacuum seal. I allow the rings to rest finger tight on jars, leaving room for the lids to unseal if the jars should lose their vacuum seal.

SELECTING THE CORRECT FRUITS

One of the easiest guarantees for keeping botulism spores away while using the HWB method is to put up foods that are naturally high in acid. Many fruits happen to fall into this category. Parts of the fruit, such as watermelon rinds, have been used to make pickled items, chutney, and even relish, but these items must meet the acidity level in order to become shelf stable. Acidity lifters such as bottled lemon juice, lime juice, or citric acid will assist in increasing the pH balance in such items.

Lettuce does not retain its flavor or shape and should be eaten fresh instead of canned. Kohlrabi becomes bitter and discolored when canned. It can be dehydrated or frozen.

INCREASING ACIDITY LEVELS IN VEGETABLES

Vegetables are low in acid, yet many can be HWB canned if the acidity level is lifted by using 5 percent vinegar, citric acid, or bottled citrus juice. In short, you are creating a pickled item or chutney when a vegetable is being HWB or steam canned. Pickled carrots and green beans are staples on our homestead as delicious and healthy snacks for the kids. Let's not forget to mention that pickled asparagus makes the perfect partner for a Bloody Mary!

BOILING WATER BATH CANNING VERSUS STEAM CANNING

When a HWB canner is selected as a means of preserving, foods that are high in acidity can be processed to be shelf stable. Hot water bath canning is extremely easy. Jars are submerged in a pot of boiling water for the appropriate length of time to ensure that all oxygen is removed from the food items.

In 2015 the FDA approved another hot water canning tool for use by home canners. World, let me introduce you to my favorite new tool—the steam canner. This tool is ideal if you are looking to minimize the amount of water being used during the canning process and during the summer months when the temperature in your home is unbearable. Not to mention, it is quite a bit gentler on the burners of your stove and ideal for those with a glass top stove. Over the years the steam canner has been my choice of tool for all items high in acidity, leaving my hot water bath canner gathering dust on the shelf. I often encourage individuals new to canning to investigate the steam canner, as the benefits outweigh a hot water bath canner.

A steam canner uses roughly 2 inches of water and preserves foods using steam. The steam reaches 212°F (100°C), thus providing the same sterilizing heat as boiling water. The processing time for goods in a steam canner is the same as for a HWB canner, yet the steam canner

LOW-ACID FRUITS

Many of the items on this list can be used in jams, jellies, marmalades, chutneys, and even salsa. Bananas can be used as an ingredient in preserves but should not be canned independently or pureed prior to canning due to how dense they become. The density of pureed or crushed bananas prevents heat or steam from penetrating through the fruit. Melons, including watermelon, should be used as an ingredient in recipes like chutney or relishes, or they should be pickled.

- Asian pears and pears
- Bananas
- Berries (including blueberries, blackberries, dewberries, huckleberries, loganberries, mulberries, elderberries, gooseberries, raspberries, currants, strawberries)
- Coconut
- Figs
- Mango (ripe)
- Melons
- Papaya
- Peaches and Nectarines
- Pineapple
- Plums
- Rhubarb

is much more efficient, saving water and energy costs. The steam canner is capable of processing foods for up to 45 minutes; anything over 45 minutes will require the use of a HWB canner.

This canner is capable of canning half-pint, pint, and quart jars, as well as, sampler-size jelly jars. The processing time for sampler jars would be the same as half pint jars.

HOW TO USE A STEAM CANNER

A steam canner is an easy canning tool to use. Here are the basic steps:

1. Place the bottom rack that comes with the steam canner into the bottom pan.

2. Fill the canner with the recommended amount of water, never exceeding above the bottom rack.

3. Place the jars onto the bottom rack and add the dome lid.

4. Allow the steamer to heat up, then vent steam from the holes in the lid until you see a solid, unbroken column of steam.

5. Once the unbroken column of steam is solid, start the processing time. The processing time will be the same as what is recommended for a hot water bath canner.

6. Make sure the column of steam is unbroken throughout the entire processing time.

7. Maintain the heat to regulate the column of steam. If the heat is set too low, you risk the chance of breaking the column of steam. If the heat is set too high, you may run out of water within 20 minutes.

8. If you should lose the strong column of steam during the processing time, you will have to begin the processing time again, starting the time once a strong column of steam is visible.

9. Upon the completion of processing, turn off the burner, allow the steam to evaporate, and remove the cover.

ITEMS THAT CAN BE PICKLED BUT NOT PRESSURE CANNED

Here is a list of items that can be pickled and then HWB or steam canned but should not be pressure canned:

- Artichokes
- Broccoli
- Brussels sprouts
- Cauliflower
- Cabbage
- Eggplant
- Olives
- Summer squash

10. Allow the jars to rest undisturbed in the canner with the cover off for 5 to10 minutes.

11. Remove the jars from the canner, and place them on a towel or dish mat for 12 to 24 hours.

12. Once cooling time has been met, check the seals, wash the jars, label them, and store the canned goods.

HOW TO STEAM FARM-FRESH EGGS IN YOUR CANNER

Freshly laid eggs can be hard to peel. Here's how to cook them perfectly in your steam canner. (Methods on how to preserve your perfectly steamed eggs can be found in later chapters.)

1. Using the steam canner, add 2 inches of water.
2. Place a vegetable or bamboo steamer onto the canning rack, making sure the water remains below the canning rack. Add those beautiful farm-fresh eggs.
3. Add the canner lid and allow the water to come to a hard boil. Once a steady stream escapes from the lid, begin the timer, allowing the eggs to steam for 21 minutes to achieve the perfect hard boil.
4. Once complete, turn off the stove, and allow the steam to evaporate. Immediately submerge the eggs in a bowl of ice water to stop the cooking process. Allow the eggs to cool prior to peeling.

Eggs can also be steamed using a shallow 8-quart pot and steaming basket. Insert the basket in the shallow pot, making sure the water remains below the basket. Bring the water to a boil and add eggs. Cover with a lid and allow to steam for 21 minutes. Immediately submerge the eggs in a bowl of ice water to stop the cooking process. Allow the eggs to completely cool prior to peeling.

STEAM JUICERS

Using a steam juicer has revolutionized how I now put up jelly on my homestead. Gone are the days of boiling the fruit and then hanging it in a jelly bag to extract the juices. Though I am thankful to have learned this traditional method, I am even more thankful to leave it in the past. Making jelly can be a daunting task, which is why I rarely made it prior to owning the steam juicer.

Oh, but wait, the liquid extracted from the fruit can also be used to make wine! We aren't wine drinkers here, but if you're interested, information on how to transform the juice concentrate into wine can be found online.

Once canning season has come to an end, utilize the steam juicer for steaming produce and meat for meals, as well as to steam farm-fresh eggs. It's a great tool and should not be reserved for canning season only!

As a homesteader, I welcome tools that allow me to get the job done in a timely, easy manner; and though time is valuable, the presentation of the overall product is just as important. Jelly should contain no fruit sediment. Rather, it should be crystal clear and have the full flavor of the fruit. This is exactly what the steam juicer provides.

Once the juice has been extracted from the fruit, what remains is called the "pulp," and it is just as valuable

HOW MUCH JUICE CONCENTRATE CAN I EXPECT?

How much juice concentrate you will be able to extract will vary based on the type of fruit you select and how ripe it is. The colander of the steam juicer can hold roughly 11 quarts of fruit. Feel free to load that baby up!

fruit	quantity needed	processing time	yield
APPLES	10 pounds	1½–2 hours	3–4 quarts
APRICOTS	1 pound	1–1½ hours	1–1½ cups
BERRIES	1 quart	60–80 minutes	2–3 cups
CHERRIES	1 quart	1 hour	2 cups
CHOKECHERRIES	1 quart	1 hour	2–3 cups
CRABAPPLES	10 pounds	1½–2 hours	3–4 quarts
CRANBERRIES	1 quart	1 hour	1½–2 cups
GRAPES	1 quart	1 hour	2–3 cups
PEACHES	1 pound	1–1½ hours	1–1½ cups
PEARS	1 pound	1½–2 hours	1–1½ cups
RHUBARB	1 pound	1½–2 hours	1½–2 cups
PLUMS	1 pound	1–1½ hours	1–2 cups
TOMATOES	1 pound	1 hour	1–2 cups

The timeframe listed above is a great guideline to follow for extracting every ounce of juice from the fruit. Once I became acquainted with the steam juicer, I shortened the processing time, allowing the pulp to retain more flavor. I transform the pulp into butters, sauce, or fruit leather.

You'll need to monitor the water level of the steam juicer. This will be difficult because the other compartments are filled with fruit and liquid. By adding a few marbles to the water compartment, you will be able to monitor the water level. When the marbles start to rattle, it's time to add water!

The most important advice I can leave you with is this: *Never* allow the water tank to run dry. It will damage your pan and leave the liquid and fruit pulp with a burnt, smoky flavor that may ruin the batch.

as the juice. If you are into creating zero waste, you can use the mush from apples to make applesauce (see page 196) or the pulp from hard stone fruit, like cherries, to make fruit leather bites.

Let's backtrack and talk about how to HWB can the juice produced by your juice steamer. The juice is considered a concentrate containing nothing but fruit juice and an optional amount of sugar. Sugar is added for two reasons. The first is to create a ready-to-drink beverage. Sugar also acts as a preservative, allowing the concentrate a longer shelf life. How much sugar to add will depend on the ripeness of the fruit and your personal preference. Generally, ¼ to 1 cup sugar is added to the fruit prior to beginning the steaming process. However, the sugar can be added to the jar as the concentrate is being released from the reservoir. How much sugar in each jar will depend on you. I add between ⅛ to ¼ teaspoon sugar per quart jar.

HOW TO USE A STEAM JUICER

The steam juicer consists of three working parts: the colander, the reservoir, and the water compartment. The process for extracting the juice from the fruit or vegetable is done using steam, producing a crystal-clear product with no sediment.

1. Fill the bottom compartment of the steam juicer with water. Allow the water to maintain a steady boil.

2. Next add the middle part, which is called the *reservoir*. Make sure the food-grade tube is facing you, allowing the juice to be extracted into pint- or quart-size jars.

3. The top part is the *colander*. Washed whole fruits or vegetables are added to this part. There is no need to peel or slice, or remove the stems, seeds, or pits.

4. Do not stir or press the fruit during the steaming process. Doing so will force the pulp and skins into the juice.

5. Use caution when releasing the juice into jars. The liquid is extremely hot and can cause injury if you are not careful.

6. Jelly can be made right away from the juice concentrate, or the jars can be processed as is.

SWEETENERS

Jam, jellies, fruit butters, and marmalades are meant to be sweet, and if they are not, then it's just fruit juice in a jar. Keep in mind, sugar is a preservative and adding sugar creates a longer shelf-stable item.

When it comes to pickled items, unless you *love* vinegar, it is good to balance the vinegar by adding a sweetener. Luckily for us, sweeteners such as refined or unrefined sugar,

Simple syrup for preserving whole fruit can be made with water and sugar.
Heat the water and sugar together, bringing them to a boil. The table below is for nine pint-size jars.
Any extra syrup can be stored in the refrigerator to be used later.

sweetness level	water-to-sugar ratio	makes
VERY LIGHT SYRUP	1 cup sugar to 4 cups water	4½ cups syrup
LIGHT SYRUP	2 cups sugar to 4 cups water	5 cups syrup
MEDIUM SYRUP	3 cups sugar to 4 cups water	5½ cups syrup
HEAVY SYRUP	4¾ cups sugar to 4 cups water	6½ cups syrup

There are many alternatives to using refined sugar; however, some can change the flavor and color of your final product. For example, coconut sugar will give the canned product a molasses flavor and will tint it slightly brownish. If this does not bother you, feel free to experiment with other options.

Substitutions for 1 Cup Refined Sugar

¾ cup honey	¼ cup maple syrup	1 cup coconut sugar
⅔ cup agave nectar	⅓–½ teaspoon stevia	24 packs Splenda

honey, or stevia help to provide natural sweetness to the items we are canning. Refined sugar has gotten a bad rap, but in truth it does a great job in providing the necessary flavor and creating a longer shelf stable item.

If you are set against using refined sugar, even an organic one, unrefined sugars are a good alternative. Sugars such as honey, agave nectar, maple syrup, stevia, and even Splenda will do an excellent job in providing sweetness in jams, jellies, marmalade, canned whole fruit, and pickled items.

Though Splenda can be used as a substitute for refined sugar, it should be reserved to use when preserving whole fruits and not in jams, jellies, or even marmalades. This is because whole fruit is canned in a sugar water solution also known as "simple syrup." Splenda should only be used to create a simple syrup in the canning process and not as a sugar substitute in a recipe.

PECTIN

Pectin is a gelatin used in making jams, jellies, and marmalade to help the item set, also known as *gelling*. Pectin can easily be found in the canning section of your local market and is available in a liquid or powder form. How much pectin is needed will be based on the type of fruit being canned and how many cups of fruit you are preserving.

Avoid presoaking fruit and vegetables in water. This will dilute the pectin and natural acid found in the fruit. Instead, quickly dunk or wipe down the produce with a damp paper towel to wash it. Keep in mind that boiling water sterilizes the product.

However, some fruits, like raspberries, are naturally high in pectin and do not require the assistance of added pectin. Fruits that are slightly underripe are high in pectin and work best if you are looking to preserve a pectin-free item. Other fruits high in natural pectin are apricots, rhubarb, and Italian prunes.

Unlike regular pectin, low-sugar pectin is available for those who wish to watch their sugar intake. Low-sugar pectin is ideal to eliminating all sugar or to minimize the amount suggested. Fruit that is on the sweeter side is a great candidate for a low-sugar pectin since a minimal amount of sugar will be needed.

Pomona pectin, which contains no preservatives, is another great option, though not a favorite of mine. I've had a hard time determining the right amount to use to get jelly or jam to set properly, and the pectin is on the pricey side. Also keep in mind, preserves processed with Pomona pectin do not last as long when they are opened versus preserves using other pectin alternatives. Even so, there are people who love it and swear by it.

As I've mentioned, unripe fruit is higher in pectin and can be added to jams and jellies to help set the product. For example, if you are canning strawberry jam, add a few unripe berries to the cooking process along with your pectin to help ensure that the product jells.

Sometimes jams or jellies will not set. Don't be discouraged. They make amazing glazes for pork, chicken, or beef!

HOMEMADE APPLE PECTIN

There will come a time when you'll want to create items rather than purchase them from the market. Luckily, making your own pectin is one of those things.

INGREDIENTS

Unripe apples or crabapples, as many as
    you can get your hands on
White vinegar
Water

METHOD

1. Wash the apples in a white vinegar and water solution (1:2 ratio), allowing them to soak for 30 minutes to clean and kill any bugs.
2. Quarter the apples, leaving the seeds and skin. These items contain high amounts of natural pectin and will assist in creating a great product.
3. Add the apples to a stainless steel stockpot, and fill with water. Add just enough water to barely cover the apples. Too much water will dilute the pectin.
4. Cook on low for about 12 hours. Avoid stirring the apples, as this will release sediment and make it difficult to strain. Once the apples begin to resemble applesauce, your apple pectin is done, or close to being done, and is ready to be tested for consistency.
5. Remove a small amount of the pectin, and allow it to cool completely. Using a small dish, add a small amount of rubbing alcohol and a small amount of the cooled pectin. If the pectin coagulates into a jelly-like consistency and can be picked up with a fork, it is done and can be used as pectin in preserves. If it remains in a liquid form, continue to boil the apples for another few hours and try the test again.
6. Using a fine mesh strainer and a coffee filter, begin straining the liquid into half-pint- or pint-size jars, leaving a ¼ inch of headspace.
7. Process the jars in a HWB or steam canner for 15 minutes.

VINEGAR AND CITRUS OPTIONS

When it comes to raising the acidity level in canned foods there is a plethora of vinegars and citrus options available on the market. The most important factor when it comes to canning is that the acidity level for these items must be 5 percent or higher. Each brand of vinegar will have its own unique flavor. Some may be stronger than others. If you have a sensitive palate, as I do, you might be inclined not to experiment with vinegar options.

Much like vinegar, there are a few options when it comes to increasing the acidity with a citrus product. There is no right or wrong way when it comes to choosing the type to use. It will depend on your preference.

CHOOSING THE RIGHT VINEGAR

When using vinegar, make sure to select one that is 5 percent or higher in acidity. There are a few brands out there that fall short of meeting this standard, and I strongly suggest you carefully read the labels on the bottles. If the acidity level is 5 percent or higher, you can choose from white distilled, apple cider, white wine, red wine, rice, and even balsamic vinegars.

There's no point in using *raw* apple cider vinegar to pickle foods. First, it's expensive, and second, the beneficial health qualities will be lost when heated. Homemade apple cider vinegar should also not be used in canning because the acidity level cannot be tested.

WHITE DISTILLED AND APPLE CIDER VINEGAR

White vinegar, also known as distilled vinegar, works well if you are planning to preserve quite a bit of a particular item. The cost is low, and overall it does a great job. Distilled vinegar works well for preserving lighter-colored fruits and vegetables (for example, cauliflower) and creates a nice presentation.

Apple cider vinegar (ACV) has a much different flavor than white vinegar, and in truth, I do not use it often unless I've run out of white vinegar. But hey, you might love the flavor, so go with it! What it really boils down to is taste preference, and to be honest, some pickling recipes work better with ACV.

BALSAMIC VINEGAR

Balsamic vinegars that are 5 percent or higher are great options to use for canning specialty items. There is nothing quite as perfect as pickled beets in a balsamic and thyme brine. Nothing. Due to the cost of balsamic vinegar you may want to reserve it for small-batch canning. Anything pickled in a balsamic brine has a very sophisticated flavor that partners well with various meats and salads.

CITRIC ACID, BOTTLED CITRUS JUICE, AND FRESH LEMON OR LIME JUICES

To help keep fruits, like apples, from browning as you are prepping them for canning, place the slices into a bowl of water with a small amount of either bottled or fresh citrus juice, or a citric acid.

Bottled citrus juice, such as lemon or lime, works well to guarantee that acid levels are met while working with sugar to assist in allowing pectin to set. How much citrus juice needed will depend on the recipe. Even if you're not a fan of citrus, I can guarantee (almost) that you will not taste the sourness of the juice as it balances the sweetness of the jam.

You may come across a few pickling brines that call for both vinegar and citrus, and that is completely okay! The citrus blends well with the vinegar, herbs, and spices in the brine while raising the acidity level.

Fresh citrus juice is lower in acidic content than bottled citrus juice. As you are searching for pickling recipes you may come across one that calls for fresh lemons, like our pickled asparagus (see page 70). Keep in mind, the brine I use in the pickled asparagus recipe also contains white wine vinegar with a 5 percent acidity level in addition to bottled lemon juice. Marmalade recipes (even though they are made of citrus) require bottled citrus juice to reach the correct pH balance.

Citric acid is a manufactured product that can be used as an alternative to bottled lemon or lime juice in the canning process. It is a powder substitute found in the canning section of your local market, and it also works as an emulsifying agent. You will see the word *emulsify* often as you are fact-checking recipes. Emulsifying agents are not only preservatives, but they also prevent food from breaking down and spoiling.

THICKENING AGENTS

There's something special about homemade pies. Well, at least that's what my husband, Justin, tells me. But if you're like me, there are times when making a pie from scratch isn't an option. What is an option? Going into the pantry and grabbing a jar of already prepared pie filling. Pie filling is a great way to put up bushels of fruit when they are in season, and making it shelf stable is quite easy to do. The trick is the thickening agent you use.

CORNSTARCH AND FLOUR

It was once common to use cornstarch or flour as thickening agents for home-canned goods due to the simple fact that it was all that was available. Pie filling and stews are canned not only to preserve the harvest but because of the convenience they provide.

> Other thickeners such as tapioca and arrowroot are excellent gluten-free thickeners for cooking, although, like cornstarch and flour, they should not be used for canning.

Even then, canners noticed that the quality of the food being canned with flour or cornstarch wasn't great. As the canned goods sat on shelves, the consistency of the food started to gum up, get lumpy, or even turn into a solid mass that couldn't be easily removed from the jars. As a novice to the canning world, I learned this lesson the hard way.

It was eventually discovered that cornstarch and flour were both too thick to allow the heat to properly penetrate through the jar, preventing the heat from killing any bacteria or removing the oxygen from within the jar. Is it risky to use these products? Yes. Is it a guarantee that botulism spores will form from using these products in canning? No. However, if there was an alternative item to use why not give it a try?

INTRODUCING CLEAR JEL

In the late 1980s, the USDA approved a thickening agent called Clear Jel for canning. In addition to Clear Jel, products such as Therm-Flo and Perma-Flo have been approved as thickeners to be used for home canned good. Clear Jel, Therm-Flo, and Perma-Flo are products known as a modified cornstarch and should not to be mistaken for regular cornstarch. Unlike regular cornstarch and flour, Clear Jel allows the heat to thoroughly penetrate the jar, making it a great option to use when canning stews, chili, soups, and pie filling.

HOW DOES CLEAR JEL WORK?

During the heating process, as the food is being prepared or while it is in the canner, Clear Jel starch remains in a jelly-like consistency. Once the canned item has cooled completely, Clear Jel reaches its maximum level of thickness, making the jars of preserved foods exactly what they were intended for—instant quick meals or fillings.

> When filling a jar that contains Clear Jel, leave roughly 2 inches of headspace. The product in the jar will expand as the jar cools.

You may have a family apple pie recipe that contains a thickener like cornstarch or flour. Don't toss the recipe. Instead substitute Clear Jel and continue to pass the recipe down for generations to come!

What if you don't want to use Clear Jel, Therm-Flo, Perma-Flo, and other thickening agents? What are your options? Is it necessary to add thickeners in the canning process? If you don't, does this affect the pH level?

Thickeners do not alter the pH balance in canned goods and they do not have to be used for canning. Instead, thickening agents can be added once the jar is opened. Regardless, the final product is just as delicious!

WHERE TO PURCHASE REGULAR CLEAR JEL

When you search for Clear Jel, you will need to make sure of one thing, the product you're looking for is *regular* Clear Jel, *not* instant. The instant version is good for cooking and to thicken meals that are *not* being canned.

Clear Jel can be hard to find and is rarely in stock at your local market. With that said you will have better luck finding in online, at an Amish market, and locations which sell canning supplies *may* also carry it. This is a bit discouraging, I know, but the product is worth having. Clear Jel keeps well for roughly a year, making a 2-pound container enough for our homestead.

CLEAR JEL CONVERSION CHART

Again, Clear Jel expands once it has cooled. Being conservative with the amount suggested is wise until you are comfortable using it.

1 tablespoon cornstarch = 1½ tablespoons Clear Jel

2 tablespoons flour/tapioca flour = 1 tablespoon Clear Jel

THE TRUTH ABOUT "HOME-CANNED" CAKES

Now that we've covered pie filling, let's talk about canning cake and other desserts. If you spend any time online, you've probably seen links to canning cake or dessert bread in half-pint jars. They are cute and delicious, and make for great party desserts, but I have to tell you that they're not actually canned items and are not shelf-stable. Let me tell you why.

The "canning" instructions for canned cake or dessert bread, like banana or zucchini, states that the batter should be baked in half-pint Mason jars until cooked. Once the jars have been removed from the oven, the lids and rings are immediately added to the hot jars using force to tighten the ring (see self-sealing on page 31). Though the jars may "ping" indicating that the lids have sealed, there are a few things to consider:

- The oxygen has not been removed from the jar since it has not been HWB or steam canned. This leaves room for bacteria to grow.
- Cake batter is too dense to properly allow the heat to penetrate through the jar, again, not properly killing any possible bacteria.
- The moisture within the jar leaves room for bad bacteria to grow into toxic spores such as botulism. Will botulism spores present themselves each time? No, not always. But is this something you want to chance? I don't.

Does this mean that these adorable little cakes in jars are unsafe? Absolutely not! Allowing the jars to completely cool prior to adding the lid and ring will minimize any possible risks of bad bacteria being present within the jar. The dessert in a jar will need to be stored in the refrigerator for short-term storage or in the freezer to be enjoyed later.

SPICES AND HERBS

Herbs and spices add flavor to foods being cooked or canned. Herbs such as bay leaf, parsley, dill, thyme, and oregano are favorites among canners. Spices such as peppercorns, mustard seeds, cloves, or blends work wonders in creating fabulous preserved items. Canned goods should have as much flavor as foods prepared fresh. There's no point to being boring in food preservation!

As a homesteader, I find great pleasure in being able to use herbs grown on our property. Picking and drying herbs is just another part of being a self-sustaining family. Those who receive our canned goods know that

most of what went into the jar was grown with love on our homestead. Adding spices and herbs to canned foods creates an overall better product. Isn't that what it's all about?

DANDELION FLOWER JELLY

The novelty of making dandelion flower jelly never seems to wear off, and I have since passed this recipe to my children, who are now responsible for making it each year. This little yellow herb, or weed depending on how you view it, produces a jelly that is very similar to honey and is quite fabulous. Pack up the kids and head down to the nearest pasture. The dandelions are calling to be picked!

INGREDIENTS

3 cups Dandelion Petal Tea
  (see recipe below)
1 (1.75-ounce) box pectin
Jalapeño peppers (optional)
2 tablespoons lemon juice
4½ cups granulated sugar

METHOD

1. Bring to boil the dandelion tea, pectin, jalapeño peppers (if using), and lemon juice.

2. Add the sugar and return to a hard boil, stirring often for 2 minutes.
3. Remove from the heat, and skim the foam from the liquid.
4. Fill half-pint jars, leaving a ¼-inch headspace.
5. Can for 10 minutes in a hot water bath canner (adjust the processing time for altitude above 1,001 feet in elevation; see page 65).

DANDELION PETAL TEA

INGREDIENTS

4-5 cups dandelion petals
Water

METHOD

1. In a heatproof glass container, place the petals and cover them with boiling water.
2. Cover the container with a clean dish towel. Allow to steep for a few hours or overnight.

3. Use a fine strainer lined with a coffee filter to sieve the petals from the tea.

Note: It is important to use only the petals of the flower head for the tea, as any green will cause the tea to become very bitter.

It's important to thoroughly clean vegetables and fruit prior to canning or dehydrating it. This can easily be done using two techniques with a little water and distilled vinegar. Fruits with smooth surfaces (apples and tomatoes) can be sprayed using a spray bottle: add 1 cup distilled vinegar to 3 cups of water. Spray the entire produce and rinse with cold water. Items such as leafy greens and produce with textured outer surfaces will need to be pre-washed in a solution of 3 cups vinegar to a sink of water. Dunk leafy greens into the cleaning solution, then rinse with cold water, whereas textured fruit and vegetables will need to be soaked for at least 2 minutes prior to rinsing in cold water.

DRIED HERBS AND SPICES

Most beginning canners are advised to stick to recipes that have been tested and not waver from them. These recipes guarantee that the pH balance has met expectations to ensure that the acidity level is correct, minimizing any possibility that bacteria will form in home-preserved jars. I'm not going to lie, this advice frustrated me when I first started out. I knew full well that my family wouldn't enjoy some of the herbs and spices listed in these recipes and would turn up their noses the minute I opened a jar.

Thankfully, Ball loosened the reins in 2014 and encouraged canners to experiment by substituting or adding dried herbs and spices to foods being canned, explaining that this would not change the pH balance of foods being preserved. The USDA and Extension Service also publicly announced that dried herbs (not *fresh*) and spices could be altered or completely left out of recipes. Can I tell you what this did to the foods we put up? We began to enjoy the foods we canned so much more because we could now season them the way we liked.

Let me give you a few tips about using dried herbs and spices. By the way, this is an ongoing discussion between Justin and me. You see, Justin loves foods that are highly seasoned and constantly insists that more seasoning be added to the foods we put up. I always disagree with him, but there is a reason why. The longer the jars are shelved, the more the dried herbs and spices amplify in flavor, and this can alter the taste of the preserved foods. To avoid this problem, I use seasoning sparingly. My rule of thumb is to use ¼ teaspoon herbs per pint-size jar, making any adjustment necessary at the time the recipe is used once the jar is opened.

FRESH HERBS

As you begin water canning, you are bound to come across recipes that contain fresh herbs. Heck, there are even approved tested recipes that contain fresh herbs. Fresh herbs contain water, which, once cooked, can offset the pH balance by diluting the acidity level of the vinegar or citrus juice, opening the door for potential growth of bacteria. In truth, we as home food preservers have no way of telling how much water fresh herbs may contain.

Canning salsa is a topic of discussion for many canners and canning sites, and these discussions often get heated. The argument consists of whether it is a viable claim that fresh herbs should not be used. Are the USDA and Extension Service being extreme in their decision against fresh herbs in canning? Maybe, maybe not. The key to making the decision to use or not use fresh herbs is to understand the science behind it. I have used fresh herbs in my hot water bath goods, and the amount I use is kept to a bare minimum. The NCHFP teaches against it, fearing that individuals will not be cautious in how they use fresh herbs in foods being preserved.

The Canadian Living Complete Preserving Book, written by a Canadian food-preserving agency, includes fresh herbs in home-canned goods recipes. The company states that each recipe in the book has been sent out for testing and has met the proper pH and shelf-stable guidelines, following USDA and Jarden (the parent company of Ball/Bernadin) standards.

With that said, there are a plethora of canning recipes using fresh herbs that have been tested, and in truth, many of them are quite good. The only way to know for sure is to try them out. If for some reason the flavor is lacking once a jar has been opened, feel free to add to it, whip out additional seasoning, or add some fresh cilantro, basil, or thyme. Anything can be made better at mealtime.

SIMPLE GARDEN SALSA

Garden salsa is an item you will want to put up every year. There is no doubt about it. When you can walk through your garden and gather up all the ingredients, you will be extremely proud that you are about to make a lot of people happy.

2 cups vinegar (5% acid)
1 teaspoon ground cumin
1 tablespoon dried Mexican oregano
1 tablespoon chopped fresh cilantro
1½ teaspoons salt (pickling, sea, or kosher)

METHOD

1. Combine all ingredients in a large, heavy-bottom saucepan and bring to a boil.
2. Stir frequently to prevent the bottom from scorching.
3. Reduce the heat and simmer 20 minutes, stirring occasionally.
4. Fill pint jars, making sure to remove all the air bubbles. Apply the lids, making sure to clean the rims of the jars.
5. Use a hot water bath for 15 minutes (adjust the processing time for altitudes above 1,001 feet; see page 65).

INGREDIENTS

4 cups peeled, cored, and chopped tomatoes
2 cups seeded and chopped jalapeño peppers
½ cup chopped onions
4 cloves garlic, finely chopped

PICKLING SALT, SEA SALT, KOSHER SALT, AND TABLE SALT

Unlike other methods of preserving (for example, fermenting and curing), using salt in home canning is for flavor and is not necessary to prevent spoilage, nor will it alter the pH balance if left out. This is excellent news for individuals who are watching their sodium intake.

Salt is required in fermentation and curing (which I will talk about later in the book) or when you're preparing a pickling brine. Much like dried herbs and spices, minimizing the amount of salt will prevent jarred foods from intensifying in flavor as they sit in the pantry.

Pickling salt (also known as canning salt), kosher salt, and sea salt are perfect choices to use in home preserving. These salts do not contain anticaking ingredients and will dissolve nicely once heated into a clear liquid, making the overall presentation picture perfect.

Table salt, or iodized salt, is an optional salt to use in home canning. It usually does contain anticaking additives, which can make a brine cloudy and produce sediment at the bottom of a jar. Moral to the story? Unless you're entering your canned items into the state fair and are worried about presentation, table salt is fine to use in canning.

EQUIVALENTS FOR 1 TABLESPOON TABLE SALT

1 tablespoon + ¾ teaspoon kosher salt

1 tablespoon coarse sea salt

½–1 tablespoon fine sea salt

1 tablespoon pickling salt

BOILING WATER BATH AND STEAM CANNER ALTITUDE CHART

Most recipes will reflect the processing time for 1,000 feet altitude or below. If you reside above 1,000 feet, adjust the processing time by adding time to the allocated processing time.

Altitude above Sea Level	Additional Processing Time
1,001–3,000 feet	Add 5 minutes
3,001–6,000 feet	Add 10 minutes
6,001–8,000 feet	Add 15 minutes
8,001–10,000 feet	Add 20 minutes

Many recipes do not work well when doubled. It's best to follow recipes to a tee to ensure the goods being preserved will set properly.

OUR FAMILY'S FAVORITE WATER CANNING RECIPES

Oh, my word, I could talk about water canning recipes all day. My family has a love for everything that can be water canned, I kid you not. Who can deny a delicious pickle that remains crunchy or the perfect preserve to be enjoyed not only at breakfast but throughout the day? We tend to put up the same items every year, but sometimes I like to throw in something new.

With that said, allow me to share with you some of our favorite HWB recipes. Enjoy, friends!

COWBOY CANDY

This sweet pickled jalapeño is fabulous! It can be added to *anything*, especially brats and burgers or goat cheese and crackers. You will not regret adding this item to your pantry, and it truly makes a great gift.

INGREDIENTS

3 pounds fresh jalapeño peppers
2 cups apple cider vinegar (5% acidity)
6 cups granulated sugar
½ teaspoon turmeric powder
½ teaspoon celery seed
3 teaspoons granulated garlic

METHOD

1. Wearing gloves, slice the jalapeño peppers into ¼-inch rounds and set them aside. We use a mandoline.

2. In a large stockpot, add the apple cider vinegar, sugar, turmeric powder, celery seed, and garlic and bring to a boil.

3. Reduce the heat and simmer for 5 minutes. Add the sliced jalapeño peppers to the hot brine and allow to simmer for 5 minutes.

4. Using a slotted spoon, scoop the jalapeño peppers into half-pint jars.

5. Bring the remaining brine to a hard boil for 5 minutes.

6. Using a ladle, add the hot brine to the jars. Leave a ¼-inch headspace, remove the air bubbles, and add the lids and rings.

7. Process in a boiling water canner or steam canner for 10 minutes. If using pints, increase the processing time to 15 minutes (adjust the processing time for altitudes above 1,001 feet in elevation; see page 65).

RASPBERRY JALAPEÑO JAM

This is not your average raspberry jam, absolutely not. This jam has a slight hint of spice and is a perfect appetizer when paired with goat cheese and crackers. Holiday gift giving? This is our most requested item.

Wondering if your jam or jelly will set properly? Dip a spoon into the jam or jelly. It should roll off the spoon in a sheet consistency instead of drip by drip.

INGREDIENTS

6 cups fresh raspberries

1-2 jalapeño peppers (sliced and seeds removed)

¼ cup bottled lemon juice

1 1.75 oz. box powdered pectin

7 cups granulated sugar

METHOD

1. In a heavy-bottom saucepan, add the raspberries, jalapeño peppers, and lemon juice.

2. Bring the mixture to a full boil (roughly 5 to 10 minutes) and then add the pectin. Stir continually until the pectin is fully dissolved.

3. Next, add the sugar and return to a full boil (roughly 1 to 2 minutes), continually stirring the jam until the sugar has completely dissolved.

4. Skim any excess foam. Don't kill yourself over this step! Simply remove as much of the foam as possible.

5. Ladle the jam into clean, warm jars.

6. Add the lids and tighten the rings finger tight. Process the jars in a boiling water canner or steam canner for 10 minutes (adjust the processing time for altitudes above 1,001 feet in elevation, see page 65).

Note: The jalapeños will naturally float to the top during the canning process. If you are looking to have the peppers suspended throughout the jelly, you can achieve this by gently rotating the jars in a seesaw-type motion after the canning process has been completed and the jars have rested at room temperature for at least 15 minutes. If the peppers continue to float to the top, perform the seesaw motion once again. Keep in mind that the more the jars are rotated, the less likely they are to set, and this can also prevent a good seal.

In order to help reduce the amount of foam when making jam or jelly, add 1 teaspoon butter during the cooking process. This is not a necessary step; it simply minimizes the amount of foam that will need to be removed prior to adding the jam or jelly to the jars.

SLOW COOKER APPLE BUTTER

Fruit butters are absolutely delicious and without a doubt should be one of the staples found in your pantry, with apple butter being the most delicious! What makes this recipe special? There is no time spent over the stove stirring the butter as it cooks. The apple butter is prepared prior to heading to bed and can cook on low in the slow cooker overnight; then it is canned first thing in the morning. The texture and flavor are absolutely incredible. Don't be surprised if you decide to lick the jar clean. There's no shame in it.

INGREDIENTS

6 large apples (we love Galas because they are sweet and cook down wonderfully)

Water

3 cups granulated sugar, or 1½ cups granulated sugar and 1½ cups light brown packed sugar

½ tablespoon cinnamon

½ teaspoon cloves

½ teaspoon nutmeg

½ teaspoon allspice

¼ cup bottled lemon juice

METHOD

1. Peel and core the apples.
2. Add 3 tablespoons water to the slow cooker to prevent the apples from sticking.
3. Mix the apples, sugar, and spices in a noncorrosive mixing bowl, making sure the apples are coated.
4. Place into the slow cooker and add the lemon juice.
5. Cook on low for 8 to 10 hours, making sure to leave the cover of the slow cooker slightly ajar to allow for the steam to vent.
6. Once the apples are thoroughly cooked, use an immersion blender to blend until the desired texture is achieved. If the apple butter appears too runny, it can be thickened easily by cooking on high until the desired consistency is met.
7. Process half pints 10 minutes and pints 15 minutes in a boiling water bath or steam canner (adjust the processing time for altitudes above 1,001 feet in elevation; see page 65).

Let a slow cooker or electric roaster oven become your best friend. Items such as fruit butters, sauces, and salsa require being cooked prior to being canned, and there is no better tool to do this than a slow cooker. I have found it to be extremely convenient to slow-cook foods overnight and then to can them first thing in the morning. It is all about working smarter, not harder!

A FARM GIRL'S OLD-FASHIONED APPLE PIE FILLING

Our good ol'-fashioned apple pie filling is pretty incredible. This recipe of mine calls for not one variety of apple but *three* varieties. Each bite is perfect. Galas are used for their sweetness, Fujis for their tartness, and Golden Delicious for their nice, soft texture. This pie filling will rock your world and will be a recipe you will pass on to loved ones.

INGREDIENTS

2½ cups granulated sugar

2½ cups light brown packed sugar

1 cup regular Clear Jel

1 tablespoon cinnamon

¼ teaspoon nutmeg

1 teaspoon kosher salt

2 tablespoons white vinegar

5 cups apple juice

5 cups water

12 pounds apples

METHOD

1. Mix the sugar, brown sugar, Clear Jel, cinnamon, nutmeg, and salt in a bowl.

2. In a stockpot, heat the vinegar, apple juice, and water on medium heat. As the liquid begins to warm, add the sugar mixture and stir well, making sure that the Clear Jel fully dissolves.

3. Add the apples, and bring them to a boil for 5 minutes.

4. Using a slotted spoon, fill quart-size jars with apples and filling, making sure to leave a 2-inch headspace. Remember that the Clear Jel will cause the filling to expand once completely cool.

5. Remove any air bubbles, add lids and rings, and process the jars in a boiling water canner or steam canner for 20 minutes (adjust the processing time for altitudes above 1,001 feet in elevation; see page 65).

BLUE RIBBON PERFECT PICKLED ASPARAGUS

Our pickled asparagus recipe is what I consider to be blue ribbon worthy! The presentation alone puts it in first place, but the flavor, oh man, the flavor soars beyond every pickled asparagus recipe out there! One day I will be brave enough to submit this recipe to our state fair, one day. Until then I will continue to eat an entire jar in one sitting or use it as a side with our homemade Bloody Mary mix. To maximize the use of the asparagus stalks, use large 24-ounce jars. Shorter jars will require too much of the stalk to be discarded. Don't forget to save the woody ends. They make an excellent ingredient for broth.

INGREDIENTS

5 pounds fresh asparagus

5 slices lemon

5 cloves fresh garlic

5 teaspoons mustard seeds

5 teaspoons dried crushed red pepper

5 teaspoons dill weed

3 cups water

3 cups white wine vinegar
   (5 percent acidity)

6 tablespoons granulated sugar

1 tablespoon sea salt

METHOD

1. Remove the woody end of each stalk, making sure what remains will fit into five 24-ounce jars. Blanch the asparagus in boiling water for 30 seconds and set aside. (Blanching the asparagus will open its pores, allowing the brine to fully seep into the stalks, which provides incredible flavor for every bite!

2. Fill each jar with 1 slice fresh lemon, 1 clove fresh garlic, 1 teaspoon mustard seed, 1 teaspoon crushed red pepper, and 1 teaspoon dill weed. Add the blanched asparagus stalks to each prepared jar.

3. In a 6-quart heavy saucepan, bring to boil the water, white wine vinegar, sugar, and sea salt.

4. Once the salt and sugar have dissolved, immediately fill the jars, leaving a ½-inch headspace.

5. Add lid and rings, and process the jars in a boiling water bath or a steam canner for 15 minutes (adjust the processing time for altitudes above 1,001 feet in elevation; see page 65).

SHELF-STABLE BRANDIED CHERRIES

Brandied cherries are one of the most popular items to preserve, and rightfully so. They make an excellent ingredient for baked goods, are delicious over vanilla ice cream, and can be used in various cocktails. Once you've devoured the jar of cherries, you will understand why they were worth the effort.

INGREDIENTS

½ cup granulated sugar
½ cup light brown packed sugar
1 cup water
½ cup lemon juice
6 pounds sweet cherries, washed, stemmed, and pitted
1¼ cups brandy

METHOD

1. In an 8-quart heavy-bottom saucepan, combine the sugars, water, and lemon juice.

2. Bring the syrup to a boil, stirring often, until the sugars have dissolved. Add the cherries, and simmer until they have heated through.

3. Remove from the heat and stir in the brandy.

4. Using a slotted spoon, ladle the cherries into 6 pint-size jars.

5. Add the brandy syrup to the jars, leaving a ¼-inch headspace. Remove the air bubbles, and top the jar with additional syrup if needed.

6. Add lids and rings, and process in a boiling water bath or steam canner for 15 minutes (adjust the processing time for altitudes above 1,001 feet in elevation; see page 65).

PICNIC RELISH

Who doesn't love a great relish? This is one of the traditional partners for hot dogs, brats, and burgers and is definitely an item worthy of putting up every year.

INGREDIENTS

3 cups granulated sugar

2 cups apple cider vinegar

1 tablespoon celery seed

1 tablespoon mustard seed

¼ cup pickling salt

2 pounds cucumbers, chopped

2 cups chopped onions

1 cup chopped green bell peppers

1 cup chopped red bell peppers

METHOD

1. In a saucepan, combine the sugar, vinegar, and spices. Bring to a boil.

2. Add the cucumbers, onions, and peppers. Allow to simmer for 10 minutes.

3. Pack six pint-size jars, and fill with the brine, leaving a ¼-inch headspace. Remove the air bubbles, and fill with additional brine if needed.

4. Add lids and rings, and process in a boiling water bath canner or steam canner for 10 minutes (adjust the processing time for altitudes above 1,001 feet in elevation; see page 65).

Use home canned pickles that are too soft for your liking to make this picnic relish recipe. That, my friends, is how you think like a sustainable homesteader, and always remember, waste not, want not.

GRANDMA'S DILL AND GARLIC PICKLES

This recipe comes from Justin's family, who, by the way, was big into preserving the harvest. My mother-in-law shared this recipe with me, and it was one of the very first items we canned. With love, I share this with you all, from our family to yours.

The longer home-canned pickles sit, the softer they tend to become. However, there are ways to keep your pickles crispy longer. Select small, young pickling cucumbers and soak them in ice water a few hours prior to canning, or can them immediately after picking. Use natural tannins such as grape leaves (as in the recipe below), oak leaves, or even ½ teaspoon black tea leaves. Ball makes a product called Pickle Crisp, which is another option for keeping pickles crunchy longer.

INGREDIENTS

8(ish) pounds pickling cucumbers

7 cloves garlic or ⅛ teaspoon granulated garlic per jar

1 tablespoon pickling spice per jar

Fresh baby dill sprigs or ⅛ teaspoon dill weed per jar

Whole dried red pepper or ⅛ crushed red pepper per jar

15 cups water

⅔ cup pickling salt

4 cups distilled white vinegar (5 percent acidity)

7 grape leaves

METHOD

1. Pack seven warm wide-mouth quart jars with pickling cukes, garlic, pickling spice, dill, and pepper.

2. In a heavy saucepan, bring the water, pickling salt, and vinegar to a boil.

3. Add the brine to the packed jars, leaving a 1-inch headspace. Remove all air

bubbles, and add more brine if needed. Cover the cucumbers in each jar with a grape leaf making sure the leaf is also covered by the brine.

4. Add lids and rings, and process in a boiling water bath canner or steam canner for 15 minutes (adjust the processing time for altitudes above 1,001 feet in elevation; see page 65).

PICKLED GARLIC

Do not even consider skipping this recipe. You have no idea what you are missing if you do! This pickled item is perfect to pair with foods or, heck, to eat straight from the jar. The garlic becomes mild over time due to the pickling process, and the white wine vinegar enhances the overall flavor. If you take the time to make this, I promise you will make it quite often. It's *that* good!

INGREDIENTS

2⅔ cups water, divided
1 cup whole garlic cloves
1 dried red chile per jar
1 dried bay leaf per jar
⅔ cup white wine vinegar (5% acidity)
2 tablespoons honey
1 teaspoon fine sea salt or pickling salt
½ teaspoon allspice (whole berry)
½ teaspoon coriander seeds
⅛ teaspoon whole cloves
½ teaspoon dried oregano

METHOD

1. In a 2-quart saucepan, bring 2 cups of water to a boil. Add the fresh garlic cloves, and continue to boil for 3 minutes.
2. Strain the garlic and divide the cloves into seven half-pint jars.
3. Add 1 small dried chile pepper and one bay leaf to each jar.
4. In a 12-quart saucepan, add the remaining ⅔ cup water, the white wine vinegar, honey, salt, allspice, coriander, cloves, and oregano; and bring to a hard boil.
5. Add the brine to the garlic, remove air bubbles, and add more brine if needed, leaving a ½-inch headspace from the top of the jar.
6. Add lid and rings and process the jars in a boiling water bath canner or steam canner for 35 minutes (adjust the processing time for altitudes above 1,001 feet in elevation; see page 65).

A GARDEN FAVORITE—THE TOMATO

Our little homestead invests *a lot* of time preserving tomatoes, and it is the most canned item in our pantry. If you are wondering why, think about how much cooking requires the use of tomatoes. Foods like soups, stews, chili, sauces, casseroles, and even frittatas are better when tomatoes are added. You might wonder why on earth you should bother canning tomatoes when store-bought canned tomatoes are so inexpensive. It's because home-canned tomatoes contain no metallic flavor, no preservatives, and no other junk. Home-canned tomatoes are ridiculously delicious, and you will more than likely never purchase a can of tomatoes again once you have put up your own.

For these very reasons, this little fruit deserves a small section all for itself. Just about every garden around the world grows some variety of tomato, yet when it comes to preserving, it is the most talked-about item by canners. Many are unsure as to whether tomatoes should be HWB or pressure canned.

We have talked a little about how air, water, soil, and seed quality have changed over the years. Many heirloom plants are not the same as what once grew in garden beds of past generations. The tomato is a great example of this. Tomatoes were once considered to be high in acidity and could be hot water bath or steam canned without question. Tomatoes, even heirloom, are no longer high enough in acidity to can through the simple process of water canning. Don't fret. With a little help, tomatoes can still be HWB canned.

How you plan to preserve tomatoes will determine if they should be hot water bath or steam canned or pressure canned. If you prefer not to use a pressure canner, keep how you preserve tomatoes simple.

Many tomato-based items will need to be pressure canned if fresh ingredients or meat have been added. Stewed tomatoes, tomatoes with garlic and basil, and spaghetti sauce with meat are a few examples of this. However, items like barbecue sauce, ketchup, tomato paste, and tomato juice can all be water canned if the pH level is met.

A word to the wise? Expand your garden to grow as many tomatoes as it can hold. If not, meet a local farmer and purchase in bulk. This is one investment you will not regret!

It is best to remove tomato skins and the core when working with larger tomatoes such as vine ripe, beefsteak, or plum tomatoes. If not removed the skins will peel and harden during the cooking and canning process, creating an undesirable product. Trust me, there's nothing worse than pulling out hardened peels from a meal.

HOW TO EASILY REMOVE THE PEEL

Cut an X on the blossom side of the fruit, just enough to cut the skin. Place the tomato into a pot of boiling water for roughly 30 to 60 seconds, allowing for the skin to separate from the fruit. Using a slotted spoon, remove the blanched tomato and place it into cold water to cool the fruit. Peel the skin, reserving it to be used to make into tomato powder to create a zero-waste product.

CANNING CRUSHED, DICED, OR WHOLE TOMATOES

Whether you plan to use a HWB or pressure canner, the acidity level for each jar will need to be lifted prior to canning the goods. A pinch of salt can be added to each jar, but this is only an option and is not needed for preserving reasons. The size of the jar (quart or pint) will depend on your family size and how you intend to use the product.

An entire chapter could be dedicated to various ways of preserving this amazing fruit, but I am going to give you the very basic techniques of how to water bath can tomatoes.

CRUSHED TOMATOES

Crushed tomatoes are extremely convenient to add to recipes. We love to use them to thicken sauces and chili. They're ideal for soups, stews, and omelets. If you were to preserve tomatoes one way, I'd say this is the option to choose.

Preparing them for jarring is extremely easy. Keep in mind that roughly 22 pounds of fruit will give you seven quarts, enough to fill a canner. For those who wish to use pint jars, 14 pounds of tomatoes will give you roughly nine pints. Make sure to meet the appropriate pH levels by adding the correct amount of bottled lemon juice or citric acid to the jars. Page 77 provides a chart on how to increase the acidity per jar of tomatoes to make them eligible for hot water bath or steam canning.

DICED TOMATOES

What are diced tomatoes good for? Well, mainly for presentation. No joke. Items like bruschetta can easily be made using diced tomatoes. Putting up diced tomatoes takes time and a lot of work. Do we put these up often? Not really. Crushed tomatoes work better for us.

An average of 35 to 45 pounds of tomatoes are needed for about seven quarts. As you can see, a few more pounds of tomatoes can fit into the jars if crushed.

WHOLE TOMATOES

I enjoy putting up whole tomatoes mainly because it takes less time than putting up crushed or diced. And goodness, the process is extremely easy: blanch in boiling water to remove the peel, cut off the stem (core), and fill the jars. How many tomatoes go into each jar will depend on both the size of the tomatoes and the jar. Just make sure to pack each jar tightly.

Roughly 21 pounds of tomatoes are needed for seven quarts, and an average of 13 pounds will fill nine pints.

HOW TO INCREASE ACID LEVEL FOR WATER CANNING TOMATOES (CRUSHED, DICED OR WHOLE)

Quart jar:
2 tablespoons bottled lemon juice, or
½ teaspoon citric acid, or
4 tablespoons 5% vinegar
(may alter the flavor)

Pint jar:
1 tablespoon bottled lemon juice, or
¼ teaspoon citric acid, or
2 tablespoons 5% vinegar
(may alter the flavor)

WATER CANNING TIMES FOR TOMATOES

Whether you have selected the raw or hot pack method, the processing times are the same:

altitude	quart	pint
0–1,000 feet	45 mins	40 mins
1,001–3,000 feet	50 mins	45 mins
3,001–6,000 feet	55 mins	50 mins
Above 6,000 feet	60 mins	55 mins

Once the hot water bath and steam canning methods have become second nature and you are comfortable with the guidelines for putting up high-acidic items, the adventure really begins. You will find yourself wanting to put up foods using your own recipes. Just remember, there are guidelines that need to be met to prevent bacteria or spoilage from occurring. My only advice is, make sure your skill set is where it should be prior to getting creative.

Home-canned food brings people joy. You know this. Who doesn't love receiving a homemade preserve or pickled item as a gift? As a mother, I love knowing that the foods my children are consuming are made from natural ingredients with no chemicals and natural preservatives. The jams, jellies, chutneys, marmalades, and pickled items you will be putting up are about to change your life. I hope you are ready for that. You have officially begun to own your foods. Welcome to the club.

Three   LET'S TAKE THE PRESSURE OFF PRESSURE CANNING

Once I became comfortable using the hot water bath canner and had more than enough jams and pickled items than I could store, the pressure canner started calling my name. Though I loved the time spent with the water bath canner, I knew there were bigger and better items to put up that would require the use of a pressure canner.

When we made the decision to homestead, our goal was to live a clean life, which included consumption of foods without chemicals or preservatives. Do you know where I am going with this? My trips down the canned goods aisle of our local market would soon be ending. I was going to say goodbye to convenience and begin to create my own kind of fast foods. Good, healthy, clean fast food. Is that even possible? Yes, it is!

Entering the world of pressure canning meant that we would not only be preserving vegetables like carrots, green beans, stewed tomatoes, and beans but also the good stuff. Yes, the *good* stuff like pork, beef, chicken, venison, elk, seafood, sauces, and soups. Your life just improved by knowing what the pressure canner can preserve, no joke.

Now, this is not to say you will *never* shop at the market again. We still usually shop in the spring, when our pantry and freezer items have dwindled. Let me be the first to tell you, *do not feel guilty about this*. It happens. To everyone. Every year. If this becomes a pattern every spring, we know we need to plan better going into next year's harvest and make accommodations for what we've used most often to ensure we don't run out.

If you're entering the pressure canning phase of home food preservation in a fearful state, I'm willing to bet you've read something somewhere that put the fear of God into you. I am also willing to bet a few of the statements you read went something like this: You can kill someone. The pressure canner will explode. You can't can everything. Forget the pressure canner exploding. Your *brain* is going to explode with these messages, which are likely the very reason you haven't begun pressure canning. Am I right?

Much like you, I heard the same horror stories when I first started. What should have been a smooth transition into the next phase of canning was extremely intimidating instead. I realized I was becoming fearful of a canning tool that I didn't even own yet, all because I took to listening to people who were afraid themselves. As a homesteader, this was not going to do if my goal was to live a self-sustaining life. I knew I needed to suck it up and begin to learn about this beastly tool.

So, I sucked it up. I hauled out the pressure canner I had been given, created a list of items to be put up, and began pressure canning before I could change my mind. The decision to start with something uncomplicated led me to putting up carrots, green beans, and corn. I had researched that the preparation would be easy and the processing time short, exactly what I needed for my first attempt at pressure canning. What I got was a product that looked like art in a jar, and the flavor was perfect! The best part? The carrots, beans, and corn did not have that metallic flavor often found in store-bought canned foods *and* no chemical preservatives. I did add a pinch of salt for flavor.

Now, let me be honest. The first time I used our pressure canner, I was a nervous wreck not to mention I was sweating like a pig. But you know what? I did it and didn't kill anyone including myself in the process. The canner didn't explode, and all was well. This allowed me to be more at ease each time the PC was pulled out.

Our pantry quickly filled with vegetables that would have normally been frozen, and I eagerly moved onto canning meat. Absolutely nothing could top the meals that were put into jars. Soups, stews, sauces, even Thai curry (minus a few ingredients) went into them. Justin was able to take healthy, ready-made meals with him to work or out of town, and the kids had meals they could heat up for lunches.

Pressure-canned dried beans should be enough of a reason to incorporate pressure canning in your food preservation routine. Truthfully, how many of us have forgotten to soak beans in preparation for a meal? Now, imagine grabbing a jar of home-canned beans and quickly reheating them for a meal. You really cannot lose on this one. It's good ol' home cooking in a flash.

Should I mention power outages, tough financial times, or natural disasters? How many of us have gone through one or more of those seasons in life? Having food in the pantry helps to alleviate the fear of not being able to eat, and during tough times, that is vital.

I succeeded in learning how to use a pressure canner without blowing up my kitchen or killing my family. So can you. It takes learning the whys and hows, then deciding what is best for your family. You see that pressure canner sitting there? Smile at it, give it a hug, and get to know it. It will soon become your partner in preserving clean healthy foods that contain pronounceable ingredients. How can you deny yourself or your family this opportunity? You can't, and you shouldn't.

PICKING THE BEST PRESSURE CANNER

If you have not yet selected a pressure canner, there are a few things you will need to keep in mind. Don't worry. It's not quite as difficult as buying a car. Choosing the right pressure canner is about preference, how much you would like to spend, and the size of canner you will need. The final decision will be choosing between a dial, weighted, or dual-gauge canner. Your stove top will also be a determining factor on the type of canner you choose.

Regardless of the brand or the size, whatever you select will do the job to create a shelf-stable item. And that, my friends, is the ultimate goal!

CAN YOUR STOVE TOP SUPPORT THE CANNER OF YOUR DREAMS?

Keep in mind how heavy a pressure canner will be once it is filled with canning jars, especially if you plan on double-stacking. Do not feel defeated. Here are other burner options:

- Camp stove (12,000 BTU or lower)
- Portable cooktop
- Butane burner
- Hot plate

BRANDS AND SIZES

Buying a pressure canner is an investment, one that you must be comfortable with whether you are a seasonal canner or a year-round one. A pressure canner is a tool that will feed your family for many years to come. You should be happy with the choice you have made.

SELECTING THE RIGHT SIZE PRESSURE CANNER

pressure canner size	jar quantity (varies between regular and wide month)
10-QUART CANNER	4 pints
16-QUART CANNER	7 quart, 9 pint, 24 half-pint (double-stacked)
20-QUART CANNER	7 quart, 7 pint, 24 half-pint (double-stacked)
21.5-QUART CANNER	7 quart, 19 pint, 24 half-pint (double-stacked)
22-QUART CANNER	7 quart, 9 pint, 24 half-pint (double-stacked)
23-QUART CANNER	7 quart, 18 pint (double-stacked), 24 half-pint (double-stacked)
25-QUART CANNER	7 quart, 18 pint (double-stacked), 26 half-pint (triple-stacked)
30-QUART CANNER	14 quart, 19 pint (double stacked), 38 half-pint (triple-stacked)

Remember that a pressure *cooker* is not a pressure *canner*. Pressure cookers are designed to cook foods and are not capable of maintaining the adequate pressure needed to preserve foods. However, pressure canners can be used as both a canner and a tool to cook with.

Pressure canners can also be used as hot water canners; however, jars should not be double-stacked when hot water bath canning, as they become unstable when the water reaches a hard boil and can easily tip.

There are many brands available on the market, but the main factor in deciding what's best for you is the size of the canner. Pressure canners are always identified in terms of quarts, which indicates how many liquid quarts the canner can hold not how many jars will fit in the canner.

I learned how to pressure can using a Presto 16-quart canner and used the heck out of it. When it was time to upgrade, the Presto 23-quart dial canner became my new best friend. I was looking for convenience and the ability to process more jars during a canning session. Double-stacking jars in the new pressure canner meant shorter times spent over the stove.

I am sure I caught your attention with the term *double-stacking*. With a larger pressure canner, you can stack jars on top of each other. Another bonus of a larger canner? No additional water is required, and there is no need to increase the processing time. Talk about convenience and the ability to save time in one canning session!

In addition to the Presto canner, there is also the All American, which has the reputation of being the king of all pressure canners and comes with a hefty price tag. It's manufactured in America and is equipped with both a dial and weighted valve. With its metal-on-metal seal (no gaskets to wear out or be replaced), this canner is built to last. These bad boys are traditionally handed down to the next generation of home preservers due to their design. But they are heavy regardless if they are empty or full. If your mind is set on getting one of these beasts, it is best to use them on a gas stove top or a sturdy camp stove. Electric burners and glass-top stoves will not be able to hold the weight of an All American, which can cause major damage to your stove top.

Pressure canners can be purchased from online shopping sites or through the manufacturer's website. The Presto 16-quart pressure canner can be purchased at locations that sell canning supplies and is a great beginner's canner.

CHOOSING BETWEEN A DIAL, WEIGHTED, OR DUAL GAUGE

Remember, selecting a pressure canner is about preference, and this holds true when deciding if you would like a dial or weighted gauge. Depending on whom you ask, some will swear that a weighted-gauge canner is the only way to go while others prefer dial gauges. Keep in mind that a dial gauge is capable of measuring pressure but cannot control pressure. That is your job. A weighted gauge can control the pressure but cannot measure it.

This may have not been what you wanted to hear, so I will offer you a third option, the mighty All American dual-gauge canner. A dual-gauge pressure canner is equipped with both dial and weighted gauges and is a failsafe method to ensure the goods are pressure canned appropriately.

When I made the decision to begin pressure canning, a close family friend gave me a dial-gauge canner, and I never looked back. There is something comforting and controlling about watching the dial gain and holding the correct amount of pressure. That's not to say that I won't switch it up and try a weighted gauge or even an All American, but I don't see it occurring anytime soon. The best advice I can give is this: be comfortable with the choice you make, and talk to others about what was the best fit for them.

THE DIAL GAUGE

Call it control, but I find comfort in knowing the pressure inside the canner. The ability to visually see how much pressure is being held during the canning process via the dial gauge can soothe the nerves of many newbies.

The amount of pressure is regulated by adjusting the heat up and down with the stove's burner knob, giving you the ability to raise or lower the pressure within the canner. Dial gauges have more flexibility when dealing with altitude adjustments, allowing for smaller increments when adjusting the psi (pounds per square inch). What does this mean? It's simple. The psi reads *each* pound of pressure unlike the weighted gauge, which reads only 5, 10, or 15 psi. Again, for me it's about being in control and knowing the exact psi in the canner.

Newer dial canners have a dead, or counter, weight built in, which assists in pressurizing by opening and closing and releasing pressure at 15 psi to prevent the top from blowing. This is what differentiates newer ones from older models.

If at any point during the canning process the psi falls below the required level, you'll have to start the processing time over again, regardless of how much time remains for the canning session. This is because the correct psi has escaped the canner, leaving room for possible food-borne toxins to eventually grow.

It is safe to have the pressure slightly higher than what is suggested. However, the food quality can turn out poorly (meat or fish can be overcooked, whereas vegetables can become extremely mushy in texture) if the pressure is kept too high for an extended period. If you find that the psi is on the high side, slowly lower the heat to bring down the pressure until it reaches its correct pressure level.

WEIGHTED GAUGE

Though I have never canned with a weighted-gauge canner, I felt the need to learn more about them. One of our Facebook followers named Mary answered a few questions I had, so I now have a better understanding of a weighted-gauge canner.

She explained that, unlike the dial gauge, the weighted gauge works with the support of three 5-pound weights consisting of the spindle and two separate weights. Using a weighted canner does not allow someone to know the exact psi within the canner. Instead, there is a rough awareness of where the pressure stands. For example, if the altitude where you reside calls for 11 pounds of pressure, the spindle (at 5 pounds) and a 5-pound weight are required to support the 11 psi needed.

DETERMINING THE CORRECT WEIGHT TO ADD

Items being pressure canned will list the exact psi required to make them shelf stable. It is necessary to add the correct weight onto the air vent to maintain the correct pressure in the canner.

weight	total psi	psi covers
5-pound weight (spindle)	5 psi	5 psi up to 9 psi
2 5-pound weights (spindle and one weight)	10 psi	10 psi up to 14 psi
3 5-pound weights (spindle and two weights)	15 psi	15 psi or more

Unlike the dial gauge, a weighted gauge measures pressure but cannot control it. The weights fits on the air vent, allowing the pressure within the canner to rise to the desired point, and then releases the excess steam by rocking, or jiggling, which prevents the pressure from going higher.

A benefit to owning a weighted-gauge canner means it will not need to be monitored as closely as the dial-gauge canner since the pressure cannot be controlled. Those who own a weighted-gauge canner become attuned to the jiggling, or rocking, which allows them to monitor the canner more easily.

DUAL GAUGE

A dual-gauge canner contains both a dial and weighted gauge, and the All American is a great example of a canner with both components. Having both types of gauges provides a backup plan if one should fail. It also gives you the ability to know the exact pressure in the canner, which is necessary for higher-altitude locations.

MAINTAINING YOUR PRESSURE CANNER

Much like any other appliance, your pressure canner will require yearly maintenance to keep it functioning well. Luckily, this will not cost an arm and a leg, and if it is done annually, it could save you from having to purchase a new canner every few years. Most of the maintenance on a pressure canner can easily be done within the comfort of your home. However, calibrating it to ensure the psi is being held within the canner can be difficult for most people to do themselves. But don't worry; there are a few options for how to have your pressure canner calibrated in this section.

Though I love my dial-gauge PC, I will tell you that I am not a fan of having to maintain it yearly. This particular canner needs regular maintenance in order to ensure the gauge is no more than 2 pounds off. The dial cover must be checked for cracks, and the rubber gasket must be inspected for dry rotting or tears. You can do this yourself, though if there is a local extension office near you, they can assist in ensuring your canner is in good shape.

CLEANING THE RUBBER GASKET

The rubber gasket can be found under the lid of both the weighted and dial pressure canner and will need to be cleaned after every use. Liquids containing grease, salt, and seasoning can siphon out of the jars into the water, which reaches the gasket as steam rises to the top of the canner. Cleaning the gasket after each use also gives you the opportunity to check for tears caused by basic wear and tear.

You should be able to remove the gasket easily from the metal lid, but if you cannot get a good grip, use a butter knife to gently separate it from the lid, making sure to not cut into the rubber.

Mild soap and water are all you need to clean it, though a dip in a water and vinegar solution will help to remove any grease that may remain due to canning meat or fish. At this point, check carefully for cracks or tears in the rubber. If any are found, discontinue using the pressure canner until a new gasket is installed. However, if you're anything like me, there's an extra gadget sitting in your drawer for an emergency such as this.

CALIBRATING A DIAL-GAUGE PRESSURE CANNER

Trying to calibrate the canner yourself can be a hassle, but it can be done. Information on how to do this can be found on the National Center for Home Food Preservation's website. Many state or local extension offices can calibrate pressure canners, but you may have to travel out of your area to find one.

Another option is to send the canner back to the manufacturer for testing, but keep in mind there is a risk of damaging the gauge during the shipping process, not to mention shipping costs will need to be covered both ways.

With that said, there is a bonus for owning a weighted-gauge pressure canner. It does not require testing or to be calibrated yearly. Checking the gasket is all you'll need to do.

WHERE TO FIND REPLACEMENT PARTS

Luckily for us, finding replacement parts for the dial, weighted, and dual-purpose pressure canners is extremely easy. Weights, dials, and gaskets can be purchased directly from the manufacturer and even from stores such as Ace Hardware or other locations that sell canning items. Also, Amazon is an easy option if you need a part within 2 business days.

THE SCIENCE BEHIND PRESSURE CANNING

The word *science* might make you nervous, but it's important to understand how pressure canning works and why certain items should be preserved through this method.

You should never preserve foods a certain way just because someone told you it was okay. You *should* educate yourself about the process as well as the precautions. If at any point you were told that Great Grammy hot water bathed jars of green beans for hours to kill any possible food-borne spores, you *should* take the time to think about it. Who has the time to process low-acidic items in a pot of boiling water for hours on end? Realistically, who wants to?

Low-acidic food generally has a pH balance of 4.6 or higher. Items such as vegetables, meats, poultry, and seafood fall under this category. Many vegetables can be preserved using a hot water bath canner if they are pickled. When pickling vegetables, it is important to use vinegar that contains an acidity level of 5 percent or higher, as well as adding bottled citrus juice or citric acid. The other method used to preserve vegetables, meat, poultry, and seafood is to utilize a pressure canner. A pressure canner does not require vinegar, citric acid, or bottled citrus juice to preserve the food being canned. Unlike a hot water bath canner, a pressure canner reaches up to 240°F in an aluminum canner. The high temperature in a pressure canner eliminates the possibility of botulism spores surviving within a jar. In short, pressure canning low-acidic foods such as vegetables, meats, poultry, and seafood creates ready-to-consume foods, also known as ready-made meals in a jar or healthy "fast foods."

Though bacterial cells are killed through boiling at 212°F, certain cells can withstand this temperature and form toxic spores that grow into botulism. These spores grow well in low-acid foods in the absence of air. Does this happen in every case? No, but to minimize the risk, vegetables, meats, poultry, and seafood must be processed at 240°F or higher. The amount of time required will depend on the type of food being preserved and the altitude in which you reside.

SYMPTOMS OF BOTULISM

I've already mentioned botulism, but it's worth discussing in more detail here. It's important to know the symptoms of botulism because there is no taste, smell, or change of texture in the foods that have it, and the symptoms can come on immediately or may take a few days to a little over a week before showing up. If anyone displays any of these symptoms after consuming home-preserved goods, please seek medical assistance right away:

- Double vision
- Blurred vision
- Drooping eyelids
- Slurred speech
- Difficulty swallowing
- A thick-feeling tongue
- Dry mouth
- Muscle weakness

Did you know you can make your own distilled water using a pressure canner? There are excellent tutorials available online as well as on YouTube for how to build an easy distiller.

THE IMPORTANCE OF A STERILIZED WORKSPACE AND CANNING JARS

There are many ways to prevent food spoilage and the spread of bacteria, but the best practice is to keep a clean workspace. Keeping your surfaces and tools sterilized and your hands sanitized will help to prevent the transfer of bacteria from one environment to the next.

In addition to maintaining a sanitized workspace, it is important to sterilize canning jars which have been in storage. New jars directly from the packaging do not require being sterilized. Jars can be sterilized through the process of hot water sterilization, which can be achieved in two ways, with the use of a dishwasher or by bringing jars to a boil in a large stockpot.

When using a dishwasher to sterilize jars, it is important to sync the wash and sterilize cycle with what you are canning. The jars can be kept in the hot dishwasher and pulled out one or two at a time to be filled.

For those of us who do not own a dishwasher, the process takes a bit more work. The jars will need to be sterilized in boiling water for a minimum of 10 minutes prior to filling them. To keep the jars hot prior to being filled, pull a jar or two at a time to work with.

If you are reusing jars, it is important to deep-clean them prior to once again canning with them. At first glance a jar may look clean; however, it is best to ensure that the jars are truly free of all food particles and bacteria with a secondary washing. This can easily be done by washing the recycled jars with mild soap and water. Once the jars have been washed in soapy water, boil them in a vinegar and water solution for 10 minutes. The final step in deep-cleaning recycled jars is to wash them a third time in boiling water for 10 minutes. Using clean water, add the super-sanitized jars and bring to a boil.

When deep-cleaning recycled jars, a ratio of 1 cup vinegar to 1 gallon water works well to remove any food particles or grime. Make sure to have the exhaust fan on or the windows open when using a vinegar water solution, as the vinegar can be irritating to some people.

I generally do not miss owning a dishwasher, although when canning season starts, it becomes a bit annoying trying to balance all that needs to happen when canning food.

Lids should not be sterilized in boiling water and realistically have no reason to be sterilized since lids should be new when used. Prior to placing the lids onto jars, you will need to soften the wax to seal the jars. This can be achieved by placing the lids into a mini slow cooker or a bowl of hot water until they are ready to be used. Boiling the lids can cause the wax found on the underside of the lid to melt away, leaving very little to adhere the lid to the jar.

THE USE OF COLLOIDAL SILVER IN CANNING

Holistic care is an important part of our homestead lifestyle, which has led us to incorporate the use of colloidal silver. Colloidal silver is thought by some to have antiseptic qualities and is used as a natural preventative for food spoilage. The use of silver can be dated back to the Roman empire and to the days when American pioneers went west. It is currently used throughout hospitals around the world. Silver is known for its antibacterial and fungicidal qualities but has become almost obsolete in food preservation.

There are many people, including us, who believe that the use of colloidal silver can assist in preventing food spoilage in home canning, specifically when it's used for pressure canned goods. Because we brew our own colloidal silver on the homestead, I will often add a tablespoon of it to a quart-size jar prior to pressure canning, hot water bath, or steam canning.

I should note that using colloidal silver as a part of home food preservation has not been studied or approved by the USDA, FDA, or the National Center for Home Foods Preservation. The use of colloidal silver should not replace the appropriate tools or appliances needed to assure that botulism spores or various forms of bacteria are destroyed during the canning or preserving process.

Let me say it this way: do your research and decide what best fits the needs of your family. Using colloidal silver is a traditional method we've incorporated on our homestead; however, we do not suggest using it in lieu of methods provided by the NCHFP.

LOW-ACID ITEMS AND PROCESSING TIME*

vegetables	pint	quart
ASPARAGUS, spears or pieces, raw or hot pack	30 min	40 min
BEANS, snap and Italian, pieces, raw or hot pack	20 min	25 min
BEANS OR PEAS, shelled, dried, hot pack only	75 min	90 min
BEANS BAKED, dry, with tomato or molasses sauce	75 min	90 min
BEETS, whole, cubed, or sliced, hot pack only	30 min	35 min
CARROTS, sliced or diced, raw or hot pack	25 min	30 min
CORN, cream-style, hot pack only	85 min	n/a
CORN, whole kernel, raw or hot pack	55 min	85 min
LIMA BEANS, shelled, raw or hot pack	40 min	50 min
MIXED VEGETABLES, hot pack only	75 min	90 min
MUSHROOMS, whole or sliced, hot pack	45 min	n/a
PEAS, green or English, shelled, raw or hot pack	40 min	40 min
PEPPERS (all varieties) hot pack only	35 min	n/a
POTATOES, SWEET, cubed or whole, hot pack only	65 min	90 min
POTATOES, WHITE, cubed or whole, hot pack only	35 min	40 min
PUMPKIN AND WINTER SQUASH, cubed, hot pack only	55 min	90 min
SPINACH AND OTHER GREENS, hot pack only	70 min	90 min
TOMATOES, whole, diced, cubed, crushed, hot pack only	10 min	15 min
TOMATOES, stewed, hot pack only	15 min	20 min

Note: Anything marked with an "n/a" under the jar size indicates that the National Center for Home Food Preservation has either not tested the food item for that particular jar size or that the result of the quality of the food is poor due to long processing times. Additionally, some foods become denser when packed into larger jars, preventing proper heat penetration to reach through the jar properly.

*Adjustment to processing times will need to be made for altitudes higher than 6,000 feet above sea level:

For 6,001 to 8,000 feet, add an additional 15 minutes.

For 8,001 to 10,000 feet, add an additional 20 minutes.

LOW-ACID ITEMS AND PROCESSING TIME*

meat and seafood

meat and seafood	pint	quart
CHICKEN OR RABBIT, cut up, without bones, raw or hot pack	75 min	90 min
CHICKEN OR RABBIT, cut up, with bones, raw or hot pack	65 min	75 min
GROUND OR CHOPPED MEAT, hot pack only	75 min	90 min
STRIPS, CUBES, OR CHUNKS OF MEAT, raw or hot pack	75 min	90 min
MEAT STOCK, liquid only, hot pack	20 min	25 min
FISH, raw pack only	100 min	n/a
SMOKED FISH	10 min	n/a

Note: Anything marked with an "n/a" under the jar size indicates that the National Center for Home Food Preservation has either not tested the food item for that particular jar size or that the result of the quality of the food is poor due to long processing times. Additionally, some foods become denser when packed into larger jars, preventing proper heat penetration to reach through the jar properly.

*Adjustment to processing times will need to be made for altitudes higher than 6,000 feet above sea level.

For 6,001 to 8,000 feet, add an additional 15 minutes.

For 8,001 to 10,000 feet, add an additional 20 minutes.

sauces, stews, soups

sauces, stews, soups	pint	quart
SPAGHETTI SAUCE, VEGETARIAN, hot pack only	60 min	70 min
SPAGHETTI SAUCE, MEAT, hot pack only	60 min	70 min
STEW, meat, raw or hot pack	70 min	90 min
SOUP, meat, raw or hot pack	70 min	90 min

*Adjustment to processing times will need to be made for altitudes higher than 6,000 feet above sea level.

For 6,001 to 8,000 feet, add an additional 15 minutes.

For 8,001 to 10,000 feet, add an additional 20 minutes.

DETERMINE THE CORRECT PSI BASED ON YOUR ALTITUDE AND CANNER

altitude	dial-gauge canner	weighted-gauge canner
1–1,000 FEET	10 psi	10 psi
1,001–2,000 FEET	11 psi	15 psi
2,001–4,000 FEET	12 psi	15 psi
4,001–6,000 FEET	13 psi	15 psi
6,001–8,000 FEET	14 psi	15 psi
8,001–10,000 FEET	15 psi	15 psi

HOW TO FIND YOUR ELEVATION BASED ON SEA LEVEL

Various websites, smartphone apps, and your local, city, or state extension office
can provide you with this information. Here are a few:
Veloroutes.org: http://veloroutes.org/
What is my elevation: www.whatismyelevation.com
Google Maps Find Altitude: www.daftlogic.com
Elevation Map with Altitude Finder: www.elevationmap.net
Google Maps found on smartphone GPS

Determining the correct processing time and psi for home recipes is based on the ingredients list. The item that requires the longest processing time will determine both psi and how long it should be processed. For example, when pressure canning stewed tomatoes, which contain onions and bell peppers, the correct processing time and psi will be based on the peppers, since they take the longest amount of time to process. Information on how to modify a recipe can be found on page 39.

ADDITIONAL HELP, PLEASE!

The manual that comes with your canner will be a resource you use often. It contains information about processing time, altitude information, and may even contain recipes. Though processing times can be found online, I find that processing can vary slightly between what the manual states and what you find in recipes online. When that occurs, I always default to the information provided in the manual.

I would also suggest bookmarking the National Center for Home Food Preservation website. This is a great resource for those who are new to home preserving.

COMMON MISTAKES YOU SHOULD NOT MAKE

Regardless if you are a beginner or a seasoned canner, it is important to be aware of each step along the process. We have all made mistakes and accidentally skipped or even rushed a step. The following are the most often neglected steps when it comes to pressure canning:

Failing to make proper adjustments for altitude levels. This is a big pet peeve of mine and usually occurs when you're following a shared recipe. Often the sharer forgets to mention that the psi may need to be adjusted according to where you live. It is important to select the correct psi based on your altitude.

Allowing hot pack foods to cool prior to placing into the jar. If the food being preserved is intended to be hot packed, it needs to be immediately filled with boiling liquid and pressure canned.

Forgetting to vent the pressure canner. I am human; I will admit it. When I first started pressure canning, the stress of doing it right often caused me to not pay attention to venting the canner. Let me explain, I did vent the canner but often would forget how long it had been venting. It is necessary to vent a pressure canner for 10 minutes prior to adding the weight. This ensures that the air is fully removed and the canner is prepared to fill with steam to build up the desired pressure.

Not performing annual checkups on your pressure canner. We have already covered this, but many home preservers skip the necessary step of annually inspecting their dial-gauge canners.

Neglecting to follow the correct headspace when filling jars. Proper headspace is needed for many reasons and should be followed. Too little or too much headspace can cause spoilage. It can also affect whether the jar seals correctly or whether the food has room to expand in the jar.

PRESSURE CANNING VEGETABLES

Remember when I said that people tend to become overloaded researching information on what can and cannot be canned? The main issue stems from conflicting information found on various websites. Does this mean these sites should not be trusted? No, it just means that you must understand the science and decide on how to proceed based on the needs of your homestead. I wanted to share some general information about other items to eliminate any possible confusion. Make sure to do your research if you question anything on a blog post, website, or even a book for that matter. That, my friend, is what helps us preserve food for our families safely.

Adding one small garlic clove to a jar of vegetables being pressure canned does not change the processing time.

Pressure canning is an incredible means for preserving many of the items that follow, but not all items should be processed in this way. Some items don't hold up well in a pressure canner, while others contain gases that could cause a jar to implode. For those items, consider dehydrating, freezing, or freeze-drying them instead.

ONIONS

Let's start with onions. They are on the "okay to pressure can" list. However, I do not enjoy them canned because they tend to get mushy. Maybe it's the 40 minutes in the canner.

CABBAGE, BROCCOLI, AND CELERY

These three items are on the "do not can" list because it is said that they do not retain their texture, become discolored, and more than likely will taste terrible when pressure canned.

I can testify that cabbage does not retain its texture during the pressure canning process, and it becomes extremely bitter, whereas broccoli loses its texture when pressuer canned, creating a mushy product. Broccoli should be reserved for pickling, dehydrating, or freezing.

Now, let's talk celery. What's a homesteader to do with an abundance of celery in the garden? This situation led me to try canning it.

I cut the stalks into 1-inch pieces and pressure canned them for 40 minutes, which is the highest time allocated for any pressure canned vegetable. How did it turn out? Like celery that has been cooked. It is perfect added to chicken and tuna salad, and since it has been cooked, I can add it to any meal that requires celery.

It is important to note that the NCHFP does not list celery as an item which is safe for canning because there was no funding available to test this item. Celery has been approved, however, as an ingredient in recipes designated for canning purposes.

SUMMER AND WINTER SQUASH INCLUDING PUMPKIN

Nothing is harder to accept than the fact that summer squash should not be pressure canned and neither should pureed winter squash. Considering how much I *love* pumpkin butter, this is a big loss for me. Fortunately, there are other means for preserving this group, such as freezing or dehydrating.

Summer squash is a low-acid item that was once on the "okay to pressure can" list, but it has since been pulled. The National Center for Home Food Preservation has stated that summer squash, once heated, packs so tightly into jars that it doesn't leave enough room for the heat to properly penetrate through the jars. However, slices of summer squash have been approved as an ingredient to be added to soup to be pressure canned.

Let's cover the hot topic of canning pureed winter squash and pumpkin. Sadly, pureed foods should not be pressure canned. Once it has been pureed, it is too dense to allow the heat to properly penetrate through the jar. Why is this considered a hot topic? Mainly because of the *Ball Blue Book of Preserving* recipes for split pea soup and pureed carrots. People have questioned why these recipes are acceptable if they're dense and pureed while pureed squash is not. For best practices, pureed squash and pumpkin should be frozen or freeze-dried.

If you'd like to can pumpkin, butternut, or acorn squash, it is best to cube them into 1-inch pieces and pressure can them. Since they have already been cooked, pureeing them after you open the jar for cooking is made simple. Or, if you are like me, you can add the appropriate pumpkin pie seasoning in the jar as it is being pressure canned. Simply open the jar, blend it, and throw it into the pie shell. Bam, the quickest homemade pumpkin pie, ready to go in minutes!

Because spaghetti squash is stringy and does not remain cubed once pressure canned, there are no canning options available for it.

PRESSURE CANNING LEAFY GREENS

As a kid I *loved* store-bought canned spinach. I could devour a can all by myself. If I had known what greens right out of the garden tasted like, I might not have loved it so much. Yes, leafy greens such as collards, kale, Swiss chard, mustard greens, beet greens, and spinach can be pressure canned. The greens should be served as a side rather than adding them to soups or casseroles. Let me warn you that it takes about 28 pounds of fresh greens to put up 7 quarts, making pints a better option for canned greens.

As with any produce being preserved, select the freshest, crispest greens available. Roughly cut the greens, including the stems. The greens will need to be steamed for 3 to 5 minutes. You want them to be wilted not cooked. The blanching and steaming process will stop the bacteria and enzymes from ruining the quality while on the shelf. Salts and seasoning are not required, but a pinch of salt will help the flavor.

Fill the jars, leaving a 1-inch headspace, then fill with boiling water, maintaining the 1-inch headspace. Remember to remove the air bubbles. Greens will take 70 minutes to process for pints and 90 minutes to process for quarts (use the chart on page 92 to determine the correct psi for your altitude).

ROOT VEGETABLES

Although root vegetables, such as beets, parsnips, carrots, potatoes, and sunchokes, can easily be stored in a cold room or root cellar, pressure canning them is the way to go. I encourage raw packing them, and the process is extremely easy. Raw packing prevents these items from being overcooked, which is not how we like our canned produce.

The ultimate question is whether to peel. The National Center for Home Food Preservation states that all root vegetables should be peeled prior to canning because the soil in which they are grown carries botulism spores, which can transfer onto the rooted vegetables.

So, what's the debate all about? If root vegetables can be consumed through regular cooking with their skins after a good washing, why can't the same be true of canning? If the botulism spores are not thoroughly destroyed while being pressure canned, they will thrive in an oxygen-free environment which will encourage them to grow. You can take this information as you see fit and do what you feel is right for your homestead.

HOW TO PREVENT JARS FROM CRACKING IN THE PRESSURE CANNER

Often jars will break in the canner, and it's usually caused by shock and stress on the jars. Placing a cold jar into extremely warm water will cause the jar to crack due to temperature shock. Older jars will also crack easily in the canner due to overuse. Here are good rules to keep in mind as you are preparing jars for the canner:

- For raw packing, use raw food and hot jars. Begin boiling when the jars are added to the canner.
- For hot packing, use blanched produce or browned meat, hot jars, and hot water. The water should be not quite boiling prior to adding the jars to the canner.

PRESSURE CANNING MEAT

Those of you who are new to canning may not fully understand why you should can meat when freezing is an option. The ability to produce a ready-made item is a necessity for many busy modern homesteaders. A ready and quick meal may consist of combining canned meat with a side of fried eggs and a vegetable from the garden, or the canned meat can be used for making an "instant" soup. Not to mention, canned meat is excellent to use when the power goes out. At our homestead, for example, we often can any older meat, game, or poultry to make room for newer meat items. Additionally, canned meat can be taken camping, hunting, or on road trips for convenience.

Pay close attention to the processing and canning times provided based on the different varieties of meat being put up; they do vary slightly.

BEEF, LAMB, VEAL, AND VENISON

Canned meat is beneficial to have on hand besides being exceptional in flavor. The final product is tender, moist, and tasty when it's allowed to cook in its own juices with a small amount of herbs, spices, and salt. Here's what you should know about pressure canning this kind of meat:

1. Excess fat will need to be removed prior to canning.

2. Meat that is strong in flavor, such as wild game, can be soaked for 1 hour in a water solution containing 1 tablespoon salt per 1 quart water. Make sure to rinse brined meat well prior to canning.

3. Remove any large bones and cut into desired pieces.

4. Meat and poultry can be canned using the hot or raw pack method. The choice is yours to make.

The process of raw packing allows the meat to cook through the canning process without drying it out. Loosely pack the jars, adding herbs, spices, and salt of choosing. Liquid is not required when utilizing this method, because the meat creates its own juices during the canning process.

When utilizing the hot pack method, the meat will need to be precooked until rare by roasting, stewing, or browning in a small amount of fat prior to canning. The meat will need to be cubed to 1-inch pieces prior to precooking. You then fill the jars with the precooked meat and hot broth or water, leaving a 1¼-inch headspace.

The processing time and psi (based on your altitude) are the same for raw and hot pack methods. Remember, trim as much of the fat from the meat as possible prior to canning.

Much like canning root vegetables, there is a lot of discussion about whether meat should be precooked prior to canning. The National Center for Home Food Preservation states that meat should be hot packed when canning soup or stews. With this information, we use the raw pack method and cover the foods with boiling water when it comes to canning soups and stews.

POULTRY

Poultry refers to chicken, duck, goose, turkey, game birds such as domestic or wild quail, and guineas. Here's what you should know about pressure canning this kind of meat:

1. Make sure to remove any skin, excess fat, and organs prior to canning.

2. Allow poultry to chill for 6 to 12 hours prior to canning.

3. Remove any large bones, though smaller wing bones can be left in, and cut into 1-inch strips, cubes, or chunks.

4. Poultry can be canned using the hot or raw pack method. The choice is yours.

There is no difference in the processing time for both hot or raw pack methods, however, make sure to follow the correct processing time for bone in or no bone found on page 91.

Additional canning time is needed for elevations higher than 6,001 feet sea level. The correct psi setting is based on the altitude of your location.

RABBIT

Rabbits are a good source of high-protein, low-fat meat, which is gaining in popularity particularly among homesteaders. Here's what you should know about pressure canning this kind of meat:

1. Make sure to remove any skin, excess fat, and organs prior to canning.

2. Soak dressed rabbits in a saltwater brine for a minimum of 1 hour using 1 tablespoon salt (kosher, pickling, or sea salt) to 1 quart water.

3. Remove any large bones, though smaller foreleg bones can be left in, and cut into 1-inch strips, cubes, or chunks.

4. Meat and poultry can be canned using the hot or raw pack method. The choice is yours to make. The processing time for canning rabbit is the same as for canning poultry.

MAPLE BOURBON BACON JAM

This recipe really needs no introduction. All you need to see is the word *bacon* and you know it's going to be good. How do you eat it? Over eggs, on homemade biscuits or bread, even in a sandwich with a bit of smoked Gouda. Oh, goodness! This recipe can also be refrigerated or frozen if you decide not to pressure can it.

INGREDIENTS
1 pound raw bacon end cuts
2 cups diced shallots
1 cup diced sweet onion
4 garlic cloves, minced
½ teaspoon smoked paprika
½ cup bourbon
½ cup maple syrup
¼ cup white wine vinegar
½ cup brown packed sugar

METHOD
1. Chop the bacon or bacon bits into small pieces, and fry until the bacon becomes crispy. Keep the grease warm in the pan.
2. Strain the bacon on a paper towel to remove the grease.
3. Add the shallots, onions, and garlic to the bacon grease. Cook on low until they are tender.
4. Add the smoked paprika and stir until fully combined.
5. Increase the heat, and add the bourbon and maple syrup. Bring to a boil, stirring and scraping the bottom of the pan often to prevent scorching. Continue boiling for about 2 to 3 minutes.
6. Add the white wine vinegar and brown sugar. Continue to boil for about 3 minutes.
7. Return the bacon to the pan, reduce the heat to low, and simmer for about 10 minutes. The mixture will thicken and look jam-like in the process.
8. Fill half-pint jars and leave a 1-inch headspace.
9. Processing time is 75 minutes. Add appropriate time for altitudes over 6,001 feet above sea level.

Preparing the pressure canner:
See page 105 for proper canning instructions.
Select the correct psi based on the altitude in which you reside, see page 92.

FOODS THAT SHOULD NOT BE PRESSURE CANNED

Ever wonder why there are all kinds of canned items in the grocery store, but home preservers are discouraged from canning certain ones? This is because a pressure canner designed for home use cannot compare to industrial canners that reach temperatures over 240°F. Here's a quick overview of foods that should not be canned and why.

Canning dairy at home raises the risk of the item going rancid and spoilage setting in, leaving room for toxic spores. You may have come across an article about canning butter, but keep in mind that a dairy item such as butter will go rancid if allowed to sit too long at room temperature.

Noodles, rice, and pasta are other items that should not be canned. They often are too thick to allow the heat from home canners to penetrate, again leaving room for possible toxic spores to settle in.

As I've mentioned previously, items such as flour or cornstarch should not be used as thickeners for stews and other dishes. They make the liquid too thick for the steam to penetrate through the jars. However, a product like Clear Jel, which stays in a liquid form until it has cooled, is an excellent choice for making ready-made meals.

Lard and bacon grease are best stored frozen. The fat used to render these items can go rancid if left out for long periods of time. There is no canning method that prevents fats from turning rancid.

In my experience, canning leftovers generally does not result into anything mouthwatering once the jar has been opened. One of the reasons is the food has been double cooked, once when it was first made and then a second time in the pressure canner. Not my idea of delicious. The second reason is the ingredients list may contain items that do not do well when canned. Pureed soups should not be pressure canned because they often contain dairy or are too thick to allow the heat to properly penetrate through the jar.

CANNING BABY FOOD

As our first grandchild made an appearance into this world, I realized the importance of talking about canning baby food. Whether you are a rebel or a by-the-book canner, you'll need to ensure that the foods babies consume are as safe as they can be.

As tempting as it is, pureeing foods for canning is not something I could advise. However, you can cube vegetables such as squash and then puree it out of the jar. Meat can also be processed in the same way with broth added afterward to make it moist.

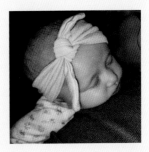

Keep in mind that canned foods for infants and toddlers should contain small amounts of salt, herbs, and spices.

Pressure canning foods for feeding your little ones should be done in half-pint and pint sizes.

PERFECTLY PICKLED EGGS IN A JALAPEÑO PEPPER BRINE

If you're new to the concept of pickling eggs, this recipe is going to convince you that it should be done. If you are already pickling eggs, I would suggest you give our pickled egg brine a try. You are going to love it! Keep in mind, this is not a canning recipe but a method of preserving farm-fresh eggs using a vinegar brine and the refrigerator. Pickled eggs can keep 3 to 4 months in the refrigerator, but I can promise you, they will not last that long. These pickled eggs are perfect with a salad or as a great protein snack, but I love them as a side with a nicely grilled steak. There is no method available for canning eggs, but this recipe is too good to leave out!

INGREDIENTS

12 medium farm-fresh eggs
Jalapeño pepper, sliced
½ sweet onion, diced

The brine:

1 cup white wine vinegar 5% acidity
1 cup water
1 cup organic sugar
2 teaspoons dried thyme
2 teaspoons mustard seeds

METHOD

1. Steam the fresh eggs (see page 50). Peel them after they have cooled.

2. In a 2-quart saucepan, combine all the ingredients for the brine, and bring to a hard boil for 5 minutes, stirring often.
3. In a large mixing bowl, mix the peeled eggs, jalapeño peppers, and sweet onions to fill a quart-size jar.
4. Cover the eggs with brine, remove all air bubbles, and top off the jar with additional brine.
5. Now the hard part. Allow the pickled eggs to marinate for 1 to 2 weeks prior to consuming.

MODIFYING RECIPES FOR CANNING

Can *all* soups and stews be pressure canned? Some of them can, but picking apart a recipe to make it "canable" should be reserved for seasoned canners. It's important to think about the following when considering a recipe:

1. Begin with the process of elimination. Those items that should not be canned, such as dairy, pasta, grains, and noodles should be taken out of the recipe.
2. Next look at the produce. Can everything withstand the high temperature of the pressure canner or will it get mushy?
3. Because the flavor of herbs, spices, and salt will intensify the longer the item sits on the shelf, you should reduce the amount in the recipe.
4. Finally, make sure to eliminate any thickening agent such as flour or cornstarch. Luckily, these can be replaced with Clear Jel.

What you end up canning is a base ingredient. Once ready to serve, the items removed can then be added back into the recipe and enjoyed.

HOW TO USE A PRESSURE CANNER

Even though it can be time consuming, pressure canning is extremely easy. Here's a little secret: when my pressure canner is going, I find other work to do in the kitchen so I can be around to watch the dial to ensure the pressure is holding. I also keep the canner's manual handy for anything that may arise. Here are the basic steps to operating your pressure canner:

1. Place the canning rack in the canner. If you plan on double-stacking jars, you'll need to keep the second rack handy.

2. Fill the canner with 2 to 3 inches of water prior to adding jars. Longer processing times, like fish, will require more water.

3. Add jars fitted with lids and ring bands into the canner, making sure to keep the jars upright. Tilted jars can cause the liquid or food to spill into the sealing area, preventing the jars from sealing.

4. Securely fasten the lid onto the canner.

5. Turn the heat setting to its highest position.

6. Allow the canner to vent a consistent stream of steam for 10 minutes. Improper venting can cause air to be trapped in a closed canner, which will affect the temperature and processing time.

7. Once the canner has vented for the appropriate length of time, place the weight on the vent port or close the petcock. You will see the canner begin to pressurize within a few minutes.

8. Regulate the heat under the canner to maintain a steady pressure. Start the processing time when the correct pressure is reached on the dial gauge or when the weight gauge begins to rock as indicated in the manual of your canner.

9. It is okay for the pressure to be slightly above the gauge level, but it should never fall below it. If the pressure falls below the correct pressure, you'll need to start the processing time over. Weight gauges will display different degrees of rocking, indicating that the pressure is being met. A dial gauge must be monitored to ensure the pressure never falls below the pressure required.

Using vodka or white vinegar to wipe down the rims of the jars prior to placing the lids will help remove any possible food, grease, or liquid. Water is not strong enough to remove the grease that may be left behind when canning meat, fish, soups, or stews.

If at any point your psi should fall below the correct pressure, it will need to be brought back up and the processing time will have to be restarted.

10. When the processing time has completed its cycle, turn off the heat, and allow the canner to cool down naturally. Do not depressurize the canner, and do not force-cool the canner by submerging or allowing cold water to flow over it. Doing so can cause the loss of liquid from jars and possible seal failures, which may lead to food spoilage. This can also cause the canner lid to warp.

11. Once the canner has been completely depressurized, remove the weight from the vent pipe or open the petcock. It is best to wait roughly 10 minutes before opening the lid to make sure no steam remains in the canner.

12. Using a jar lifter, remove the jars, making sure not to tilt them. Place the jars on a towel or cooling rack, leaving at least 1 inch of space between the jars.

13. Allow the jars to sit undisturbed as they cool for 12 to 24 hours.

14. After cooling, remove the rings and check that the lids have properly vacuum-sealed. Any unsealed jars will need to be refrigerated and used first.

15. Wash jars and lids to remove all residues that may have leaked from the jars.

16. Label the jars and store them in a cool, dry place out of direct light.

17. Rinse and dry the canner, lid, and gasket, or take off the removable petcocks and safety valves before storing.

Keeping in mind the following tips when you put up foods will help calm your nerves and remind you of what's important:

- **Use proper canning techniques.** It's important to understand both the science (and rules) for pressure canning foods. It's also important to be familiar with old-world methods or how the rest of the world preserves food. This allows you to make an informed decision on why and how foods should be pressure canned.
- **Use the right equipment.** Choose the right tool based on what is being preserved, whether it's a pressure canner, steam canner, or hot water bath canner.
- **When in doubt, throw it out.** If a preserved item smells funky, has mold growing on it, has a questionable texture, or the lid has popped, do not hesitate. Toss it out.
- **Keep everything sterilized.** Make sure jars are sterilized before you start canning. The working space and any tools must be kept clean.

FARMHOUSE RECIPES

Whether we are homesteaders or suburbanites, convenience foods are big in our culture. Because we can preserve ready-made meals on our homestead, our "fast food" is much healthier and tastes a million times better than what you'd get from a drive-through restaurant. There is really nothing more rewarding than for my husband to be able to grab a ready-made jar of stew or soup from the pantry for lunch or for our kids to cook a nice spaghetti dinner with jars of home-canned sauce. No one said meals must be made from scratch every day.

CORNED BEEF AND POTATOES

Corned beef is a favorite around our homestead. We love to can it straight up to be used later fried with farm-fresh eggs or as a ready-made meal of corned beef and potatoes, sometimes adding carrots if there are any around. Pressure canning the meat will leave it tender and melt-in-your-mouth delicious. Enjoy!

INGREDIENTS

4–5 pounds corned beef
1 tablespoon lard or vegetable oil
Pickling spice
12 cups peeled and cut russet potatoes
8–10 cups peeled and cut carrots
   (optional)

METHOD

1. Remove as much fat from the meat as possible. Cut the meat into 1-inch cubes, and brown them in the lard or vegetable oil.

2. Strain the meat from the juices.

3. Add ¼ teaspoon pickling spice to each jar.

4. Layer raw pack vegetables and the browned meat, leaving a 1-inch headspace.

5. Fill the remainder of the jar with boiling water, leaving a 1-inch headspace. Remove all air bubbles.

6. Using white vinegar or vodka, thoroughly clean the rims of each jar.

7. Place the warmed lids and rings on each jar and finger tighten.

HEADSPACE IN JARS

Many meats, vegetables, and bean recipes require at least 1-inch headspace, measuring from the top of the food and liquid to the rim of the jar.

Preparing the pressure canner:
See page 105 for proper canning instructions.
Select the correct psi based on the altitude in which you reside (see page 92).

BONE BROTH

Homemade bone broth is packed with minerals and calcium that help to boost the immune system while working to reduce inflammation. It also makes for excellent cooking. Any type of bone can be used, raw or cooked. Roasting bones for 30 minutes at 350°F will provide amazing flavor to the broth, and cooked bones can be kept in the freezer until you are ready to use them. You can also add poultry feet and vegetable scraps. Adding poultry feet increases the medicinal qualities found in broth while creating a delicious gelatinous product. Vegetable scraps, herbs, and spices amplify the flavor. The bonus? Bone broth is excellent for dogs and cats. If you're not making bone broth on a regular basis, I strongly suggest you start!

INGREDIENTS

2 pounds bones, preferably from grass-fed livestock
2 chicken feet (optional)
Water
2 tablespoons apple cider vinegar
Fresh herbs
1 small head garlic
1 tablespoon whole peppercorns
Onions, carrots, celery (optional)

METHOD

1. In a large stockpot, slow cooker, or roasting pan, add the bones and poultry feet. Cover the bones with water.
2. Add the vinegar, herbs, garlic, peppercorns, and vegetables.
3. Bring the pot to a boil. Once it reaches a vigorous boil, reduce to simmer. Simmer on low for 12 hours.
4. The broth will be done once it is deep brown in color and tastes delicious.
5. Using a fine-mesh strainer, separate the broth from the ingredients into pint- or quart-size jars.
6. Using white vinegar or vodka, thoroughly clean the rims of each jar. Place warmed lids and rings on jars, and finger tighten.
7. For canning purposes, this recipe is for broth only.
8. Processing time is 20 minutes. Add appropriate time for altitudes over 6,001 feet above sea level.

Preparing the pressure canner:
See page 105 for proper canning instructions.
Select the correct psi based on the altitude in which you reside (see page 92).

CANDIED SALMON

We take advantage of living in the Pacific Northwest, and one of the benefits is having access to beautiful wild salmon. Smoked and pressure canned salmon make for great meals when salmon season ends. Of all the seafood you can put up, salmon and tuna are the better choices.

INGREDIENTS
2 fillets salmon, scaled (leaving on skin is optional)

1 cup granulated sugar

1 cup brown packed sugar

1 cup fine sea salt

2 quarts water

METHOD
1. Cut the salmon into 8-ounce portions, or small enough to fit into half-pint jars. Remove as many bones as possible; however, any remaining bones will dissolve during the pressure canning process.

2. Mix together the dry brine ingredients and add water. Allow the sugars and salt to fully dissolve.

3. Add the salmon to the liquid brine and allow to marinate for 1 hour. Remove salmon from the brine and rinse.

4. Fill half-pint jars with the salmon, leaving ½-inch headspace.

5. Processing time is 100 minutes. Add appropriate time for altitudes over 6,001 feet above sea level.

Preparing the pressure canner:

See page 105 for proper canning instructions.

Select the correct psi based on the altitude in which you reside (see page 92).

STEWED TOMATOES

Every year we put up stewed tomatoes, and each year I think I've overdone it. But by the spring, the pantry is empty, which is a sad, sad moment around here. What can you do with stewed tomatoes? Everything, and soon they will be your favorite tomato product to put up each year.

INGREDIENTS

25 large tomatoes, any variety, blanched and chopped
1 cup diced yellow onion
½ cup diced celery
½ cup diced green bell pepper
Salt (optional)
Sugar (optional)
Lemon juice

METHOD

1. Blanch the tomatoes to remove the skins. Reserve the skins to be made into tomato powder. How to dehydrate tomato skins can be found on page 131.
2. Chop the tomatoes, removing the hard core. Removing the seeds is optional.
3. Combine the remaining ingredients, except the lemon juice, in a nonreactive pot. Cook for 10 minutes over medium heat. Remember to stir often to prevent scorching.
4. Fill the jars, leaving a 1-inch headspace. This recipe makes roughly 4 quarts or 8 pints.
5. Add lemon juice to each jar, 2 tablespoons per quart, 1 tablespoon per pint.
6. Process pint jars for 15 minutes, quart jars for 20 minutes. Add time for altitudes above 6,001 feet sea level.

Preparing the pressure canner:
See page 105 for proper canning instructions.
Select the correct psi based on the altitude in which you reside (see page 92).

My goal from this chapter was to help you understand the science behind pressure canning. Remember, an educated preserver seeks to know as much as possible about preserving the harvest. Give that pressure canner of yours a pat on the lid. Soon it will become one of your best friends.

Four DEHYDRATING EVERYTHING GOOD

I am going to start by saying that I have come a long, long way from the first time I ever dehydrated food. I had an awakening when I discovered how much a dehydrator can preserve. It can preserve not only fruits, vegetables, herbs, flowers, roots, and nuts, it can also be used to make dog treats, jerky, to help dry pasta, even to assist in getting bread to rise. And what if I told you a dehydrator is great for making cottage cheese and yogurt? Do you see how amazing and valuable a dehydrator can be?

As much as I love my dehydrator, there's something charming, romantic, and old world about being able to hang herbs in the house for drying, not to mention the amazing smell of the natural essential oil released from the plant or flower during the drying process. It honestly doesn't get better than this. For this very reason, you will often find herbs and various medicinal flowers hanging throughout our farmhouse.

There truly isn't anything more rewarding than reaching into the pantry and grabbing a homemade herb mix that you grew, gathered, and dried. The ability to give our dogs, who are on restricted diets, treats that are specific to their needs makes my heart happy. But nothing, absolutely nothing, beats providing my children with healthy snacks.

Foods available for drying can come from the garden, farmers' market, and even from the supermarket. Yep, from the supermarket. A good tip to keep in mind when you are purchasing items to be dehydrated is to purchase large quantities at a time if you can. It is much more efficient to run a full dehydrator of the same produce than to run a few smaller batches with various items. Trust me when I say that one half-gallon jar is easier to store than four quart-size jars. And it uses only one oxygen absorber for keeping moisture out instead of four, creating minimal waste and maximizing storage space.

When you start exploring the world of dehydration, you are going to be floored at the endless options. This is also a great opportunity for children to begin learning how to preserve the harvest. Allow them to work with you, explain the step, and give them control to work the dehydrator, especially when you are making treats for them.

HOW FOOD DEHYDRATING WORKS

Although dehydrating is much simpler than canning, there are techniques and precautions that need to be followed to guarantee that the food item has been preserved properly and to prevent any mold or bacteria from forming.

Remember, food spoilage is always a risk when trying to dry items in less than ideal circumstances. Let's take the Pacific Northwest, for example, which is one of the wettest parts of the country. Dampness is a huge issue for us, and air drying is very difficult from November to May. When industrial tools such as a dehydrator are used, the food must be immediately packaged with an oxygen absorber and vacuum-sealed to prevent moisture from forming in the foods.

Think about it like this: when you're drying off from a swim in the lake, the sun and breeze work together to evaporate the moisture. The same concept applies to dehydrating. When moisture is being removed from food, it must be exposed to warm, moving air regardless of the dehydrating technique being used. The water in food evaporates by being exposed to heat, and then the airflow draws the moisture away, allowing the foods to dry.

If the drying process has been successful and no moisture remains in the food, harmful bacteria, fungus, mildew, or mold have nothing to adhere to. That is why rice and beans are excellent items for long-term storage. Also, keep in mind that spoilage can occur during the dehydrating process if it takes an extended amount of time for the goods to dry. When using standard ovens (we will talk about convection ovens later) for drying, spoilage can occur if the drying process takes too long. Though the oven may provide enough heat, there may not be enough airflow to move the heat.

Foods packaged before being fully dried can cause an entire container to go bad. The food should never have a soft and moist texture before being stored. Dried apples should have a pliable, leather-like consistency, while bananas should harden once they have cooled. Herbs, flowers, and leafy greens will have a brittle texture if they've been dried properly. Your dehydrator's manual will indicate how the final product should appear upon completion.

Dried food can be eaten as is. However, reconstituting dried foods will bring it back to its original glory. There are various methods to reconstitute the dried item: soaking it in broth or water, boiling it, or cooking the item in various liquids or sauces.

The biggest misconception is that all foods which are dehydrated become brittle when completely dried. Most vegetables will finish with either a leathery or brittle texture. Dried fruits are generally brittle, leathery, or pliable. Herbs, when completely dried, are brittle regardless of the type of herb being dried. Fruit or vegetable peels can also be dried and will be brittle upon completion, making them easy to grind into powder.

We have been successful in dehydrating turmeric and ginger then grinding them to make powders. The trick is to slice the roots thinly and dry them on the herb setting for roughly 12 hours. To test dryness, the root should easily snap in half.

Herbs such as lavender should be harvested before their flower buds open. Chamomile, nasturtium, calendula, pansy, roses, bee balm, feverfew, and echinacea can be harvested before they start losing petals. Harvesting herbs before the sun is at its peak and once the dew has been dried ensures their essential oils are most potent.

METHODS FOR DRYING FOODS

There is a plethora of methods for drying foods. Some of these methods are quicker than others, while some need the right weather conditions to properly dry the goods. You will find that there are specific methods you will resort to often. In truth, during prime drying season (spring to fall) you are likely to utilize more than one of these methods. There's nothing quite as romantic as hanging herbs in your kitchen while the dehydrator is running.

Many home preservers enjoy utilizing natural methods for drying. Heck, I do. We have drying racks both on the back deck as well as inside and love using the warmth of the sun to dry goods. When we begin to run out of hanging space but still have a large amount of herbs to dry, a brown paper bag comes in handy.

I have even tried drying things in the microwave and the oven. Not what your typical homesteader would do, but I thought it was worth testing. Since I consider us to be modern homesteaders, I can proudly state that my dehydrator is one of my most-used appliances.

Pick the methods that work best for you. Many begin by drying items in the oven since it is readily available. Those who live off the grid only air- or sun-dry foods. Give each method a try, especially if you live in a warmer, drier part of the world.

SUN-DRYING IS THE OLDEST METHOD FOR DRYING FOODS

We are constantly talking about learning the old ways. Drying food in the sun has been used for centuries and is still used today.

Herbs are not ideal candidates for sun-drying, as volatile oils found in the thin leaves will burn the plant, leaving very little flavor in the final product. Selecting a location that receives either morning or late afternoon sun is best when drying herbs.

The right weather conditions are vital for success. If you reside in the same part of the world as I do, this may not be the best method for you. To successfully sun-dry food, you'll need an average of 3 to 5 days, with a minimum of 8 hours of sunshine, and a temperature of at least 90°F with low humidity to successfully dry the food item. Something as minor as cloud formation or a cool breeze for an extended period can keep the food from drying properly, so check the weather forecast prior to putting foods out to be sun-dried. Additionally, if you live in a place that has bad air pollution or heavy traffic nearby, your dried foods run the risk of being contaminated due to airborne emissions.

Hot, dry, and sunny weather is best for sun-drying. However, some foods can get scorched. Humidity, regardless of how high the temperature gets, can also cause the food items to dry inadequately.

Not to deter you from sun-drying, but I am going to warn you that it can be a long, drawn-out process. The goods cannot be left out overnight because they could absorb too much moisture; they must be brought in each evening. Then you repeat the process for 3 to 5 days until the food is dried. Are you prepared to commit to this?

In addition to monitoring the weather, keep in mind that bugs and pests like chipmunks, squirrels, and birds may be a problem when it comes to drying outdoors. Covering the food trays with a light mesh netting can help the problem, but a persistent bird is a persistent bird that will often find a way to get to the food. If you are not willing to wage war on any critters or bugs, try sun-drying indoors in a sunroom or a greenhouse. Just make sure the trays are near doors and windows for proper airflow. Turn off the air-conditioning and keep fans away from the items being dried. This method of drying requires high temperatures to effectively dry foods.

I've listed quite a few cons regarding sun-drying food, which is quite ironic since our ancestors and those living off the grid did it successfully and without complaining.

Drying foods using a solar panel is another excellent method. You can find information on how to build a solar dryer at motherearthnews.com.

AIR-DRYING

Air-drying takes the longest amount of time for drying goods, but it works extremely well when drying herbs and thinly sliced fruit and vegetables. This method requires no direct sunlight or intense heat to complete the job, making it easy to dry items inside the house or outside on a drying rack. Hanging herbs near a kitchen window almost always guarantees air circulation, but if for some reason you should be concerned about airflow, simply place a fan in the area to create proper air movement.

HOW TO MAINTAIN AIR MOVEMENT WHILE SUN-DRYING

Drying trays are easy and inexpensive to make. With the use of a stainless steel screen and a large recycled picture frame from your local thrift store, you can easily make a drying tray. The stainless steel helps to ensure that the foods do not become contaminated during the drying time. The drying trays can be placed on sawhorses to allow for proper air movement under the food items.

HANGING RACKS

We hang our herbs from old metal rakes, curtain rods, or ceiling hooks in the kitchen and dining room. We'll hang them anywhere we can, even from the dining room chairs if the season proves to be abundant! When tying your herbs with twine or fishing line, tie them tightly. Herbs will shrink in size when they dry and may fall out of the bundles. To prevent any possible mold from forming on the leaves, herbs with high water content, like basil, tarragon, or mint, should be bundled in smaller bunches when hanging.

When summer ends and the air begins to get damp, those of us who reside in older homes tend to light our wood-burning stoves early to dry out the interior of the house. You can take advantage of this time by hanging herbs or other food items next to the wood stove to dry. Make sure they're far enough away from the stove to prevent scorching and overheating. Additionally, make sure there is proper airflow from a ceiling fan or a stand-up fan. And because I'm a little compulsive, I wrap cheesecloth around the drying items to protect them from wood stove dust.

There are a few drawbacks to air-drying. You never know how long it will take to complete the drying cycle. Herbs need to dry until they are brittle, and fruit and vegetables need to dry until they are leathery or brittle, which will depend on what is being dried. Because of the long drying time, you could have an issue with mold or mildew forming. This happened to me when we first moved to the homestead. The house was extremely moist and cool due to the amount of rain; this caused the herbs hanging in the kitchen to remain moist and get moldy.

When hanging herbs for drying, you will want to keep the bunches small—about four to five stems per bunch. Too many stems tied together will prevent proper airflow and can cause the bunches to get moldy. The only exception to this rule is rosemary. Because rosemary branches are stiff, there is plenty of air space between them. For this reason, I generally tie five to eight branches together.

ELECTRIC FOOD DEHYDRATOR

All dehydrators are equipped with a heating element, fan, air vents, and food trays. Additional items such as drying sheets, clear doors, and additional trays can often be purchased through the maker. Make sure to dry foods according to the setting dictated in the manual that accompanies the dehydrator. Foods dried at a temperature higher than necessary will result in uneven drying. These items generally have a drier exterior and a moist interior, allowing for bacteria to grow.

Although it is another preserving tool to add to the items you already have, an electric food dehydrator is an item I strongly believe in and will always have on our homestead. It is not only capable of preserving herbs, fruit, and vegetables, but it can also assist in making jerky. And who doesn't love the idea of making jerky at home? Also, depending on the type of dehydrator you select, you may be able to use it to help raise bread, dry pasta in large batches, and make yogurt or cheese.

Regardless of the brand, electric dehydrators are designed to dry foods. The exterior design will vary. There are models that are stackable much like a box, while others resemble a cabinet. If you are considering a stackable model, keep in mind that additional trays can be purchased to increase the amount of food

being dried at a given time. If you go with a box or cabinet model, you can remove the trays, which will allow you to use the dehydrator for such things as raising bread and making yogurt and cheese.

An electric dehydrator is designed to produce heat. Once food is heated, it naturally releases moisture into the dehydrator. The built-in fan then pushes the moisture away from the foods and out of the dehydrator through vents. The fan is also designed to generate

CREATING RAW DEHYDRATED FOOD

Raw food enthusiasts can benefit from using a dehydrator to preserve fruits and vegetables, as well as make items such as raw granola and pureed fruit leather, while maintaining the essence of raw fruits and vegetables.

Consuming raw foods maintains the enzymes, vitamins, and minerals found in the foods. Though any dehydrator can be used for this, a good-quality dehydrator will not expose the foods to high temperatures, thus causing the food to become cooked. Raw foods should be dehydrated at no higher than 140°F to allow for the enzymes to be retained in the raw foods.

To enjoy dehydrated foods in their raw form, selecting the right dehydrator is crucial. The dehydrator must have an adjustable thermostat. Also, rear-mounted fans are valuable in circulating the air efficiently, whereas stackable dehydrators generally have poor air circulation, requiring the trays be rotated.

If preserving foods in their raw form is something you wish to do, I would suggest you spend the money on a higher-quality dehydrator, which will allow for everything noted above.

air circulation inside the dehydrator, preventing the foods from gathering bacteria or even possibly cooking due to the heat.

Depending on the type of dehydrator you select, the location of the fan will vary; it can be located either on the top, bottom, or rear. Over the years we have owned dehydrators with top- and rear-mounting fans, and in truth, we found that the rear-mounted fan worked better for drying goods. Rear-mounted fans allow for the air to be dispersed evenly throughout the dehydrator, reaching every tray. Again, this is necessary to prevent spoilage. The brand we owned with a top-mounting fan required the trays to be rotated throughout the drying process, because the fan circulation could not reach the bottom trays.

Foods such as herbs, most vegetables, and fruit can easily dry between 95°F and 145°F. Drying meat requires a higher temperature setting of 160°F to 165°F to discourage bacterial growth. The dehydrator manual contains valuable information such as the proper temperature setting, the best methods for preparing foods, and how the product should look and feel once completed. It is a valuable resource, so be certain to refer to it often.

A common misconception that many people have about dried foods is that they should always have a crunchy or brittle texture. In truth, the texture of a dried item will depend on the item being dried and will vary from pliable or leathery to tough or brittle.

BROWN PAPER BAGS

I love this method and have taught my kids about drying herbs using this technique as well as the air-drying method. The process is extremely easy; all that is needed is a brown paper lunch bag or a brown paper grocery bag and of course freshly harvested herbs.

I tend to err on the side of caution. It is better to have foods be slightly overdry than underdry when using this method. Any remaining moisture will encourage mold and rot, and no one has time for that!

1. Using a pen or pencil, poke some small holes throughout the paper bag.

2. Gently add the freshly harvested herbs. Do not overstuff the bag. It's important to ensure airflow can occur between the stems and leaves.

3. Staple or tie the bag shut using twine or yarn. Allow the herbs to be stored in the brown bag for approximately one to three weeks.

Make sure to check the bags often during the drying time for signs of mold and mildew. Using a paper bag will draw out the moisture from the herbs more quickly than will occur if hanging them to be air-dried. Keep in mind, there is no precise timeframe when using this method, as the drying time will vary depending on the moisture in your home, the herb being dried, and how filled the paper bags are.

This method is excellent for preventing dust from settling on the items being dried, although you don't get to enjoy the charm of seeing herbs hanging and smelling the natural essential oils being released.

OVEN-DRYING

Let me start by saying that this is my least favorite method for drying foods. On our homestead, this method is simply not practical. Oven-drying requires more electricity than a dehydrator. Not to mention, the oven cannot be used until the drying period has been completed, and for some that can create a hassle when preparing meals.

To successfully utilize the oven for drying, the temperature will need to reach as low as 140°F, with the understanding that various foods will need to dry at different temperatures. There is still the issue of proper airflow. To resolve this, the oven door must remain slightly open during the drying period. Even if you have a convection oven, you should keep the oven door slightly ajar during the drying time to draw the warm air out.

A fan can also be used to circulate hot air away from the foods being dried.

Additionally, the foods will need to be cut uniformly, as any variations in size can affect the drying time. Drying time using this method will vary greatly depending on what is being dried and the size of the food. Generally, it can take up to 12 hours to completely dry certain items. Overcrowding the oven can also slow the drying time, causing the pieces at the edge to dry more quickly than those in the center.

Keep in mind that using this method during the summer months will add heat to an already hot house, making this an impractical option.

Plan to dry strong-smelling items, such as onions, garlic, peppers, and leeks, outside or in the garage if you can. Not only does this prevent the strong oils from filling your home, it also prevents the transfer of smells to other foods. This tip also applies to meat, seafood, or organs dried as treats for dogs and cats.

MICROWAVE-DRYING

Microwave-drying is an unconventional method and not one I use. Microwaves are notorious for not cooking foods evenly. Can you imagine how difficult it would be to maintain an even temperature for dying foods? I felt the need to test this theory, and I will say that in a pinch, herbs dry pretty well in the microwave, but *nothing* else does.

Though this process is faster than any other method, it requires some effort. When drying herbs using this method, you must work in short bursts, generally 1 to 2 minutes at a time on the high setting for roughly three to five cycles. After each cycle, open the door to allow the moisture out and the herbs to cool. If the herbs are not brittle after the first cycle, repeat the process in 30-second increments until they have dried. I once tried this on apple slices, and let me tell you, I lost patience after 25 minutes. Overall, the microwave is not an ideal tool to use for drying.

SELECTING A DEHYDRATOR

Picking out a dehydrator is a bit easier than selecting a pressure canner. There are quite a few options available, and you should do some research before purchasing one. I have owned two different brands of dehydrators and would recommend both in a heartbeat. The first served its purpose as an ideal beginner's tool, but it was on the smaller size. Also, the fan was located on the top of the appliance, causing me to have to rotate the trays every hour.

The second dehydrator to grace our homestead was the "king of dehydrators," and I absolutely love it. I will tell you that I had to sell fifty-four cartons of eggs to justify buying an Excalibur, but it has been worth every penny.

For each square foot of tray space, 1 to 2 pounds of fresh foods can be dried.

Here's a list of what you should consider when making your decision.

SIZE AND WEIGHT

Dehydrators come in various heights and widths. Some are stackable, and others are box types. Weight is also a factor when considering the best one for your home. Depending on the time of year, a dehydrator may become a temporary fixture in your kitchen. Larger appliances are especially difficult to move, and the more they are jostled, the more likely they are to become damaged. Because of how often we use our dehydrator, Justin built a custom cabinet so we don't have to move it every time we use it.

Selecting the best model and size will depend on how much food you plan to preserve each year.

THERMOSTAT CONTROL AND FAN PLACEMENT

When our first dehydrator finally bit the bullet, it was time to select another. This time I spent quite a bit of time researching what brand would best fit the needs of the items we would be preserving and how to get it done efficiently. A thermostat was an important factor as it would allow for an even temperature during the drying cycle. Our goal was not only to dry herbs, fruits, vegetables, and pasta but also to make dog treats, jerky, kefir grains, and yogurt treats. Based on experience, we knew that fan placement was the most important factor, so a rear-mounting fan was a requirement.

IT'S ALL ABOUT THE BENJAMINS

Let's face it, cost is the number one factor when making such an investment on appliances. And if you are new to dehydrating, then the thought of spending a couple hundred dollars on a dehydrator may not seem practical. Smaller starter dehydrators can range from fifty dollars to one hundred dollars. Middle-of-the-road dryers will be one hundred fifty dollars to two hundred dollars, while higher-quality dehydrators can be a few hundred dollars. I believe we made the right choice in deciding to begin with the Nesco Square dehydrator. It allowed me to become acquainted with how to work a dehydrator while monitoring how often we used it in a year. That bad boy lasted us 3 years, and we got our money's worth out of it for sure.

THE WONDERFUL WORLD OF DRIED FOODS

Dried foods have been a part of your life from the moment you were able to chew and swallow foods. Dried herbs seasoned your meals, and fruit leather and dried fruit were probably some of your favorite snacks. Fast forward to adulthood and learning to cook. You may have felt overwhelmed by the selection in the dried spice aisle of your local market.

When you preserve herbs from your garden, you can create your own blends to season your foods. You can also dry medicinal herbs and flowers to treat ailments, make soap, or for cleaning purposes. For many of us, there is nothing more rewarding than creating healthy snacks for our children or our faithful "fur babies."

By now you've narrowed your choice of dehydrator, so it's time to get to work. Ready to begin?

PRETREATING

Unlike the hot pack method in canning, it is not necessary to pretreat produce that is intended to be dried. This means that you *do not have* to blanch, steam, marinate, or salt food items for them to become shelf stable.

Not to confuse you, but there *is* a benefit to pretreating items. Pretreating food helps to slow or inhibit enzymes while adding flavor to the foods being dried. But again, it is not necessary.

Since pretreating is an option for drying fruits and vegetables, don't be afraid to dry foods in their raw form; you'll end up losing fewer vitamins and nutrients this way. There are a few items such as artichokes, broccoli, carrots, and turnips that benefit from being blanched or steamed prior to drying. The full list and necessary blanching or steaming times can be found in the manual of your dehydrator.

What's my advice about pretreating using salts and seasonings, marinades, and sweeteners? Absolutely, a million times, yes. Have fun with it, and create flavors you and your family will enjoy!

HOW TO PREVENT BROWNING DURING THE DRYING PROCESS

Blanching, steaming, and applying an acidic solution to fruits and vegetables will help to prevent browning as well as slow or inhibit enzymes from allowing the food items to go bad more quickly. Now, for those who do not know, there is a difference between blanching and steaming. I prefer blanching over steaming when it comes to preparing foods for the dehydrator.

When fruit and vegetables are blanched, they're dipped into boiling water for roughly 30 to 60 seconds. Then they're removed from the boiling water and immediately submerged in ice water to stop the cooking process. Steaming foods is done using steam, creating a product that is slightly cooked. The food item is never submerged but instead is placed into a steaming basket or colander that sits just above boiling water. The lid is placed onto the pot to allow the steam in the pot to build. As with blanching, an ice water bath is necessary to stop the cooking process.

Blanching and steaming removes many of the vitamins and minerals found in raw foods. Most dehydrator companies believe in maintaining as many vitamins and minerals as possible in food items. On the other hand, the National Center for Home Food Preservation suggests blanching and steaming for the sake of keeping food items longer. If you are seek-

ing to store dehydrated foods for a long period of time, I would suggest blanching or steaming. Though if you'd like to retain as many of the vitamins and minerals as possible, simply skip it. Just know the dried foods will not last quite as long. Also note that the drying time is shortened for all food items that have been blanched or steamed.

Apples, bananas, and potatoes are great examples of fruits and vegetables that will brown quickly if not pretreated with an acidic solution such as lemon juice or citric acid. If a fruit does not normally turn brown once exposed to air, such as grapes or plums, there is no need to pretreat it with an acidic solution.

MARINATING

Anytime the word *marinate* is mentioned, I drool slightly. I'm not ashamed to admit that everything tastes better when it is marinated. This includes items being dried. Jerky and dog treats are the most common items that use marinating as a pretreatment.

What is used to create your marinade is up to you. Something as simple as sugar, vinegar, soy sauce, minced garlic, and ginger can make the most delicious marinade. How long items are marinated will depend on the thickness of the cut. The longer the items can marinate, the better the flavor you will get out of the final product.

SALTING AND SEASONING

Salting and seasoning can transform a simple item into a delicious one. Sea salt on dried tomato slices, or an herb and salt seasoning on green beans and carrots makes tasty and healthy snacks. Additionally, foods pretreated in this manner make excellent gifts for some lucky individual.

SWEETENING

Sweetening typically applies to fruit or fruit leather. The dehydrating process generally draws out the natural sugar of fruit when it is dried; unripe or fruit with little flavor is a great example of this. However, even ripe items may need to be sweetened if you are seeking to preserve them a certain way.

Fruit dipped in honey or a simple syrup made of sugar and water prior to being dried provides a sweet flavor to every bite. Cranberries dipped in honey and then dried are a great example of this.

No extra drying time is needed for fruits pretreated with a sweetener; just remember the sugar on the exterior of the fruit will be sticky. This can be somewhat annoying as you're consuming the food.

Fruit leather is generally made with ripe fruit, which means that the item will have a naturally sweet flavor because of its ripeness. A sweetener is not always necessary, but it can be used if the fruit you're transforming into leather is bland in flavor. How much sweetener to use is up to you, but a little goes a long way.

SELECTING FOODS TO DRY

Over the years I have tested the limits of what can be dried, and what I have learned is this: just about anything can be dried, though not everything *should* be dried.

I know that's hard to hear, but it's the truth. Some foods are better preserved using other methods. Zucchini is an item worthy of being dehydrated. Since it cannot be canned, and freezing requires it to be shredded, zucchini that is quartered and sliced makes a great candidate for being dehydrated. It reconstitutes well and can be used in soups, stir-fries, and casseroles without being overly tender when cooked.

The most important factor of consuming foods that have been dried for the sake of cooking is knowing how to properly reconstitute them. Vegetables can be added to soups, stews, and casseroles in their dried form and will soften during the cooking process. When reconstituting dried tomatoes to make salsa, for instance, lime juice mixed with a little water will give the tomatoes the texture necessary.

WHAT'S NOT WORTH DRYING

Let me give you an example of what I mean when I say not everything should be dried. We consume a lot of mushrooms around our homestead, and they do dry and reconstitute quite well. However, I feel that canned mushrooms are easier to work with. Cabbage is another example. It can be dried by slicing it into ⅛-inch strips, which really do not give you many options for cooking. It also doesn't reconstitute well. I find that freezing cabbage wedges or putting them in cold storage provides me with more cooking options.

Leafy greens, spinach, kale, collards, and chard dry well and make excellent chips for snacking, but storing them long term is not practical. The dried leaves tend to crumble when they're packed in jars. I suggest blanching and freezing leafy greens to make them more versatile for cooking, or they can also be pressure canned.

Blanch asparagus before you dehydrate it. Pat dry to remove excessive moisture, and then dehydrate the stalks with some garlic salt or seasonings to create a nice snack or leave plain to be used in soups.

Lettuce and cucumbers are best consumed in their fresh form. These items do not reconstitute well and really have little flavor when dehydrated. Remember, cucumbers can be made into pickles, relish, or chutney and hot water bath canned.

Also, keep in mind that overly ripe fruits and vegetables do not dry well. The enzymes create a less than desirable product. Overripe fruits can be made into jelly, whereas many vegetables can be blanched and frozen to be used for cooking.

HARVESTING, PREPARING, AND DRYING PRODUCE

As I wander through the garden or visit our local farmers' market, I never stop thinking about what can be done with the beautiful fresh produce in front of me. Though we'll eat much of it fresh, we'll also dry and use it when the gardens and farms stop producing for the season. With our limited freezer space, dried food allows us to enjoy the harvest deep into the winter months.

It is important to make sure the produce is thoroughly clean prior to preserving it. This can be done by soaking it in the vinegar and water solution found on page 62. Depending on your preference, many of the items being dried will need to be peeled, cored, and seeded prior to drying. Fruit is often sliced about ¼ inch thick, and dense items, like carrots, are sliced even thinner to allow for adequate drying time.

DRYING HERBS

The best time to harvest herbs is midmorning once the dew has dried and before the sun has hit its highest point. This retains the essential oils in the herbs, adding more flavor when you dry them. It is also beneficial to harvest before the herbs begin flowering. Herbs need very little preparation for drying. Simply give them a good washing and discard any dried or diseased leaves. I like to dry herbs in a salad spinner prior to patting them down with a paper towel.

Flowers such as echinacea, chamomile, and feverfew can be dried as is. When drying rose petals, it is best to remove them from the stem. This helps to ensure the petals do not turn brown during the process.

Other than air-drying, another option for drying herbs is to use an electric dehydrator. Using a dehydrator speeds up the drying time and allows for more herbs to be dried at a quicker rate than when air-drying. The leaves are removed from the stem and placed on the drying trays. If the tray screens are too large for drying herbs, place a paper towel or parchment paper on the trays prior to adding the leaves. Once completely dried, the leaves will be brittle to the touch. It is best to store the leaves whole, crushing them as you need them; this will provide the freshest and strongest flavor when used.

HERB MIXES

When you create your own herb blends, you know how old the dried herbs are, how they were grown, and the joy it brought you to grow them. There is no right or wrong way to create blends for cooking, so enjoy being creative.

Generally 1 teaspoon crushed dried herbs is equivalent to 1 tablespoon fresh herbs.

Italian Seasoning
Equal parts dried oregano, basil, rosemary, marjoram, sage, thyme, Italian parsley

Poultry Seasoning Mix
7 tablespoons dried sage
5 tablespoons dried thyme
3 tablespoons dried marjoram
4 tablespoons dried rosemary

Pork Seasoning Mix
Equal parts of the following dried herbs: sage, parsley, thyme, rosemary
Garlic powder can be added per your preference.

DRYING ROOTS AND SEEDS

Drying turmeric, ginger, and dandelion roots is extremely easy. They will keep for quite a while in their whole form and can be stored in Mason jars, mylar bags, or vacuum-packed to be preserved. If the root system is small and thin, like dandelion roots, they can be bundled together using twine or rubber bands and placed into a brown paper bag with holes for air circulation. The drying time for this method can take a few weeks. Thick roots such as turmeric, ginger, chicory, or thicker dandelion roots should be evenly sliced into strips or into coins. The strips or coins can then be air-dried or dried with the use of an electric dehydrator.

DELICIOUS TURMERIC MILK TO HELP REDUCE INFLAMMATION

There are days when something warm and soothing is greatly needed and much appreciated, especially when it contains beneficial ingredients such as turmeric, ginger, and black pepper. You know there is nothing but goodness in the mug. Turmeric milk, also known as golden milk, helps to soothe sore and tired muscles when your body is overworked. Turmeric works to reduce inflammation, and when partnered with black pepper, the curcumin from the turmeric can be absorbed into the body. Black pepper also assists in combating coughs and colds and promotes good digestion and intestinal health. Ginger helps with digestion and nausea, fights the flu and common cold, helps to reduce muscle pain and soreness, and is also anti-inflammatory. The warm milk? It will bring you comfort and help you relax as you sit by the fire.

INGREDIENTS

2 cups milk, coconut milk,
  or raw milk
1 teaspoon turmeric powder
1 teaspoon ginger powder
Small pinch freshly ground black
  peppercorn
Honey (optional)

METHOD

1. Slowly heat the milk in a 2-quart saucepan over the stove.
2. Add the turmeric, ginger, and peppercorn to the milk, and bring it to a gentle boil.
3. Remove the saucepan from the heat, and let it sit for roughly 5 minutes.
4. The turmeric milk can be sweetened with honey if desired.

Seeds from herbs such as oregano, mint, or basil are tiny, but collecting them is not difficult at all. Simply bundle the stems together, and cover the flower head with a brown paper bag or tie a muslin cloth around it, then hang the bundle upside down as if you were air-drying herbs. Once the flower bundle is thoroughly dry, shake the seeds from the stem or pick larger seeds from the dried flower head.

DRYING FRUITS

Drying fruits is extremely easy, and the flavor is delicious. As a matter of fact, my husband enjoys dehydrated fruit more than when it is freeze-dried because the concentrated sugar content creates an intense fruit flavor, not to mention he loves the chewy texture. Drying fruits that are not quite ripe will draw the concentrated sugar contained within, making them perfectly sweet and delicious. Dehydrating watermelon with little flavor is a great example of this.

As with all items being dried, the slices should be uniform in size, as the thickness and the shape of the cut will affect the drying times. I don't make it a habit to peel the skins of fruit such as apples, kiwi, or pears mainly because we don't mind consuming the skins, even if they get slightly tough during the drying process.

PRETREATING FRUIT WITH AN ACIDIC SOLUTION

Use one of the acidic solutions below to pretreat fruit such as apples, pears, bananas, peaches, and apricots to prevent browning, reduce vitamin loss, lengthen shelf life, and destroy potentially harmful bacteria:

1 teaspoon powdered ascorbic acid to 1 cup water for 10 minutes
½ teaspoon powdered citric acid to 2 cups water for 10 minutes
Equal parts lemon juice to water

Another item to prevent browning in fruit is honey. Honey works as well as the options above, and it provides a sweetness to items too.

Honey Dip: ½ cup sugar to ½ cup hot water; allow to cool to lukewarm and add ½ cup honey

DEHYDRATING TIPS FOR FRUIT

Dehydrating berries is an all-time favorite of ours. We enjoy them as snacks, as well as add them to baked goods or breakfast items such as yogurt, oatmeal, and granola. Since many fruits do not necessarily need to be pretreated to preserve well, there are a few tips that will help you achieve an excellent product.

Blanching berries without a core, such as blueberries, cranberries, or grapes, for 30 seconds allows the skin to crack, which drastically shortens the drying time. Though berries and grapes do not need to be pretreated with an acidic treatment, we love to honey dip cranberries prior to drying. The flavor is amazing, and the kids seem to prefer them this way.

Here's a guide to preparing and pretreating various fruits for drying:

PREPARING AND PRETREATING FRUITS

fruit	preparation	pretreatment
APPLES	core and cut into ¼-inch slices	acidic solution
APRICOTS	cut in half and remove pit	acidic solution
BANANAS	slice ⅛ inch thick	acidic solution
BERRIES	dry whole or cut in half	not necessary
CHERRIES	remove stems and pits	not necessary
CITRUS	slice ¼ inch thick	not necessary
CRANBERRIES	blanch 30 seconds	Honey Dip (optional)
DATES & FIGS	slice ¼ inch thick	Honey Dip (optional)
ELDERBERRY	blanch 30 seconds	Honey Dip (optional)
GRAPES	puncture skin and remove stem	not necessary
KIWI	slice ¼ inch thick	not necessary
MELONS	slice ¼ inch thick	not necessary
NECTARINES & PEACHES	remove pit and slice into ⅛-inch pieces	acidic solution
PAPAYAS & MANGOES	cut into ⅛- or ¼-inch slices	not necessary
PEARS	slice ¼ inch thick	acidic solution
PINEAPPLE	remove core and slice ¼ inch thick	not necessary
PLUMS	cut in half and remove pit	not necessary
RHUBARB	remove tough ends and cut 1-inch pieces	not necessary

DRYING VEGETABLES

The National Center for Home Food Preservation states many vegetables should be blanched prior to being dehydrated. This step is often missed by many, but there is a reason for it. Blanching allows moisture to escape, softens the cell structure, assists in helping foods dry and rehydrate faster. Again, the drying time will depend on how uniform the cuts are, as well as the thickness and shape of the cut.

The exceptions to this rule are garlic, onions, spicy and sweet peppers, and herbs. Keep in mind these items air-dry extremely well. When drying bell peppers, you'll need to slice, seed, and core them prior to drying. Spicy peppers such as Thai chile and cayenne can be dried whole, whereas jalapeño and serrano can be sliced into coins or quartered and dried. I would suggest removing the white membrane from the interior of the peppers; if left, it can cause the pepper to become bitter in flavor once dried.

Garlic and onions can be dried as whole bulbs or using one of the drying methods suggested in this section. If air-drying garlic and onions whole, they must be cured prior to storing them for the winter months. Information on how to cure onions and garlic can be found on page 211. Aside from being dried and stored whole, they can be sliced and dried in a dehydrator as well as in the oven, with the drying time varying based on the size of the slices. Once dried, they can be stored as is or ground into powder. To store for long periods of time, add an oxygen absorber and vacuum-seal the lids. Reserving small quantities for use in half-pint or pint-size jars allows these food items to be stored longer.

AIR-DRYING ON THE VINE

Shelling peas and beans such as white, fava, lima, kidney, soybeans, or other legumes can be field-dried. This is also known as drying on the vine. Though this method is practiced often, there are a few challenges. The pods must be picked prior to the first frost and before they overdry. Overly dry pods will break open on the vine, causing the seeds to drop to the ground. If squirrels or chipmunks are in your area, be prepared to lose a few seeds. But more importantly, if you reside in the Pacific Northwest, harvest the dry pods prior to the rainy season. Leaving them too long on the vine can cause mold and even rot to set in. The pods can be finished by drying them in a dehydrator or oven.

DEHYDRATING TIPS FOR VEGETABLES

Many people will not invest a lot of time dehydrating vegetables, but in truth, it is an excellent method for preserving foods from the garden or farmers' market. Utilizing an electric dehydrator gives you the ability to create a zero-waste product. Celery leaves and fruit peels (including tomato) can be dried and ground into powder, which can then be used to create celery salt, tomato powder (which can be reconstituted to make tomato paste), for flavorings for yogurt, oatmeal, or baked goods, and so on. You can also transform vegetables into delicious snacks by adding seasoning salts to kale, chard, green beans, or peas. Your options are endless!

Celery Salt

1 tablespoon fine sea salt
6 tablespoons dried celery leaves

TOMATO POWDER

Though technically not a seasoning, dried tomato peels are useful when ground into a powder. The powder can be reconstituted to make tomato paste, as well as to add flavor to soups, casseroles, and egg dishes. It also creates a zero-waste product when you're putting up tomatoes.

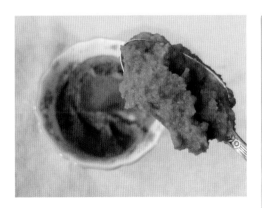

METHOD

1. Lay the tomato peels evenly on the dehydrator trays; slightly overlapping the peels is okay.

2. Set the temperature to 135°F, and dry for 4 to 10 hours. The drying time will depend on the type of dehydrator being used and how thickly the peels are laid on the trays.
3. Once complete, the peels will be brittle.
4. Blend them into a powder and store in an airtight container with an oxygen absorber for up to 6 months at room temperature. If you do not plan to use the powder right away, vacuum-seal the lids with a lid sealer.
5. To make tomato paste, slowly add water to the powder, balancing between powder and liquid until the desired consistency has been achieved.

PREPARING AND PRETREATING VEGETABLES

vegetable	preparation	pretreatment
ARTICHOKES	Cut hearts to ⅛-inch strips	Blanch 6–8 min
ASPARAGUS	Remove woody end and cut in half	Blanch 4 min or Steam 4 min
BEANS	Cut into 1-inch pieces	Blanch 2 min or Steam 2½ min
BEETS	Cut ¼ inch thick	Cook until fork tender
BROCCOLI	Cut florets and dry whole	Blanch 2 min or Steam 2½ min
BRUSSELS SPROUTS	Cut in half lengthwise	Blanch 5½ min or Steam 6–7 min
CABBAGE	Quarter, core, and cut ⅛-inch strips	Blanch 2 min or Steam 3 min
CARROTS	Peel and cut into ⅛-inch circles	Blanch 3½ min or Steam 3½ min
CAULIFLOWER	Prepare as for serving	Blanch 3–4 min or Steam 5 min
CELERY	Slice stalks ¼ inch thick	Blanch 2 min or Steam 2 min
CORN	Blanch cob 3 min	Cut kernels from cob
EGGPLANT	Same as summer squash	Blanch 3 min or Steam 3½ min
GARLIC	Peel, finely chop bulbs	Not necessary
GREENS, LEAFY	Trim into strips	Blanch 1½ min or Steam 2½ min
MUSHROOMS	Slice, peel larger mushrooms	Not necessary
OKRA	Slice ¼-inch circles	Not necessary
ONIONS	Slice ¼ inch thick	Not necessary
PARSNIPS	Slice ⅜-inch slices	Blanch 3½ min or Steam 3½ min
PEAS (SHELLING)	Shell	Blanch 2 min or Steam 3 min
PEPPERS & PIMIENTOS	Remove seeds, white membrane, stem	Not necessary
POTATOES	Peel, slice ⅛-inch circles	Blanch 6 min or Steam 6–8 min
PUMPKIN	Remove seed & pulp, slice ⅛ thick	Blanch 1 min or Steam 3 min
SQUASH, SUMMER	Slice ¼ inch thick	Blanch 1½ min or Steam 2½–3 min
SQUASH, WINTER	Cut to small chunks, slice ⅛ thick	Blanch 1 min or Steam 3 min
TOMATO	Slice ¼ inch thick	Not necessary
TOMATO, CHERRY	Cut in half, skin side down	Not necessary
TOMATO, STEWING	Blanch to remove skin	Not necessary
TURNIPS	Peel, cut ⅜ inch thick	Blanch 3½ min or Steam 3½ min
YAMS	Peel, slice ¼ inch thick	Blanch 6 min or Steam 6-8 min

Once the vegetables have been blanched, immediately submerge into ice water to stop the cooking process. The food items will need to be patted dry with a paper towel prior to dehydrating them. Blanching and steaming times are provided by the National Center for Home Food Preservation.

Some dehydrated vegetables can easily be reconstituted in liquid. We find it easier to add them to what's being prepared, allowing the liquid from the foods to slowly bring them back to life. When using dehydrated carrots, celery, and onions in a roast, adding a small amount of water to the bottom of the pot helps the reconstitution process.

I want to bring your attention to a discrepancy between what you will find in your dehydrator's manual versus what can be found on the National Center for Home Food Preservation website in terms of blanching and steaming vegetables. The NCHFP states, "Blanching stops the enzyme action which could cause loss of color and flavor during drying and storage. It also shortens the drying and rehydration time by relaxing the tissue walls so moisture can escape and later re-enter more rapidly." However, a top-brand dehydrator company states that only dense root vegetables should be blanched or steamed prior to being dehydrated.

Blanching and steaming are not required for food safety in dried goods. However, they do help create foods that will store longer and they do reduce the drying time. The choice is yours to make. The chart on the facing page provided by the NCHFP is specific regarding which vegetables should be pretreated and how they should be prepared prior to blanching or steaming.

I love manuals and refer to them often, even prior to searching the NCHFP website. In truth, the manufacturer knows the best practices for their appliances. The manual will clearly state which vegetables should be steamed or blanched and which should be dried in their fresh form.

DRYING NUTS

If you are one of the lucky individuals who has access to harvesting almonds, walnuts, Brazil nuts, cashews, chestnuts, peanuts, pine nuts, or even pistachios, you need to get those babies dried prior to consuming them. Nuts preserved at home will keep them at their peak up through 4 months.

Raw nuts have enzyme inhibitors, which prevent the body from absorbing their healthy enzymes. Additionally, raw nuts contain phytic acid, which is indigestible and prevents the minerals from being absorbed by the body. Because of this, all nuts need to be pretreated prior to being consumed. Once they have been removed from their shells, soak the nuts in warm water for 30 minutes. Much like blanched or steamed vegetables, the nuts will need to be dried by patting them with a towel to remove any water prior to adding them to the dehydrator. Shelled nuts have successfully dried when the surface is leathery but the inside is tender.

Nuts and seeds such as pistachios, sunflower seeds, pumpkin seeds, and peanuts can be home-dried in their shells, although these items must still be soaked in warm water for 30 minutes prior to drying them. A saltwater soak is ideal for these items, making them salty in flavor and excellent for snacking. Once the nuts are thoroughly dried, the shells will be hard and easy to crack. The seeds will be tender and should not be wrinkled.

SALTED NUTS AND SEEDS

INGREDIENTS

1 cup raw nuts or seeds

2 cups water

2 teaspoons salt

METHOD

1. Prepare the nuts and seeds by soaking them in the saltwater brine for 3 to 6 hours.
2. Spread them on a baking sheet in a single layer.
3. Preheat oven to 200°F and bake for 4 hours, or dry in a dehydrator at 100°F for 2 to 4 hours.

DRYING DAIRY AND EGGS

If you are living the life of a homesteader, this section may be quite useful for you. The idea of preserving dairy goods and eggs isn't always appealing or even necessary to many people, but having these items on hand allows you to be equipped in emergency situations or when you have an abundance of dairy and eggs. One does not need to own a cow, goats, or chickens to preserve dairy or eggs. You can buy extra when they are on sale and preserve them for later use.

PRESERVING FARM-FRESH EGGS

If you are being overrun with eggs from your loving hens, consider dehydrating them. Keep in mind that dried eggs are nothing like fresh, and you are limited in what can be done with them. They reconstitute well and make pretty good scrambled eggs or they can be used for baking, but that's about it.

METHOD

1. Wash eggs well, and crack them into a bowl or directly into a blender.
2. Mix the eggs using a hand whisk, immersion blender, or regular blender.
3. Place parchment sheets on dehydrator trays, and create a well to contain the eggs by folding the ends of the parchment paper. Place the mixed eggs into the well in the parchment paper.
4. Set the temperature to 135°F to 145°F (make sure to check with the dehydrator manual for the correct setting).
5. Generally, raw eggs will dry between 8 to 10 hours. However, drying time will vary based on the thickness of the raw eggs in the drying tray and the type of dehydrator being used.
6. The eggs are dried once the mixture appears to be cracked and dry looking. They can be ground into powder with the use of a blender or food processor.
7. Store the powdered eggs in an airtight container with an oxygen absorber. Dried eggs will last 1 year at room temperature. If they are not used right away, it is important to vacuum-seal the jars using a jar sealer to maintain freshness. Make sure to add an oxygen absorber or two to maximize freshness.
8. To reconstitute, add 1 heaping tablespoon powder eggs to 2 tablespoons water in a bowl. Allow to sit for 5 minutes, making sure to mix the eggs and water well prior to cooking.

It gets better. Milk and eggs are not the only dairy items that can be dried at home. Items such as yogurt, cheese, cottage cheese, and ricotta can also be dried and made into a shelf-stable item. The shelf life of these goods is not as long as it would be if they were to be dried using a freeze-dryer, but they will generally store well for a few months. Freeze-dried dairy items have a 25-year shelf life. Learn more about long-term food storage utilizing a freeze-dryer in Chapter 8.

You might remember that dairy should not be canned due to its high fat content, which can cause the milk to turn rancid within a short period of time if not instantly once canned. I am an adventurous canner, but canning dairy is something even I won't touch. Drying it? Yes, most definitely!

Choosing milk with the lowest fat content will help when it comes to storing dried dairy. If you are a lucky individual who raises a dairy cow, it is important to remove the fat (or cream) prior to drying the milk. Keep in mind that goat's milk should not be dried due to its high fat content; the cream does not separate from the milk.

All right, let's begin! If you are nervous about drying milk, feel free to move to the yogurt section. You will be happy to know that dried yogurt makes for excellent yogurt bites and leather. If you're not ready to dry dairy products, at least you'll now know how to do it if the need should arise.

DRYING MILK

Home-dried milk isn't something to ooh and aah over, but it does serve its purpose. The texture when reconstituted is somewhat odd, and there is no way our kids will drink it. However, if you are looking to use it for cooking, baking, or adding to coffee or tea, it really does the job nicely. Home-dried milk tends to not have the same texture as store bought, though the taste of freeze-dried milk is actually very similar to dried milk purchased at the market.

With that in mind, if you happen to stumble upon a great sale on milk at the market or are currently heavy in milk from your milking cow, or maybe you just use a lot of dried milk, this might be something you may want to try. If you're purchasing milk from the market, select one that contains very little fat, like skim milk, although 1 to 2 percent will work too. Drying milk is an extremely long process, and the dried milk must be packaged immediately upon completion to ensure that moisture does not re-enter what has been dried. You will know the process has been completed when the dried milk begins to flake away from the drying tray. At this point, you can store it as flakes or grind it into a powder-like consistency. Don't forget to include an oxygen absorber and to vacuum-seal the jar when storing.

If you don't own a dairy cow, raw milk is available for purchase in certain states. It is excellent for drying. Removing the heavy cream from the milk is extremely easy and can be done in minutes. By allowing the milk to rest in the refrigerator overnight, the cream will naturally rise to the top. Using a turkey baster, gently and slowly draw out the cream, making sure to keep the cream from mixing with the milk. If too much cream mixes with the milk during the withdrawal process, allow the milk to once again rest in the refrigerator, and repeat the process.

RECONSTITUTING POWDERED MILK

½ cup powdered milk mixed with ⅔ cup water = 1 cup milk

Use a whisk, immersion blender, or blender to ensure the powder dissolves and mixes well. When powdered milk is used for baking, the powder can be added directly to the dry ingredients and the water to the liquid ingredients.

DRYING TIMES FOR MILK

Oven: Set at 130°F, dry for 26–32 hours
Dehydrator: Set at 130°F, dry for 24–30 hours

DRYING YOGURT

Dehydrated yogurt makes an excellent snack for kids. We love to take it on camping and hiking trips or pack it in their school lunches. Heck, we've also been known to eat it straight off the dehydrating trays (we, meaning my children and Justin).

You can use your dehydrator to make delicious yogurt bites or yogurt leather, and many dehydrator brands sell reusable nonstick sheets specifically for this project, though the sheets tend to be on the expensive side. The easiest and most economical way to prevent a mess in the dehydrator is to use waxed paper to line the trays. This also works well for making yogurt leather, as the waxed paper can easily be cut into strips, then rolled and stored. See how to properly store dried yogurt below.

Simply spread homemade or store-bought yogurt on the drying trays, and let the dehydrator do its thing. If you are making your own yogurt, which I suggest you do, use fruit puree rather than chunks to flavor the yogurt; the chunks will cause uneven drying. I've been known to use pureed homemade jams or fruit peels that have been dried and ground to powder as flavoring. Yes, the jam increases the sugar content in the yogurt, but don't knock it until you try it. It's really quite good!

DRYING TIMES FOR YOGURT

Oven: Set at 125°F–135°F, dry time 8–10 hours
Dehydrator: Set at 125°F–135°F, dry time 6–8 hours

Keep in mind: spread yogurt no thicker than ⅛ inch when adding to trays to allow for even drying. If you're adding pureed fruit, dry time will need an additional 4 hours. The dry time for yogurt bites will require an additional 6 to 8 hours due to the thickness of the yogurt. Also, the degree to which the yogurt is dried will depend on the type of oven being used and the brand of dehydrator.

STORING DRIED YOGURT

Storing dried yogurt is easy. What you'll need is a Mason jar, oxygen absorber, and a vacuum sealer if storing long term. I highly suggest storing yogurt bites in small jars such as pint or even half pint. This allows the freshness to be maintained as the jars are opened. Yogurt leather strips can be stored in either pint or quart jars, depending on how quickly they are devoured. For easy storage, roll the cut leather strips and place as many as possible into a jar, making sure to add an oxygen absorber. Vacuum seal jars that will not be consumed right away.

Dried yogurt is a shelf-stable item. If it's stored longer than a week, though, it tends to become sour. It will keep for a few months in the refrigerator. So, why bother with all this work if it will only keep for a week stored on the shelf, you might ask? If you are making yogurt yourself, it is a healthier item than what you will purchase from the market, and that, my friend, is the ultimate reason.

HOMEMADE YOGURT

If you have never tried making homemade yogurt, you are really missing out. The flavor is outstanding and much better than anything you will find at the market. It can be made in the oven, a cabinet-style dehydrator, a slow cooker, and even in an electric pressure cooker. You need to try it!

INGREDIENTS
½ gallon milk (raw is better, but pasteurized is good)
4 tablespoons starter (premade yogurt with live cultures or yogurt starter)

METHOD

1. Heat the milk in a stainless steel pan over medium heat until it reaches 180°F.

2. Pour the heated milk into clean Mason jars of choice, and allow to cool either by setting them on the counter or by placing the jars in a cool water bath until the temperature drops to 110°F, never exceeding 115°F.

3. Add 2 tablespoons live culture for each quart-size jar. Gently stir until the cultures are incorporated into the milk.

4. Place the jars with lid and rings on into the oven with *only* the light on for 12 to 24 hours, allowing the culture to incubate. The light provides constant heat at about 110°F, never exceeding 115°F.

5. After 12 hours of incubating, taste a small amount of the yogurt; if it is tangy in flavor (much like store-bought yogurt), it is done. Do not be afraid to allow the yogurt to incubate up to 24 hours.

6. Once the yogurt has completed the incubation period, place the jars in the refrigerator to allow the yogurt to cool and set.

7. Once the yogurt has set, pour off the whey from the top or strain the yogurt for a thicker consistency.

Note: There is a big difference in the incubation time whether you're using an oven or an electric dehydrator due to the heat source. Yogurt that incubates in the oven with just the bulb generating heat will take a while to complete. Twelve hours is the minimum amount of time yogurt should be incubated; however, if it incubates up to 24 hours, the lactose in the milk is generally fully absorbed, creating a true yogurt flavor.

If an electric dehydrator is used to incubate the live culture, follow the steps as noted above. Place the quart jars in the dehydrator with the heat set to 115°F for 8 to 10 hours. The heat set at 115°F speeds up the incubation period.

Never allow the temperature to exceed 115°F. If so, the live beneficial bacteria are killed, which means no yogurt for you.

WHAT IS WHEY AND WHAT IS IT USED FOR?

Whey, also known as whey protein, is the water part of milk that appears once yogurt has set or curds have formed in the cheese-making process. Sweet whey occurs when making yogurt, hard cheese, milk kefir, or buttermilk. This type of whey is used more often in helping to ferment foods, in many drink items such as milkshakes and fruit juice. It can also be added to make lacto-fermented drinks such as ginger ale. If you do not plan to consume it, feel free to feed it to livestock. Acid whey is left when soft cheeses such as ricotta, feta, chèvre, or paneer are made. There is not much that can be done with this type of whey other than feeding it to livestock. Be careful, though, as this can upset their digestive systems.

OTHER DAIRY ITEMS

Aside from milk and yogurt, cottage cheese, ricotta cheese, and sour cream can also be dried. Each of these items are dried using the same method for drying yogurt, though the texture will be brittle. Once dried, these items can be crumbled into flakes for easier storage. Just make sure to include an oxygen absorber to minimize moisture within the jar. They can be used to flavor sauces and soups, but they can't be reconstituted to their original forms.

As cheese connoisseurs, otherwise known as cheese heads, we find no purpose in drying block or shredded cheese, mainly because we eat it a lot quicker than I care to share. Just know that if you have an abundance of shredded cheese or hard cheese from the market on hand, it can be dried to make it shelf stable. However, cheese is another item that does not reconstitute well. Turning it into powder once it is fully dried is the best use for it. Powdered cheese is an excellent ingredient for making macaroni and cheese or casseroles that call for cheese. Start by using 1 part liquid to ½ part powder, and increase the amount as needed to achieve the desired consistency.

MAKING RICOTTA CHEESE AT HOME

The first time I consumed homemade ricotta cheese, I could have eaten the entire batch. No joke. A friend showed us how to make it, and I was blown away by how easy it was. All that is needed are a few ingredients and a bit of patience. Her technique is flawless, and I hope you enjoy it as much as I do! Keep in mind that 1 gallon of milk should yield about 1½ pounds of ricotta.

INGREDIENTS

1 gallon whole milk (avoid homogenized and ultra-pasteurized)

1 teaspoon citric acid dissolved in ¼ cup cool water (or use 1½ to 2 tablespoons bottled lemon juice)

1 teaspoon finely ground kosher or sea salt to taste, preferably cheese salt

2 tablespoons heavy cream (optional, but it provides such a wonderful, silky texture to the finished ricotta)

EQUIPMENT

Stove or induction cooktop (avoid using a hot plate, as it offers no temperature control)

Large pot

Slotted spoon or ladle

Thermometer

Colander

Butter muslin

Measuring cup and measuring spoon

METHOD

1. Pour the milk into a large, heavy-bottomed pot.

2. Add the citric acid solution or lemon juice to the milk and stir thoroughly.

3. Gradually heat the milk to 185°F to 195°F. Use a food thermometer to check the temperature often. The heat will need to be medium to medium-low to avoid scorching the milk. Make sure to stir often. Do not allow the mixture to boil, as your milk may take on a "cooked" flavor.

4. As the milk heats up, it will begin to set a curd from the milk solids, and the whey (the liquid that separates from the curd) will become visible around the edge of the pot. Do not allow the milk to go above 195°F.

5. Remove the pot from the heat. Allow the curds to set for at least 10 minutes. (At this point, the whey should no longer be milky in appearance but should look clear with a slight greenish or yellow cast.)

6. Place a colander over a large pan. Line the colander with a butter muslin, which has a finer weave than cheesecloth.

7. Ladle the curds into the colander. Allow the curds to drain to desired consistency and texture. (Reserve the whey for another use such as the base for soups, stew, sauces; for making bread; as a ferment starter; or even feed to livestock.)

8. Add salt to the drained ricotta and mix well.

9. The ricotta is ready to be consumed at this point, though cream can be added to create a creamier flavor, if desired.

Note: If you plan to make cheese on a regular basis and would like to try making it with cheese salt, know that this particular type of salt can be purchased online through various sites.

Butter muslin should not be confused with cheesecloth. It is woven much tighter, with no holes in the material, unlike cheesecloth. It is often used to strain whey from cheese. It can be washed and reused often.

STORING DRIED GOODS

When you spend hours drying foods, it is a shame to lose them due to moisture and exposure to air. With a few precautions, your dried goods, depending on the content, can be stored for quite a while, up to a few years in fact, maintaining the same consistency as when they were first dried.

If you are planning to consume the dried goods within a few weeks, sealing jars for long-term storage isn't necessary. However, if you are not planning to eat the foods or herbs quickly or if you have dried a large batch, then add an oxygen absorber and vacuum-seal the jars immediately. Storing jars in a cool, dark location away from light also helps the goods keep longer. There is nothing worse than opening a jar or mylar bag and finding that your goods have spoiled. Before you begin drying fruit, vegetables, and jerky, I advise you to invest in the following items necessary for storage:

Jars. I find that wide-mouth jars, which are available in half pint, pint, quart, and even half gallon, work best when storing dried foods. Nothing is more difficult than trying to fit apple rings or orange slices into a regular-mouth jar.

Mylar bags. We generally use mylar bags for freeze-drying purposes, though storing meat items like jerky in resealable mylar bags makes snacking much easier. Mylar bags also work great for storing large quantities of dried items. Trust me, one large mylar bag is much easier to store in the pantry than four quart-size Mason jars.

Vacuum sealers. A vacuum sealer is a must-have for those who are preserving foods. However, a vacuum sealer can crush brittle dried food, so it's best to use for items like jerky, fruit, and vegetables. Most vacuum sealers can vacuum-seal Mason jars with the use of a jar sealer, which may come with the vacuum sealer or can be purchased as an attachment. The vacuum cap, which fits over the lids, and the cable, which attaches to the cap and vacuum machine, can be purchased online if they do not come with the machine. It is necessary to have both the cap and the cable to properly seal jars.

Oxygen absorbers. Oxygen absorbers are necessary for storing dried food, regardless if the foods are being used immediately or much later. Generally, one absorber per Mason jar, vacuum bag, or mylar bag is needed to absorb any moisture within the jar or bag. These little bags contain an iron powder that allows oxygen and moisture to enter but not to leak out, and as odd as it may seem, they are safe to use with food.

LET'S MAKE MAGIC

Let me now encourage you to be creative with the foods you dry. You can create granola, trail mix, and veggie chips that your family will enjoy or powder mixes that you would normally purchase from the market. I promise that you'll become more adventuresome as you continue preserving the beautiful bounty of your harvest. Here are some of our favorites.

JERKY MIX

A good jerky mix is hard to come by, but a great jerky will have friends and family lined up to be the receiver of something awesome. Beef jerky by default is incredible, but if you can create a jerky mix for fish and wild game, consider yourself made in the world of jerky making. Remember, there is no right or wrong when it comes to creating flavors; it is an art. If you are not ready to create your own mix, find a recipe you like, and fine-tune it to your family's taste.

A jerky gun (see page 23) is an excellent tool for making jerky; however, we prefer to use cuts of meat, poultry, or fish instead.

BASIC TERIYAKI JERKY

This recipe calls for 5 pounds of meat and is what we consider to be the most basic of recipes. When jerky is completely dried, it will have a leathery texture. At this point turn off the dehydrator, and allow the jerky to cool within the dehydrator. Jerky should be stored in an airtight container with an oxygen absorber. It will keep for 1 month at room temperature and 6 months in the refrigerator. If you are looking to store it long term, place it in a vacuum-sealed bag, and store it in the freezer for up to 1 year.

INGREDIENTS

3 cups teriyaki sauce
2 tablespoons olive oil
2 tablespoons brown packed sugar
1 tablespoon minced garlic
1 tablespoon freshly cracked peppercorns
1 tablespoon kosher salt, sea salt, or
   pickling salt
1 tablespoon Liquid Smoke
1 tablespoon finely grated fresh ginger
5 pounds red meat of choice, cut to ¼ inch
   thick

METHOD

1. Combine all of the ingredients except the red meat, and blend well.
2. Add the meat and blend well again. Marinate for a minimum of 1 hour. For a longer marinade, place the bowl in the refrigerator.
3. Place parchment paper on the drying trays, and then lay the strips of marinated meat onto the trays, making sure the strips don't touch each other.
4. Dry in the dehydrator at 145°F for 6 to 8 hours.

COWBOY'S WHISKEY JERKY

This jerky mix is for Justin, a diehard Dallas Cowboys' fan who enjoys his whiskey! Unlike my husband, who's rough around the edges, this jerky has a mild disposition and one that the older folks around the homestead truly enjoy. Feel free to play with the type of alcohol being used—rum and bourbon make excellent options. If you did not think that adding alcohol to a liquid brine would be delicious, you have no idea what you are missing. Let me help you resolve that problem.

INGREDIENTS

2 cups whiskey, nothing fancy
1 tablespoon soy sauce
1 tablespoon brown packed sugar
1 tablespoon olive oil
1 teaspoon kosher salt, sea salt, or
   pickling salt
½ teaspoon Liquid Smoke
½ teaspoon minced garlic
¼ teaspoon freshly ground black
   peppercorns
1 pound red meat, sliced ¼ inch thick

METHOD

1. Reduce the whiskey to ⅓ cup in a pot with high sides, as it may flame. The flames will subside once the alcohol burns off.
2. Allow the alcohol to cool, then add the other ingredients and stir well.
3. Marinate the meat for at least 1 hour. For a longer marinade, place the bowl in the refrigerator.
4. Place parchment paper on the dehydrator trays, and lay the marinated meat on the trays, making sure the strips do not touch each other.
5. Dry in the dehydrator at 145°F for 6 to 8 hours.

DOG TREATS

I wouldn't be a good dog momma if I didn't share our dog, Ms. Harley Quinn's, favorite treat! This treat made from chicken strips, turmeric, crushed black peppercorn, and dried parsley not only makes her happy, but it also meets the guidelines of her restricted diet while helping to reduce inflammation. Turmeric and black peppercorns are excellent aids for reducing swollen joints. If you are wondering, the parsley will help with bad breath and digestion.

INGREDIENTS

1 pound chicken strips, sliced to ¼ inch thick

½ cup organic turmeric powder

1½ teaspoons freshly ground black peppercorns

2 tablespoons freshly chopped parsley

METHOD

1. In a bowl, place the raw chicken strips and dry ingredients.

2. Allow the chicken to marinate for 1 hour. Place parchment paper on the dehydrator trays, and lay the marinated meat on the trays, making sure the strips do not touch each other.

3. Dry at 155°F for 6 to 8 hours.

STONE FRUIT LEATHER

Each year the golden plum tree at my mother-in-law's homestead becomes filled with amazing golden balls of sweetness, and each year we stuff our faces full of what we can eat fresh, then reserve the rest for fruit leather or golden plum jam. Any fruit or combination of fruit can be used to make fruit leather, for example, a berry mix of blueberries, strawberries, and blackberries. Remember to add an acidic solution if needed to prevent browning. This can be achieved with bottled lemon juice, orange juice, honey, or a citric acid and water solution. To package, leaving the parchment paper intact, cut the leather into strips, rolling to fit into mylar bags or Mason jars. Fruit leath-

er will keep for 1 month at room temperature or longer when stored in the freezer. However, I will warn you that fruit leather will not last long if you have young children, and more than likely, much of it will be consumed as you are packing it to be stored. Yes, it is *that* good.

INGREDIENTS

8 cups stone fruit, such as plums, peaches, apricots

1 cup pulp-free orange juice

METHOD

1. Wash the fruit well and remove the leaves and stems. Remove the fruit from the pit.

2. Using an immersion blender or blender, blend the fruit, skin, and orange juice until a pureed texture has been achieved, being careful not to overblend, which will make it watery.

3. Place parchment paper on the drying trays.

4. Slowly spread the fruit on the parchment paper, no more than ⅛ inch thick.

5. Dehydrate at 125°F for 5 to 8 hours. The completed product will have a leather-like texture. Fruit leather dries from the outside in. To check for completion, push down in the center. No indentation should be visible.

APPLE RINGS

Cinnamon apple rings are the most desired item to dehydrate during apple season, so we reserve roughly six half-gallon jars for these delicious treats. They make perfect snack items for home, work, or school lunches. There is not a lot that goes into them, but the reward of producing a healthy "chip" option for the family does this momma good. Apple slices are best stored in a cool, dark space. If you are not planning to eat the apple rings right away, store in a Mason jar with an oxygen absorber. This will keep them for a month. If you are looking to store them longer, vacuum-seal the jars using a lid sealer (see page 23).

INGREDIENTS

5 pounds apples, organic (which do not contain the waxy film)
¼ cup lemon juice
1 cup water
3 tablespoons ground cinnamon
Pinch of ground cloves
Pinch of allspice (optional)
3 tablespoons organic cane sugar (optional)

METHOD

1. Slice the apples ⅛ inch thick using a mandoline or apple slicer/corer.

2. Combine the lemon juice and water. Immediately submerge the sliced apples into the lemon and water solution for a minute or two to prevent browning.

3. Mix the spices and sugar in a bowl, and lightly sprinkle the apple slices with the mixture.

4. Place the apple slices onto dehydrator trays, making sure they do not touch.

5. Set the temperature of the dehydrator to 135°F.

6. Allow to dry for roughly 12 hours. You will know when they are done when the slices are pliable.

HERBED TOMATOES IN SEA SALT

If you have a love for tomatoes, you will enjoy dried tomato slices topped with sea salt. Though tomatoes are a great item to be rehydrated for cooking, these tomatoes are reserved for snacking and are generally paired with pepperoni or salami. They make one of the best veggie chips around. Tomatoes in sea salt should be stored in a cool, dark location and will keep up to 6 months at room temperature. If planning on storing longer than a few weeks, the jars should be vacuumed-sealed in order to preserve freshness (see page 23).

INGREDIENTS

6 firm tomatoes

1 tablespoon finely ground sea salt

1 tablespoon each dried oregano and
   thyme

METHOD

1. Slice the tomatoes ½ inch thick. If using cherry tomatoes, cut them in half.

2. Combine the sea salt and herbs, mixing well.

3. Lightly sprinkle the herbs and salt on the tomato slices.

4. Place the slices on dehydrator trays, making sure the pieces do not touch.

5. Set the temperature to 135°F.

6. The tomatoes will dry in roughly 8 to 10 hours and should have a leathery texture.

If you were to ask me which method of preserving is the easiest, I'd tell you it's drying foods. Drying foods is a marriage of old-world traditions and modern appliances, which works well for those of us who are modern homesteaders. Modern appliances are our friends. Let's utilize them to their fullest capacity!

Drying foods allows you to create healthy snacks that are preservative-free and contain ingredients your family will enjoy. This method of preserving is truly about creativity in utilizing herbs and seasonings, and there are very few restrictions on how it can be done.

Additionally, drying foods allows us to preserve items that cannot be canned or just don't preserve well when frozen. What I am specifically referring to are foods such as zucchini and sweet peppers. And did I mention this method of food preservation is easy?

Five — THE ART OF CURING AND SMOKING MEAT AND FISH

When we first started homesteading, our goal was to raise a few chickens for eggs and maintain a small garden that could be enjoyed during the season, keeping us out of the grocery store for a few months out of the year. Then, like anything in life, our plan evolved the more we became educated about produce that had been treated with chemicals and meat that was not humanely raised or was filled with hormones. Suddenly we realized that the labels on these foods weren't always honest about the ingredients.

In that moment we took control of the foods we consumed and began thinking about what type of small livestock we could raise and whether raising rabbits would be beneficial for our two-acre homestead. By bartering with local hunters in our area and fishing for salmon in season, we expanded our options in the variety of foods we could preserve. And if the salmon wasn't running, a quick trip to Pike Place Market and the Ballard Locks in Seattle allowed us to cure and smoke seafood year-round.

As I write this book, we are making plans to begin raising pigs and meat goats. You see, once we became comfortable preserving meat such as rabbits, guineas, quail, ducks, and chicken, we realized that we could indeed control our food sources. More importantly, we are able to control how we like the meat to be cured. If we choose not to use nitrates, then

this is our prerogative. We create the herb blends, brines, and salt mixes based on what we enjoy, not on what the market offers.

By curing and smoking meat, we are proudly resorting to a method our forefathers used. It's a method that not many people understand today, nor do they have the desire to learn. Smoking and preserving meat is on its way to becoming a lost art, but there are a few who still find value in it.

Homesteading with livestock may not be an option for many, but this should not stop you from smoking and curing your own meat. Learning this skill will provide you the opportunity to make your own bacon, duck breast pancetta, or smoked fish. Even the simple art of brining chicken or quail to be smoked is a method of preserving that can be done in an urban setting. All that is needed is patience, a cool spot for hanging cured items for a short period of time, and a smoker. You see, pork belly or back cuts for making bacon, duck breasts for making pancetta, fish, and chicken can all be purchased at your local market or through a small farmer in your area.

Of all the home preservation methods available, curing and smoking food is truly an art and one that takes patience and time. Once you have mastered this method, you have pretty much come full circle to being a self-sustaining homesteader.

Are you ready to begin?

UNDERSTANDING THE PROCESS

Much like the other methods of food preservation, it's important to understand what can or can't be done. I will not lie: learning about the risk can deter some people from curing meat. Meat, more so than any other foods, runs a greater risk of causing illness. Bacteria are present in all meat, and unless it has been prepared correctly, the preservation methods cannot kill these microorganisms. By knowing these risks, you will understand the necessary steps to preserving these items properly.

As with drying foods, moisture is the main culprit in food spoilage. The growth of mold, bacteria, and other organisms occurs when the moisture is not properly removed or the fat in the meat becomes rancid.

It is not uncommon for some meats to contain parasites, although they are generally found in wild game, fish, and home-raised pigs. These parasites can be destroyed by using caution when preparing these items for preservation.

USING CAUTION WHEN PREPARING MEAT

I am sure this is a given, but when dealing with raw food, it's important to keep the work area contamination-free. Make sure your knives, tools, and hands are cleaned between tasks. Having running water and mild soap near the workstation will help prevent the transfer of additional parasites and bacteria.

If you are butchering your own meat, do not cut into the intestine or bowels of the animal, because accidental cuts in these areas can contaminate the meat.

Again, this is not meant to scare you off; this is simply to remind you that working with raw food, especially meat not being cooked, requires a strict sense of cleanliness. Additionally, remove as much fat as possible prior to beginning.

TECHNIQUES FOR CURING MEAT AND FISH

Curing refers to the process of preserving raw red meat, pork, poultry, and fish, and depending on the type of curing method you select, the process can take days, weeks, or even months to complete. For raw meat to be preserved properly, the moisture must be completely removed. Preserving agents will prevent the growth of bacteria and decay.

The moisture found in raw foods can be removed through a saltwater brine, a dry salt and herb rub, or by smoking it. Nitrates, curing salts, and rubs are also used, but they are not necessary for preserving meat. At some point you will come across the term *pickling*. Don't crinkle your nose! Pickling uses a salt brine to create such items as corned beef and ham. You know, the good stuff.

There are a few items that can help prolong the shelf life of foods. When food is smoked, the heat, along with preserving agents such as salt, sugar, maple syrup, or a marinade, allows the finished product to be kept longer. For foods such as pepperoni, salami, and sausage, the hanging (drying time), along with salts, herbs, and even the casing will assist in the preserving process and longer storage time.

Vinegar, citrus juice, or alcohol such as whiskey or bourbon, can enhance the flavor of foods being cured. The National Center for Home Food Preservation states these items can also help preserve the foods if added in sufficient quantity. The vinegar, citrus juice, or alcohol can be made into a brine or can be injected into the food item being cured. Keep in mind, these items should not replace the use of salt as a preserving agent.

HOW TO FLAVOR CURED MEAT

We all crave flavor in our food, and that is no different for foods that have been cured. Some cured foods are delicious when kept simple, like ham, while others need spices and herbs to showcase their true flavors, like sausages. There are no strict guidelines to adding sugar, herbs, and spices; it's all based on how you like the final product to turn out. Here are the basics:

• **Salt.** This is necessary in the curing process and will always be present in the meat or fish being preserved.

• **Sugar.** The use of sugar or brown sugar, even maple syrup, not only adds sweetness to the item, but it also helps to balance the salt.

• **Spices and herbs.** The combination of spices and herbs will elevate the flavor and can be customized to suit your taste.

• **Fermentation.** The goodness of fermentation enhances cured foods! Some of the best cured foods are fermented. Who would have guessed?! Examples of cured and fermented items are salami, pepperoni, and summer sausage.

• **Smoking.** Smoking adds flavor to eggs, meat, garlic, and fish. The variety of wood being used will determine how smoky the flavor will be (see page 161 for selecting the right wood chips).

BRINING

Brining is an excellent method for tenderizing and flavoring food. Brining can be done in a water solution consisting of salt and water or by injecting meat with a salt and water solution. Adding herbs, sugar, and spices to the solution will enhance the flavor, but the key is to allow

the meat to soak for a minimum of one hour to overnight. Some recipes will call for the meat to be soaked up to a few weeks.

Traditional, and still practiced, methods call for preserving salted pork and fish in a saltwater brine for up to 1 year and just pulling out what is needed a little at a time. It is important that the meat or fish be cut into uniform pieces and fully submerged into the liquid. It will always need to be completely submerged with a weight of some sort. A heavy plate works well. The vessels for brining should be nonreactive, such as crocks or stainless steel and glass containers. Aluminum containers are reactive, meaning there is a probability that the metallic flavor could alter the taste of the food.

A salt and water brine can also create fabulous fermented items. Foods such as corned beef and pepperoni are excellent examples of fermented foods created by brining.

WHAT *REALLY* IS PICKLED MEAT?

I'm sure you've heard of pickled pigs' feet. You may absolutely love them, as I do, or not, and that's okay! What really is pickled meat all about? And why would anyone even consider it?

Pickling is a term used for preserving red meat and pork and has been around for centuries. It is having a resurgence as people become more educated on the traditional methods for preserving foods, especially meat. Though it is commonly known as *pickled meat,* it isn't really. Yes, there is a brine that consists of salt, water, and herbs; but unlike pickled vegetables, the meat cannot be consumed raw and has to be cooked prior to serving.

Well, what is it if it's not "pickled"? The correct term is *curing*. The meat or fish is preserved in the brine for up to 1 year. It must be completely submerged to prevent spoiling. The Morton Salt Company states that meat cures best between 36°F and 40°F. Anything over 40°F prevents the meat from curing properly, whereas anything under 36°F can cause the meat to spoil.

The National Center for Home Food Preservation has a recipe for pickled pigs' feet on its website. Truth. In this case, the pigs' feet are in fact cooked, the brine is heavy in vinegar, and the final product will need to be pressure canned to make it shelf stable. Even pickled fish is usually slightly cooked prior to pickling it in a vinegar brine and will need to be kept refrigerated. Unlike with pickled pigs' feet, the first step in pickling fish is to cure it in a saltwater brine.

FLAVORING BRINE WITH HERBS AND SPICES

Feel free to use whatever herb and spice combination you'd like for your brine. There are no guidelines for what cannot be used. We love creating a combination of spices, sugar, and herbs such as rosemary, bay leaves, garlic, coriander, peppercorns, oregano, thyme, or sage.

MARINATING

Marinating should not be confused with brining, though both acts require the meat or fish to be submerged in a liquid of some sort. Marinating meat or fish is done to add flavor to it, and the marinade created is one of personal preference. A marinade consists of at least one of these acidic items: vinegar, orange juice, or wine. This allows the protein in the meat to break down and become tender. Jerky is a great example of a food item that can be marinated prior to being smoke cured.

COMBINATION CURING

This method uses a dry rub (see opposite) in combination with a brine injection. It is used often when curing ham or a thick-cut of red meat, as it shortens the processing time and reduces the risk of spoilage. The meat will need to cure in the refrigerator and can be frozen once the process has been completed.

THE USE OF NITRATES AND NITRITES

Nitrates are used to cure foods as well as to act as a long-term preserving agent by preventing the growth of bacteria such as *Clostridium botulinum* spores from forming. Nitrates also work to prevent fats from going rancid quickly. Sodium nitrate can be found naturally in foods and can be used in a liquid brine or a dry rub in a pinch. For example, celery juice can be added to a saltwater brine, and spinach powder can be used in a dry rub, both acting as sodium nitrate. The concentrate is not as high as the actual product, but they will both work in a pinch.

Nitrites are the chemical alternative to nitrates and are approved to use in measured small amounts when curing meat. They are also commonly known as curing salts or pink salts. Nitrites not only preserve meat, they also provide the pink color found in ham, corned beef, and bacon and are used to add flavor to deli meat. Sodium nitrite is also used for raw curing foods such as dry pepperoni, dry salami, sopressata, and dry coppa. Curing salts or nitrites are not needed when brined meats are smoked or cooked.

Without the addition of nitrites, meats and fish can still be cured, but their appearance takes on a grayish color, and the flavoring is not that of cured meat but of seasoned, roasted meat. If you decide to cure meat without nitrites, you can add herbs and seasonings to help flavor the meat instead.

DRY RUB

A dry rub using salt, herbs, spices, sugar, and even nitrites helps to remove moisture from the meat or fish while also seasoning it. The use of salt and sugar works as a preservative and slows the growth of bacteria. Any type of meat can be cured, but it is best to remove the bone, fat, skin, and gristle because these items do not cure well and can slow the drying process, as well as cause the meat to spoil.

Meats such as bacon and ham require a dry rub mixture to be applied directly on the surface. Additional applications will need to be made until the meat is completely cured.

Be warned, I am a little of this and a little of that kinda farm girl. I can thank my momma for that! When you create mixes, feel free to make them your own. The rubs listed below consist of dried items but you can use fresh as well. Once you create a blend you like, make enough to store for later use. This will make it easier the next time you set out to cure some foods.

Herbal Dry Rub for Poultry

Salt, sage, thyme, paprika, rosemary, sugar, tarragon, garlic powder, ground peppercorns, parsley, cilantro, savory, and marjoram.

Jerk Seasoning Rub

Allspice berries, powdered garlic, hot chile peppers, cayenne pepper or red pepper flakes, and thyme.

Prior to applying the rub to the chicken, add brown sugar to the mixture.

Herbal Dry Rub for Pork

Sage, thyme, garlic powder, onion powder, salt, cinnamon, rosemary, peppercorns, allspice, basil, cloves, ground ginger, marjoram, oregano, paprika, parsley, Chinese five spice, Italian seasoning, and lemon pepper.

Herbal Dry Rub for Beef

Peppercorns, sage, thyme, nutmeg, dried onion, marjoram, basil, parsley, dried or powdered celery leaves, summer savory, and bay leaves.

Herbal Dry Rub for Fish

Dill, marjoram, paprika, peppercorns, curry powder, and dry mustard.

If you choose to use fresh herbs instead of dried, here is a conversion equation to determine the amount you'll need:

1 tablespoon finely cut dried herbs equals 1 teaspoon dried leafy herbs or ¼ to ½ teaspoon ground herbs.

DRY-CURING MEAT AND FISH

Before applying a dry rub mix, prepare the meat by trimming the fat and gristle and removing the bones. When preparing fish, remove the scales and internal organs prior to applying a rub mix. Using your hands, gently massage the dry mix over the entire surface of the meat, making sure no area has been missed.

The meat can then be hung (between 50 to 60 degrees Fahrenheit with the humidity between 65% to 80%) or set aside uncovered in a cool, dark location to rest for a few days. The dry mix will need to be reapplied, and this will most likely continue for a few weeks. How long it takes for the meat to cure will depend on the size of the cut, which means larger cuts can take up to a few months before they are thoroughly cured.

HOW TO DETERMINE IF MEAT IS DONE CURING

When salt-cured meat is done will vary based on what is being cured and the cut of the meat. I know that this is not really the answer you want to hear, but in truth, there's no absolute answer. Duck breast can take roughly 4 to 5 weeks to cure, bacon can take a week or two, and a large cut of pork may take a few months! The best method for figuring out if meat is cured is to measure it. Once fully cured it should lose 30 to 45 percent of its weight at the end of the process. Just remember, you will need to weigh it prior to beginning the curing process to know if it's lost enough of its weight. Another tip on completion will be how it feels. Many cuts will feel firm when they're ready. Salted fish is a great example of this.

SAUSAGE CURING

This method is by far my favorite. The curing method is completed in the refrigerator, and unlike other methods, once the curing process is done, the salt and spices remain in the ground meat. Preserving the meat in a casing not only makes for an amazing sausage, but it enables the item to be preserved for a longer period. If you are not equipped to make sausage, patties can easily be made and kept frozen. For curing, sodium nitrite will be needed. Otherwise, the sausage can be prepared and frozen.

Homemade Sausage

Sausage making is another method of preserving meat, regardless of the type used. The trick? Working with partially frozen meat will make grinding and filling the casings much easier. Here's what you need to make homemade sausage:

- meat grinder
- sausage casings, hog or sheep
- sausage maker, holds and fills the casing
- pork fat (optional)
- meat of choice
- herbs, seasoning, salt (kosher or pickling) to taste

PIZZA SAUSAGE

This recipe is for the pizza lovers around the world (well, mainly for Justin, who would eat pizza every day if he could get away with it). Ground sausage is made with a combination of the most perfect blend of herbs and spices. Since there are no casings involved, package your sausage according to how much you'll need for each serving.

INGREDIENTS

1 pound ground pork

1 pound ground turkey or chicken

2 teaspoons fennel seed

2 teaspoons kosher salt (or pickling)

1½ teaspoons crushed red pepper (optional)

½ teaspoon dried oregano

½ teaspoon freshly ground peppercorns

3 garlic cloves, minced

3 tablespoons dried parsley

METHOD

1. Mix all ingredients well.
2. Divide into serving sizes, generally 1 pound per package.
3. Freeze using a vacuum-sealer or butcher's paper.

TIPS FOR CURING MEATS AND FISH

- How long it takes to cure meat will depend on the thickness and the amount of bone and fat in a cut. Thicker cuts of meat will take longer to cure.
- Meat must be brined using a noncorrosive container (glass, plastic, stainless steel, or pickling crocks) and weights. A weight can be something as simple as a heavy plate, a glass weight, or a stone weight. Weights can often be purchased on fermenting websites.
- Experiment with different herbs and spices to create a great brine, but do not exceed the curing levels in the recipe. Exceeding the curing level means too much nitrite or pink salt (a combination of salt, sodium nitrate, and sodium nitrite) is added to the brine or rub, which can be poisonous when consumed in high quantity.
- Make sure the salt and sugar are thoroughly dissolved prior to adding the meat. After preheating half of the water, add the salt, and stir until fully dissolved. Then add the remainder of the water.
- One quart of brine is needed for every 4 to 6 pounds of meat. Keep in mind the brine needs to fully cover the meat. Mix additional brine if needed.
- Always chill brine thoroughly prior to adding meat.
- Meat cures best between 36°F and 40°F. Anything cooler will prevent the meat from curing properly, while warmer temperatures will encourage spoilage.
- Flip brining meat once a day to help cure the meat evenly.
- Make sure to rinse the salt prior to smoking. Not doing so can cause the meat to become excessively salty. If the meat is excessively salty once it is done curing, soaking or boiling it in water will help to remove the excess salt.

SALTING

Salting is accomplished using salt, pink salt, or curing salts (both known to contain sodium nitrite and nitrate). Salting meat or fish items can be accomplished by applying the salt directly to the food by dry rubbing or by creating a saltwater brine. Salted pork is a popular item in this category, making it excellent to cook with. The salts are used to remove moisture from the food in order to preserve it. The timeframe on how long this will take to complete will depend on the size and cut of the meat or fish being cured; dry curing is a longer process than using a saltwater brine.

When curing items, such as dry pepperoni, nduja (a spicy, spreadable salami), or dry salami, sodium nitrite or nitrate are used during the curing process to prevent bacteria spores from growing.

Curing meat that will be smoked or cooked can be done without the use of a chemical alternative such as nitrite, though keep in mind that those items will not keep as long.

If you're not too keen on using a synthetic item such as nitrite, consider using natural nitrates such as celery juice or powdered spinach. Both options can be used in a liquid brine though the spinach powder is best used in a dry rub. Many like to use heavier salts such as kosher, sea, or pickling salt to create a salt dry rub. A cup of table salt weighs much less than these items, which means more of it needs to be used.

Salting takes time; it is a procedure that cannot be rushed, nor should it be. Remember, curing is an art, and to create an excellent product, time and patience are needed.

Kosher and pickling salts are the best forms of salt to use for salting meat. Iodized or table salts have additives that can affect the curing process. Though sea salt is natural, it may contain other trace minerals that could affect the final product. I have used sea salt as a salt for curing meat and fish and have yet to notice a difference in the final product.

SALT-CURED EGG YOLK

Whether you are a self-sustaining homesteader who raises poultry or a city dweller who purchases farm-fresh eggs from a local farmer, salt curing egg yolks is something you'll want to try. The process is extremely easy and the taste is fabulous! To serve, simply grate these little disks of golden delight onto foods such as salads or pasta. Heck, use them on whatever you wish. Trust me, this is a great way to use up eggs when your poultry are producing well.

1¾ cups kosher salt
1¼ cups sugar
4 egg yolks

METHOD

1. Mix the salt and sugar, and place half of the mixture in a small baking dish.
2. Using the back of a spoon, gently create indents in the salt and sugar mixture, making sure the indent is wide enough to hold the egg yolks.
3. Separate the egg yolks from the whites, and gently place the yolks into the indent spots in the salt and sugar mixture.
4. Gently sprinkle the remaining salt and sugar mixture over the yolks, cover the baking dish with plastic wrap, and place them in the refrigerator to rest for 4 days.
5. Once cured, remove the egg yolks, and gently brush the mixture off of them. Wash the cured egg yolks under cool water to remove the remaining salt. Pat dry. Once rinsed, the yolks will have a gummy texture.
6. Preheat the oven to 150°F. Place the washed yolks onto a baking sheet and allow them to dry for roughly 1½ to 2 hours. If your oven does not drop to 150°F, you have two options: (1) allow the egg yolks to air dry for 2 days, or (2) use a dehydrator at the 145°F setting for 1 to 2 hours. Once completely dried, the yolk will have a hard texture.

When it comes to mold, we've been taught that it is dangerous and should avoid it at all cost. However, that is not necessarily true when it comes to meats that are hung and are dry curing.

White mold is a powdery white mold that is actually a good mold, known as a form of penicillin, and it smells like ammonia. However, furry or hairy white mold is not safe, and the food should be discarded immediately.

Green, blue, or black mold are not safe. Discard the hung meat immediately.

SMOKING

The process of slow smoking dries meat or fish without cooking it. The use of low, slow heating allows the meat to cure slowly with smoke created by wood chips placed into a smoker or grill with the door or lid closed. The creosote from the wood smoke is deposited on the food being smoked and acts as a natural preserving agent.

The best cuts of meat to smoke are briskets, pork bellies, roasts, breast meat from poultry, even fish. To allow for a consistent drying time, the meat or fish should be cut into uniform pieces. When smoking fish, the skin can be left on and the bones do not have to be removed, unlike with poultry or meat.

Though it is not commonly done, whole poultry can be cured and smoked. The curing method used would be a saltwater brine, allowing the bird to brine completely submerged for roughly 24 hours in the refrigerator at 35°F. Smoking a bird the size of a chicken or duck can take about 5 hours, and longer for a larger bird such as a turkey. Smoked meat can be kept in the refrigerator for up to 4 days or kept frozen for up to 6 months prior to being consumed.

If you are looking to purchase a smoker, the price will vary quite a bit. We have two smokers on the property. One is a small aluminum smoker designed to do smaller jobs. The second smoker is a large, multishelf unit with room to hang meat.

It is always wise to have two working thermometers to check the meat or fish being smoked. Larger, more expensive smokers will have built-in thermometers, while smaller smokers may not have one at all. A hand-held meat thermometer is excellent for checking that the accurate temperature is being maintained.

Depending on the type and cut of meat being smoked, a smoker will need to stay between 200°F and 300°F throughout the entire smoking process in order to ensure the food items are being dried properly. Seafood, fish, veal, and chicken tend to be smoked around the lowest temperature available.

Selecting the Right Wood Chips

Wood chips are selected based on the flavor they provide. Keep in mind, hardwoods burn longer and create more smoke. They also tend to have a stronger flavor. I encourage you to try smoking with every type of wood chip you have available to discover the flavor you like best.

FINAL TEMPERATURE FOR SMOKED FOOD

meat	minimum temperature
BEEF, VEAL, LAMB	145°F
BEEF, VEAL, LAMB, PORK (GROUND)	160°F
PORK	160°F
HAM	160°F
BACON	124°F
POULTRY (WHOLE, THIGHS, WINGS)	180°F
POULTRY (BREASTS, ROAST)	170°F
POULTRY (GROUND)	165°F
DUCK & GOOSE	180°F
SEAFOOD (FINNED FISH)	Done when the meat flakes easily with a fork
WILD GAME (VENISON)	160°F

Alder. We do a lot of smoking with alder because it's readily available on our property. The flavor it provides fish, especially salmon, is light and sweet. Alder is a great wood chip for those who do not like their foods to have a heavy smoke flavor.

Apple. By far my favorite, apple wood is excellent for smoking chicken, wild fowl, and pork. It lends a mild, sweet flavor. Note that it will take several hours of smoking to permeate the meat.

Cherry. When smoke curing poultry or ham, this is a great choice. It leaves the cured meat with a mild, fruity flavor and pairs well with other hardwoods.

Hickory. Large cuts like pork shoulder, red meat, and poultry smoke well with hickory. It leaves a sweet and savory flavor on the meat, and some say it has a bit of a bacon flavor.

Maple. Maple is another mild and sweet wood for smoking and pairs well with poultry, especially quail, and pork.

Mesquite. If you are looking for wood chips that pack intense flavor, this is the one for you. When used to smoke red meat, it leaves a strong flavor behind.

Oak. Oak is a very popular choice for many and partners well with lamb, beef, brisket, and sausage, carrying a medium to strong flavor.

Pecan. Briskets and roasts smoked in pecan are infused with a nutty, sweet flavor. If you are concerned with how sweet it can be, mix the chips with a hardwood to balance the flavor.

How to Make Wood Chips for Smoking

It is easy to make your own wood chips from whatever trees you have on your homestead or in your backyard. With an abundance of alder trees available on our property, we find it quite rewarding to make our own chips for smoking. Here's how to do it:

1. Gather some branches from the trees around your property. Strip off the leaves, and check each branch to make sure it is not infested with bugs or worms.

2. Using a wood chipper, select the setting that allows for the smallest possible wood chips. If you do not own a wood chipper, a hand-held wood planer will do the job. A wood planer is excellent for single batch smoking. The bark should not be used when smoking meat, so discard chipped pieces that contain large amounts of bark.

3. Branches can also be cut to 2-inch rounds and used for smoking. Again, the bark should be removed prior to smoking.

4. For long-term storage, dry the chips prior to storing them. The easiest way to dry a large amount is to sun dry them. However, a small amount can be dried in the oven at 200°F until fully dried.

5. Once fully dried, they can be stored in a vacuum-sealed bag for long-term storage.

To prevent excessive amounts of smoke, cured wood works best. However, if you are in dire need, uncured wood can be used, although green, unseasoned wood creates a lot of smoke and creosote. This can be minimized if the fire is extremely hot.

WHEN TO UTILIZE THE HOT OR COLD SMOKE METHOD

Hot smoking must maintain temperatures between 165°F to 185°F, though Elizabeth Karmel, author of *Taming the Flame: Secrets for Hot-and-Quick Grilling and Low-and-Slow BBQ,* will argue that the optimal temperature should be 275°F to 300°F. The goal for hot smoking is to cook the foods at the same time it takes to smoke it. Cold smoking occurs at temperatures between 90°F to 120°F, though 100°F is the most common recommendation. This method does not cook the food; rather it adds flavor to fish, salami, and other cured meats before they are hung up to dry. There is a slight disagreement about what the best temperature for items being cold smoked should be.

HOW TO SMOKE FARM-FRESH EGGS

When you raise poultry, you learn to become creative in how to use up those little golden eggs. If you have never smoked eggs, let me be the first to tell you that you're missing out! Just imagine a perfect steamed egg with a mild smoked flavor, or robust, depending on your taste. If you're anything like me, you will simply peel and eat them straight from the smoker, but you might also enjoy them sliced in a fresh green salad or added to macaroni salad for a smoky flavor. You can thank me later, but I'll say "You're welcome" now.

SUPPLIES

Farm-fresh eggs, as many as you would like

Wood chips; we prefer apple or hickory

METHOD

1. Steam the farm-fresh eggs for 21 minutes, or boil store-bought eggs for 9 minutes.

2. Lay the eggs in a prepared smoker at 225°F. Smoke the eggs for 2 hours.

3. Store in the refrigerator for up to 2 weeks.

CURING METHODS BASED ON THE TYPE OF MEAT

When you cure meat at home, you are privy to creating foods based on the flavors your family will enjoy. Feel free to experiment with spices and herbs, as well as to try new methods for curing and smoking meat and fish. The nice part about preserving foods through curing and smoking? You do not have to raise livestock to enjoy this method of home food preservation. Various meat cuts can be purchased from a local farm, butcher shop, or even at the market near you. You become the creator who transforms a basic cut of meat into something that suits your desired taste. That's what it is all about—create, preserve, and enjoy. These are the benefits of having this skill.

Here are your curing options for various types of meat and fish.

POULTRY

Poultry such as chicken, turkey, duck, goose, or game bird (including domestic quail) are delicious when smoked and can either be brined, dry rubbed, or marinated prior to placing them into the smoker. Much like red meat, poultry will need to be skinned, and the fat will need to be removed to prevent it from going rancid as it is stored. There is a lot of discussion as to whether poultry should be smoked with the bones in or if they should be removed. Ultimately the decision is yours to make, and in truth we enjoy smoking chicken with the bone in. When smoked with the bones included, it seems to have more flavor than when smoked without the bones.

Depending on the size of the cuts, it can take from 3 to 8 hours to complete the smoking process. Smoked poultry is complete once the thermometer reads 165°F or higher. When testing for doneness, test the thickest section, but do not allow the thermometer to touch the bone. Once smoking has been completed, there are three options for storing the poultry. The first option is to refrigerate it for up to 4 days. The second option is to freeze it for up to 3 months. The third option, which works well for those who have a root cellar or who live off the grid, is to wrap the meat in a cheesecloth or any other breathable cloth, and place it in a cool, dark area where the temperature does not exceed 40°F for up to 3 months.

HAM

Ham is made from the front and rear legs of the hog and is usually cured with the bone in, but it can also be cured without the bone. Remove the skin and as much of the fat and gristle as possible to prevent the meat from turning rancid.

There are two methods for curing ham: using a salt and water brine or dry curing. A salt and water brine is the easiest method for beginners. The brine generally consists of salt and water, though it is not uncommon to add sugar, spices, and nitrites. The sugar and spices are added to create flavor, whereas the nitrites are used to extend the storage time and add color to this cured item. Curing ham can take between 1 to 2 weeks depending on the weight of the cut, with the rule of thumb being for every 2 pounds of meat you'll need 1 day of curing. Not only is a saltwater brine easy to do, but the final product is quite a bit more tender than it would be if dry cured. Decide what you like best.

Dry curing is achieved by rubbing salt, sugar, nitrite, and seasoning on the ham, covering the entire surface. The moisture found in the ham is drawn out due to the ingredients found in the rub, specifically the salt and nitrites (also known as curing salt or pink salt). This method will need to be repeated several times throughout the curing process and can take up to 1 month to complete. Once the pork is quite firm to the touch, the curing process is complete. The weight of the ham should be reduced by 18 to 25 percent, indicating that the moisture has been thoroughly removed.

Remember, as the pork is curing, it will need to be stored between 36°F and 40°F, which can be done in a refrigerator as well as in a root cellar, basement, or garage.

SALTED PORK

Salted pork makes my heart happy and my stomach full. It is comfort food for the soul, and if you haven't tried it, here is your opportunity. We love to use it to season greens and to flavor soup or beans. When cooking Thai food, my mother would add it to curry to be served over rice. My absolute favorite way to consume it is fried and served over a bed of rice with fermented green beans. Is it salty? Yes, but it really hits the spot.

When you're ready to make this cured item, you will find quite a few methods on how to do so. On our homestead we like to keep it simple and stick to the traditional method for preserving it using salt, water, and a bit of sugar. That's it.

To make salted pork, you will need pork belly, and either kosher or pickling salt are our choices. Cut the pork belly into 5- to 6-inch squares and rub each square with salt and sugar. For 2 pounds of pork belly, use 10 ounces salt and ⅓ cup sugar (the sugar can be omitted and is not necessary for curing the meat). Rub the salt and sugar mixture into the pork, making sure to not miss any section of the meat. Next, pack it tightly in a crock,

plastic container, or stoneware, and allow it to sit overnight in the refrigerator or a cool location such as a root cellar. The salt will draw out much of the moisture from the pork overnight, though the curing process does not end there.

The next day, rinse the pork and soak it in water to draw out some of the salt. This step can be repeated a few times. The final step to making a traditional salted pork is to create a brine with a mix of 6 cups salt and 4 cups water, allowing the salt to fully dissolve prior to pouring over the pork belly. If you'd like, add spices and sugar to the brine. If you were to ask me, though, that would make it a glorified version of what salted pork truly should be.

Allow the pork belly to soak in the brine completely submerged for roughly 3 weeks before consuming. If the brine should become slimy, rinse the pork well and change the solution, making a new one. The salted pork can be kept in a cool, dark spot and in the same container up to 4 months.

If you are concerned about storing salted pork the traditional way (in a liquid brine), the NCHFP states that salted pork can store for 2 weeks in the refrigerator and up to 1 year in the freezer.

BACON

To cure bacon, you will need the belly cut (both meat and fat strips), which is fatty. Canadian bacon comes from the loin or back cut, containing more meat with less fat. If you want to try your hand at curing bacon and Canadian bacon, these cuts can be ordered through a local

butcher or market if you do not raise your own pigs. The high fat content in bacon increases the risk that the meat could turn rancid, so follow the steps for curing precisely.

Bacon can be cured through a wet brine or by a dry rub, using salt, sugar, spices, and nitrites (optional). Our best bacon brine consists of freshly cracked peppercorns and maple syrup. The brined meat is then smoked using apple wood chips. Feel free to play with the spices and various types of sugar. Only goodness can come from it.

It's important to know the difference between what nitrite and nitrate are. Also, remember that though they are not needed for curing, they do provided color and additional flavor to foods being cured.

Sodium nitrite is a salt not found naturally but created in a lab.

Sodium nitrate is a natural salt found in Peru or Chile, though it can also be manufactured in a lab.

HOMEMADE BACON

If you don't love bacon, I am sorry. If you love bacon, well, enjoy curing and smoking it in the comfort of your homestead. Let's make some bacon 'cause I promise, once you've mastered this method of curing, you will never return to store-bought bacon again. Ever.

This recipe contains no curing salt or pink salt and is nitrate-free. For a longer preserving time, you can add nitrates. A good beginner's recipe can be found on the National Center for Home Food Preservation's website.

INGREDIENTS
2½–3 pounds pork belly
¼ cup sea salt
¼ cup brown packed sugar
2 teaspoons black peppercorns
2 teaspoons smoked paprika
½ teaspoon garlic powder
3 whole bay leaves, dried and crushed

METHOD
1. Place the pork belly in a roasting pan.
2. Make a dry rub using the salt, sugar, and spices. Apply the dry rub to the entire surface of the pork belly. Place the pork belly uncovered in the refrigerator.
3. Allow the pork belly to cure for 5 to 10 days. (Note: The longer the pork belly cures, the saltier it will be.) Liquid will be released from the pork belly, which is normal. Just drain the liquid daily.
4. Thoroughly rinse the rub from the pork belly and its pan.
5. Place the pork belly back in pan and return to the refrigerator. Allow the pork belly to air dry for 12 to 24 hours in the refrigerator.

6. Remove the pork belly from the refrigerator. The pork belly should now be firmer and smaller in size than when first beginning the process.
7. If you do not plan to smoke the cured bacon, slice it to the desired thickness and freeze it in vacuum-sealed bags or butcher paper. If you do not plan to freeze it, consume homemade bacon within 2 weeks since it doesn't contain nitrates.

Smoke the Bacon (optional)

In a smoker, set the rack to the highest setting away from the heat source. Remember, your goal is to smoke the bacon rather than to cook it. If your smoker has a temperature gauge, aim for 175°F to 200°F. Smoke the bacon anywhere from 30 to 75 minutes. How long is up to you. The longer the bacon is in the smoker, the more smoked flavor the bacon will take on.

FISH

Smaller fish can be preserved whole; however, larger fish can be filleted, removing the head, tail, scales, and viscera. The pickling brine will help to dissolve the bones in smaller fish, though it is necessary to remove as many of the bones as possible in larger fish such as herring and pike if you plan to pickle them. Larger fish like salmon are excellent salted, seasoned, and smoked.

Salting fish is another means of preserving it. Fish such as salmon, flounder, and cod are great salted, but the process does take some time to complete. The fish is covered entirely with coarse salt and stored in the refrigerator or a cool, dark location for roughly 2 days. The salt-cured fish is then rinsed, dried with a towel, and wrapped in a cheesecloth to dry in the refrigerator for 2 weeks. Once the cured fish is stiff, the drying process is complete. It can be stored in the refrigerator for 3 months or in the freezer for up to 1 year.

A more traditional method of storing salt-cured fish would be to preserve it in a saltwater brine for up to 9 months after the initial salt dry rub has been completed. The only concern is if fermenting should set in, which can be resolved by creating a new salt and water brine.

BEEF, GOAT, AND WILD GAME

Red meat such as beef, goat, and wild game can be cured using every method mentioned in this chapter. It can be smoked, salted, dry cured, or brined. In general, the cheaper, less

desirable fatty cuts of meats are the ones preserved. Remove as much of the fat as possible when preserving to prevent the meat from going rancid.

As already mentioned, red meat without the bone will cure faster and a lot more evenly than when it contains the bone.

You may try dry-aging to achieve a cut of meat that is more tender and flavorful than the "average" cut. The art of dry-aging can be done using harvested or purchased beef, goat, and wild game.

Though it is fairly easy to do, be prepared to lose space in your refrigerator until the process is completed. We do not currently have the refrigerator space to sacrifice when our cow share is delivered, though it doesn't stop me from thinking that I may one day give this method a try.

I would rather not preserve red meat using any method other than freezing it. There's something amazing about a nice medium rare cut of meat that makes me extremely happy. However, when it comes to preparing brisket for corned beef? That I will do!

When we first began curing meat, it was overwhelming. However, as we became more sustainable, we sought to own this method of preserving food. The journey of curing is truly an art form, and over a long period of learning, we've come to truly value it.

The ability to raise your own meat is incredible, though to maximize the many ways you can preserve it takes you to a new level. For example, we raise ducks for meat, and our freezer can only hold so many of them for roasting. So now we also make duck breast pancetta, duck confit, or "duck ham," all by curing it.

Let's not forget the ability to customize your own bacon or flavor ham with your signature brine. For fishermen and women, salting, smoking, and pickling are all great options that allow you to enjoy a variety of fish throughout the year.

Out of all the methods used to preserve foods, I truly find that curing meat is the most creative. There's no better way to describe what curing meat and fish is all about.

Six   THE BASICS OF FERMENTATION

Maintaining good health requires exercise, clean eating, and a healthy gut. Luckily, as sustainable homesteaders, we have all three covered. We maintain a garden that is chemical-free with organic seeds, meat humanely raised and containing no hormones, and a focus on cooking from scratch based on the foods we grow and raise. Healthy, right? Yet more times than not, many forget that to maintain good health, it all starts with a strong digestive system. If your gut is imbalanced, you are imbalanced, and what comes from that? Absolutely nothing good.

The public understands that probiotics are necessary to maintain a healthy digestive system but tends to resort to a synthetic probiotic option readily available over the counter. This type of probiotic is easy to consume with the instruction of "just add water." What most people don't understand is that a synthetic probiotic should only be consumed for a course of ten days at a time, whereas natural probiotics found in foods and drinks can be consumed daily without any restrictions. If the thought of fermented tea, water, vegetables, and even condiments is not appealing to you, then how about sauerkraut? Sadly, in our culture, consuming fermented foods is foreign to many, even to homesteaders, though throughout

FRESH VERSUS CANNED SAUERKRAUT

Do not can sauerkraut that you've spent the time fermenting. Just *don't* do it. Kraut, of any variety, should be consumed in its fresh fermented form because it contains live healthy bacteria and is packed full of beneficial probiotics. When canned, the heat of a hot water bath or steam canner kills the beneficial bacteria. What you are left with is the same as the product found on grocery store shelves. If stored at the right temperature, home fermented sauerkraut can keep for months in the refrigerator, root cellar, or cold storage.

Asia, Europe, and Africa, these foods are consumed daily and are credited for maintaining good health. What is more beneficial than natural probiotics and healthy enzymes? I can't think of anything.

If you are not quite ready to jump into making your own fermented goodies, the health food section of your local market will carry fermented foods and drinks. I really encourage you to give them a try, but I will warn you, they can be a bit expensive to purchase and not as good as what can be made in the comfort of your home.

Fermented foods and drinks are not only beneficial to your health; they are also good for livestock and pets. Since goats have a sensitive ruminant digestive tract, natural probiotics are great for them. Our goat Pepe often enjoyed snacking on fermented green beans, but he wasn't the only one! Our dogs and poultry often receive leftover fermented foods. They also love to snack on extra SCOBYs (which stands for symbiotic culture of bacteria and yeast) from our kombucha brews. Raw apple cider vinegar is another fermented drink we provide our livestock and pets in their drinking water.

Ideally, foods selected for fermenting are those in season. As you are planning your garden each year, consider committing a part of the yield to fermented foods. When stored in the correct temperature, these items will keep for quite a long time, allowing you to enjoy the harvest while building a healthy gut.

Being half Asian, I grew up consuming fermented foods, and I have watched my mother ferment items such as various types of kimchi and blue crab throughout my childhood. I ate these foods because they were placed in front of me but did not realize they were so beneficial until we started our homesteading journey. Soon fermented foods and drinks became not only a way of preserving the harvest, but also part of our holistic health care regimen. Our kids took a bit more time to get on board, but they now tolerate a shot of kombucha and actually enjoy flavored water kefir and fermented pickles, green beans, and even kimchi. Hey, you take what you can when it comes to kids.

Whether or not you are a homesteader, this method of preserving the harvest is one that is beneficial to your health. Learning how to create fermented items is easy, and your digestive system will thank you for it.

WHAT'S YOUR CUP OF TEA? LACTO-FERMENTATION, CULTURING, OR WILD FERMENT?

For years, the only term I knew for foods and drinks that contained healthy beneficial bacteria and probiotics was *ferment*. Regardless if it was kimchi, sauerkraut, kefir, or kombucha, it was all fermented. I am sad to report that I still use the generic word *fermenting*.

As my knowledge grew, I learned the correct terms to use and what they referred to. This became extremely helpful when I was interested in trying a new ferment. So, before you go any further, let me make learning the process of fermenting much easier.

LACTO-FERMENTATION

Lacto-fermentation, also known as *lactic acid fermentation,* refers to a specific bacteria called *Lactobacillus*. These bacteria can be found on all fruits, vegetables, herbs, spices, and nuts, basically anything grown from the earth.

Fermented pickled items such as pickles, carrots, and green beans are some of the more well-known lacto-fermented items. The *Lactobacillus* bacteria found in these items, in combination with salt, creates an anaerobic (oxygen free) environment, which allows items to naturally ferment.

When lactic acid is present in foods that have been fermented, it will have a sour taste. Lactic acid improves the microbiological stability of foods, making them safe to consume and be preserved.

CULTURING

The process of *culturing* means that a microbial starter is used to initiate fermentation. The most common microbial starters are SCOBYs, kefir grains, whey, brine from vegetable ferments, sauerkraut starter, pickle brine, and powder starter cultures. These microbial starters are used to make kombucha, water kefir, fermented foods, and condiments such as salad dressing.

WILD FERMENTATION

The easiest way to describe wild fermentation is when wild yeasts found in the air meet the *Lactobacillus* bacteria found in raw foods. The two collide, creating what is known as a *wild ferment*. Wild fermenting was the last phase I tried. For some reason this process intimidated me to no end. Over time I became more comfortable, and sourdough became my first accomplishment.

Items like sourdough, sauerkraut, and kimchi are excellent examples of food items that use wild fermentation. Mead, old-world beers, and boozy drinks created with herbs, fruit, and spices are also fermented through wild fermentation. Wildcrafting boozy beverages in this form is a lost art, though in truth it is not hard to do. As with anything in home preservation, the flavors can be customized to your liking.

Lacto-fermenting, culturing, and wild fermentation are three completely different processes, even though some foods and drink items overlap (for example, sauerkraut and kimchi). Over time, as you become more acquainted with the process, it will be easier to identify the correct method to use when preserving foods through fermentation.

NAME THAT LIVE CULTURE

Live cultures vary based on the type of ferment being done and can be quite confusing to many at first. Keep in mind that these cultures are very specific to the item being fermented and should never be cross-used.

ferment type	type of culture needed
RAW APPLE CIDER VINEGAR	mother
KOMBUCHA	SCOBY
KEFIR (WATER AND MILK)	water kefir grains, milk kefir grains
SOURDOUGH	wild ferment (use of flour and water) or sourdough starter
FERMENTED VEGETABLES & FRUIT	starter culture, whey culture, wild ferment (use of salt and raw food)
MEAD	wild culture ferment (use of honey and fruit)
GINGER BUG	wild culture ferment (use of ginger and sugar)

WHAT MAKES FERMENTED FOODS AND DRINKS BENEFICIAL?

When fermented foods and drinks are consumed, the healthy bacteria, also referred to as probiotics, head directly to the gut. The beneficial bacteria then encourage the growth of additional healthy bacteria to line the gut, allowing for nutrients to be absorbed.

By consuming small amounts of fermented foods daily, you help the digestive system become stronger when colonies of healthy bacteria (flora) in the gut can thrive. Not only do the gut flora benefit, so do the stomach and intestines. But more incredibly, it has been said that consuming fermented foods helps to lessen or reduce allergies and addresses issues such as arthritis by reducing inflammation. On the flip side of the coin, the lack of probiotics can cause issues such as digestive disorders and skin conditions and contribute to autoimmune disease and a weakened immune system.

Our son Jacob has chronic skin issues, though what causes them is still unclear. He sought medical assistance for *years*, and no prescription seemed to help cure or even soothe the condition. At the age of 21, he began consuming 3 tablespoons of raw apple cider vinegar (ACV) daily. Within a week his skin began to show major improvement, the inflammation decreased, and much of the itchiness went away. Through consuming raw ACV, he was able to find relief that no prescription medicine could provide.

When I state that consumption of natural probiotics daily is important, you need to understand why. The gut is the largest organ in the immune system and is responsible for nearly half of the body's immune response. It is often referred to as the second nervous system. Microbes found in the gut promote good digestion, and they can even activate the immune system, allowing for healing. Also, when the flora found in the gut is off balance,

It is important that once a round of antibiotics has been completed, good bacteria is returned to the digestive system. This can be done by incorporating natural probiotics through fermented foods or drinks into your diet.

the natural defense against harmful bacteria is weakened, making it difficult to combat bad bacteria. Have I convinced you yet as to why it is important to consume fermented foods?

Fermented foods also retain their vitamins, minerals, and healthy enzymes, which are greatly lessened during the canning, freezing, or dehydrating process. As homesteaders, we rely on various methods for home food preservation, though there are many who believe that fermenting is the only method needed. I should note that fermented foods require cooler temperatures than canned and dried goods for long-term storage.

FERMENTED DRINKS—PERFECT FOR THE BEGINNER

Fermented drinks can often be purchased in the health food section of your local grocery store. There are various flavors of kombucha as well as water kefir. The benefit of brewing these types of probiotic drinks at home is how much money can be saved over time. Home-brewed kombucha or flavored water kefir costs a fraction of what it does at the store. Additionally, flavors can be customized based on what your family will enjoy, and who doesn't love a carbonated drink? What if it were a healthy carbonated drink packed full of natural probiotics?

TYPES OF WATER TO USE IN FERMENTING

Whether you are fermenting a beverage or food, the type of water being used does matter.

Good options:
- *Bottled water:* labeled spring, collected from rivers or streams
- *Spring water:* straight out of the ground, bottled or from a community spring
- *Well water:* generally high in minerals, which is good for water kefir but not for kombucha

Bad options:
- *Distilled water:* all traces of minerals have been removed during this process
- *City (tap) water:* generally contains chlorine and fluoride, as well as other chemicals

Treating water (water containing chlorine can be treated, and in some cases, fluoride can be removed):
- *Boiling* will remove the chlorine but not the fluoride.
- *Basic charcoal filtration* removes chlorine but not fluoride.
- *Enhanced filtration* removes chlorine; certain models may remove fluoride.
- *Reverse osmosis* removes chlorine and most minerals and fluoride.

It is said that carbonated kombucha often settles soda cravings and lessens the need for coffee. Being a caffeine/carbonation addict myself, I find that as long as there is a bottle of kombucha around, I can keep my soda and coffee addiction under control. The website Kombucha Kamp states, "Kombucha is generally considered to have ⅓ the amount of caffeine as the tea it is made with, so for example black tea, which might have 30-80mg of caffeine per cup may yield a glass of kombucha with 10-25mg of caffeine. Green tea kombucha might have just 2-3mg of caffeine."

KOMBUCHA

In short, kombucha is a fermented tea, which tends to not be appealing for many people. The word *fermented* is foreign to many, causing them to often turn up their noses in disgust. However, I propose changing the name to *healthy flavored tea,* which may draw more people into trying it. There is a stigma that home brewing such items as kombucha is difficult to do and that creating flavored brews is even more difficult. What if I were to say that all it takes is time, the right temperature, and a creative mind?

What exactly is kombucha? It's a sweet tea that's fermented with the help of good bacteria and yeast, also known as a SCOBY. Once it's finished brewing, the tea has a fizzy, *slightly* sour or vinegary flavor. It is not unpleasant in any way, though if a batch is allowed to brew too long, it will become more vinegary.

If you are ready to begin brewing kombucha, you'll need a SCOBY (a symbiotic culture of bacteria and yeast). The SCOBY is an odd-looking, blobby kind of thing. Don't let that scare you off. A SCOBY can be purchased through many sites online, shared between friends, or even grown in the comfort of your home. As a matter of fact, my SCOBY was gifted to me and is over 10 years old, not to mention it has been shared many times with family and friends over the years.

How to Grow a SCOBY

If you are interested in science or want the thrill of making your own kombucha from start to finish, try growing your

The most commonly asked question about kombucha is whether it contains alcohol. Because it is a fermented item, it can contain up to 1 percent alcohol in a one-gallon crock. The sugars, which would have caused the ferment to become alcoholic, are consumed by the SCOBY, hence the small amount.

own SCOBY. It takes roughly 3 weeks, and depending on the temperature of your home, it may or may not grow. Here's how to do it:

1. Purchase a bottle of raw, unflavored kombucha from your local market.
2. Brew 1 cup of either black or green tea, and add 1 to 2 tablespoons of white or unbleached sugar to the tea.
3. Once the tea has cooled to room temperature, add the raw, unflavored kombucha, and pour into a half-gallon Mason jar, glass vessel, or brewing crock.
4. Cover the jar with a dish cloth or coffee filter, securing the cover with twine, a rubber band, or the metal ring from a half-gallon Mason jar.
5. Allow the mixture to ferment between 68°F and 85°F for 7 days.
6. By day 7, a baby SCOBY should appear. If nothing is present after 3 weeks, discard the brew and begin again.

A baby SCOBY will look like a clear floating cloud on top of the fermented liquid. A lot of people mistake it for mold; don't toss it! Allow it to grow until it is about ¼ inch thick before using it to brew your first batch of kombucha. As it grows, you will notice that it will go from being transparent to almost cream in color.

If you use a wood stove to heat your house, you know the struggles to maintain a steady 68°F to 85°F in your house. Using LED lights wrapped around the vessel will help to keep the liquid warm. This is also how you can brew during the winter months.

SCOBY Sharing

Sharing a part of your SCOBY is easy to do, and if done correctly, it will thrive in its new home. There are two ways to share your SCOBY: either remove the new growth when it is roughly 7 days old, or remove a piece from your existing SCOBY. To have more than one brewing vessel active at a time, divide an existing SCOBY. Here's how:

1. Wash your hands very well to protect the SCOBY from outside bacteria. Remember that a SCOBY is a live organism. Then sterilize your hands by washing them in white vinegar. Wearing food grade rubber gloves will work as well.
2. Next, using kitchen shears sterilized in vinegar, cut the desired piece of SCOBY.
3. Place the new SCOBY in a crock with starter tea. How much starter tea to use will depend on the vessel size being used. A one gallon vessel will require one cup of starter tea.

If you are looking to share your SCOBY with friends and family:

1. Follow steps 1 and 2 above.
2. Place the cut SCOBY into a plastic zipper bag with 1 cup starter liquid.
3. To help prevent leaking, vacuum-seal the bag or double bag it.

Selecting the Right Tea

For fermented tea, you of course need tea, but what kind? Green, white, oolong, red, and black teas are the best to use when brewing kombucha, and all can provide enough nutrients to feed the SCOBY. These teas can even be mixed to create a unique flavor. When mixing teas, it is usually best to add a few bags of black tea to ensure enough nutrients are being provided to the SCOBY.

Herbal teas add amazing flavor to a brew but are generally low in nutrients. When using herbal teas, be sure black tea makes up 25 percent of the tea being used.

Teas that have been pan-fired (Earl Grey is the most common) should not be used. Pan-fired teas release an oily substance once they have been added to water. In addition to pan-fired teas, flavored teas should not be used. Ginger-peach tea is a good example of what not to use.

> For those brewing kombucha with teas other than black, it is best to heavily feed your SCOBY after a month or more of brewing. This will ensure your SCOBY remains in good form and does the job it needs to do. To do this, brew a batch of kombucha using black tea instead of the typical tea you would normally use.

The teas listed here all contain caffeine. Black tea has the most, oolong is a close second, and green tea is third. Not into caffeine? That's okay. Decaffeinated tea can be used as well for brewing kombucha!

Feeding Your SCOBY

Brewing kombucha takes a lot of sugar, more than what some people are comfortable using. The most frequently asked question is whether a full cup of sugar is needed for a 1-gallon brew, and the answer is yes.

The sugar feeds the SCOBY, and without it, the living culture will starve and die (think of Audrey II, in the musical *Little Shop of Horrors* when she cries, "Feed me, Seymour!"). Though there are a variety of sugars available on the market, a SCOBY thrives on white cane sugar or unbleached sugar. Keep in mind that a large amount of the sugar is consumed by the SCOBY and will not remain in the fermented tea.

Brown, raw, or whole cane sugars can produce a yeasty brew that alters the overall flavor. Additionally, they can shorten the lifespan of the SCOBY. Honey (raw or filtered), agave, coconut, and palm sugars are hit or miss when it comes to feeding a SCOBY properly. Sugar substitutes such as stevia, xylitol, and artificial sweeteners contain no nutrients and will starve a SCOBY.

Bottling Your Brew

You will learn more about how to brew your first batch of kombucha in the pages to follow, but I first want to talk about bottling a brew once it's completed fermenting.

Upon the completion of a ferment, the fermented tea will need to be transferred from the brewing vessel into bottles. Swing-top bottles work best for this, though Mason jars with plastic lids can be used in a pinch. The swing-top bottles allow for a tight seal that enables the natural fizz in the kombucha to stick around longer. For those interested in a second ferment, swing-top bottles are needed since carbonation is part of this process.

Using a funnel designed for swing-top bottles, ladle the fermented tea from the brewing vessel into the bottles, and leave a one-inch headspace. The headspace allows for the fermented tea to carbonate. Any less than one inch can cause an excessive amount of carbonation, which could cause the bottles to explode due to the buildup of gas within the bottle. An exploding bottle can be avoided by burping the bottle every few days.

Burping a bottle is easy. You simply open the top slowly to release any pressure and then quickly shut it. Do this over a sink, as carbonation buildup is unpredictable. Ask me how I know this.

If you are seeking more than a little fizz in your fermented tea, allow the swing-top bottles to sit at room temperature for 3 to 7 days. Bottles in temperatures cooler than 68°F may take 7 days to carbonate. If this is the case, I would strongly advise burping the bottles every 2 to 3 days.

Once the desired carbonation is reached, store the individual kombucha bottles in the refrigerator to slow the fermenting process.

Flavoring the Ferment

I would be lying if I said my children love kombucha, especially in its original form. It is a battle to get them to drink a small shot glass a day unless I have a flavored kombucha readily available. In truth, many adults also do not like traditional kombucha and prefer it flavored.

For those who like unflavored kombucha but seek more carbonation, a teaspoon of sugar or honey can be added to each 8-ounce swing-top bottle to help increase carbonation.

The method of flavoring a completed kombucha brew is known as a second ferment, or an *F2*, as you will often see it referred to. A second ferment not only lets you add flavor to the fermented tea, it also helps to create carbonation, which makes it easier to consume for many people who do not like a vinegar-flavored drink.

The general rule of thumb to adding ingredients to kombucha is 10 to 30 percent fruit, 10 to 20 percent juice per bottle of fermented tea, ¼ teaspoon extract per cup of kombucha, and herbs and spices to your liking.

A second ferment begins as you are bottling a completed batch. Fresh, dried, or frozen fruit such as apples, peaches, and pineapple add amazing flavor to fermented tea. There are certain fruits that help to ensure carbonation is met. Pineapple and oranges are great options for this. In addition to fruit fresh, herbs such as mint or ginger can be added. Spices, dried herbs, and even extracts can create a more intense flavor.

Ingredients such as bee pollen, aloe vera, avocado, astragalus, ginger, and black pepper can be added for their immune-boosting properties. There are master brewers in the world of kombucha who can take beets, bacon, tomatoes, and even mushrooms to create something fantastic. I do enjoy a nice beet and thyme brew, but that's about as daring as I get.

The options on how to flavor your home-brewed kombucha are endless! Make sure to use fresh ingredients that are not bruised or rotted in any way.

HOW TO BREW A GALLON OF KOMBUCHA

If you are just being introduced to the fermenting world, brewing kombucha is the easiest place to begin. Once you become comfortable with brewing a batch, move on to a second ferment. The flavors you can create will inspire you to keep brewing. Enjoy it; your gut is going to thank you!

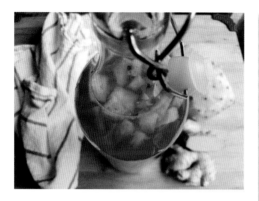

INGREDIENTS

3½ quarts water

1 cup sugar or unbleached white sugar

8 tea bags or 2 tablespoons loose green or
black tea

2 cups starter tea (a store-bought bottle
of raw unpasteurized, original flavor
kombucha or 2 cups from the last batch)

SCOBY

EQUIPMENT

1-gallon vessel (glass or ceramic crock)

6 (16-ounce) swing-top bottles

Tightly woven cloth to cover the vessel

Small funnel

METHOD

1. Bring the water to a boil and remove from burner.

2. Add the sugar and stir with a plastic or wooden spoon until fully dissolved.

3. Add the tea bags, and allow to steep in the pot until the liquid has fully cooled.

4. Transfer the cooled tea to the glass vessel or crock and add the starter tea (store-bought or from previous brew).

5. Place the SCOBY into the brewing vessel. Cover the top of the vessel with the cloth and secure it with a rubber band.

6. Allow the tea to ferment for 7 to 10 days at room temperature and away from direct sunlight.

7. After 7 days, test the brew using a reuseable plastic straw. Once it has completed fermenting, it will taste fizzy, tart, sweet, and slightly vinegary all at once.

BOTTLING THE BREW

1. Gently remove the SCOBY from the fermenting vessel and place it in a clean dish.

2. Using a funnel, fill the swing-top bottles, leaving a 1-inch headspace.

3. To slow down the fermenting process, store the kombucha in the refrigerator.

4. Kombucha is best enjoyed if consumed within a month.

Optional Second Ferment (or F2)

If you wish, you can do a second ferment once the fermented tea has been transferred to individual swing-top bottles for storage. Follow the tips provided on the opposite page.

ASTRAGALUS AND FRUIT JUICE SYRUP

Astragalus kombucha is designed to be an immune-boosting drink, but not a medicinal herbal remedy. It also contains probiotics that are beneficial to a healthy digestive system. The astragalus provides great flavor, balancing sweetness from the juice and a slight hint of bitter from the astragalus.

INGREDIENTS

1½ cups dried astragalus root

5 cups fruit juice, such as pineapple, pear, or cherry

1 cup sugar

METHOD

1. Add astragalus root to a two-quart saucepan and cover it with fruit juice.

2. Bring to a boil and reduce the heat to simmer for 20 minutes to create a decoction.

3. Strain the astragalus root from the decoction, leaving liquid in the pan.

4. Add the sugar and simmer on low for 5 minutes, or until the sugar has completely dissolved.

5. Allow the syrup to completely cool to room temperature prior to using.

THE SECOND FERMENT

Once the astragalus syrup has completely cooled, add 3 to 4 tablespoons to a 16-ounce swing-top bottle of kombucha (see page 181 on how to brew 1 gallon of kombucha). Any remaining astragalus syrup can be saved for additional brews or used on pancakes and waffles.

Allow the F2 to ferment between 3 to 7 days to obtain carbonation, making sure to burp each bottle every few days. Once the desired flavor is achieved, store in the refrigerator to slow the fermenting process.

KEFIR

Kefir is a cultured fermented beverage and can be made using various types of milk, water, coconut water, goat's milk, coconut milk, and rice milk. Kefir grains are what allow milk products and water to be transformed into a fermented beverage. Much like a SCOBY used for brewing kombucha, the kefir grains are a form of symbiotic culture of bacteria and yeast.

Milk kefir grains are used to create a watery yogurt-like beverage, whereas water kefir grains ferment water like items listed above.

Be warned, kefir grains grow rapidly and will multiply after each use. You'll want to share the grains with family and friends or preserve them to use later. You can learn how to preserve grains on page 184.

The word *kefir* comes from the Caucasus Mountains. People of this region would carry milk in leather pouches, and it would occasionally ferment, turning into kefir. The correct way to pronounce it is kuh-fear.

Much like the process for kombucha, the fermenting process for kefir is based on the temperature within your home, with between 68°F and 85°F being best. Within 24 hours of beginning, you will receive a deliciously fermented beverage.

To maintain the beneficial probiotics, milk kefir should never be heated. Once heated, the live beneficial bacteria die, and you're left with a flavored yogurt beverage.

How to Use Milk Kefir Grains, and How to Put Them to Rest

Milk kefir has the consistency of a yogurt drink, not thick like cultured yogurts, and can be made from cow's milk, goat's milk, or coconut milk. Aside from drinking it, you can use milk kefir to make dressing, dip, and cold sauces. Our kids enjoy it best as a simple, yogurt drink, and I'm happy to oblige. We also use it as a replacement for milk or yogurt in smoothies. The consistency is thinner, but it tastes fabulous.

HOW TO SUCCESSFULLY CULTURE MILK KEFIR GRAINS

Transforming milk into a fermented item requires a few simple steps and a little patience. Remember, a cultured item cannot be rushed.

1. Place the grains and 4 cups milk into a half-gallon Mason jar.
2. Cover the top of the jar with a clean cloth or a coffee filter, securing the cover with twine or a rubber band.
3. Place the glass vessel in a warm location between 68°F and 85°F.
4. Allow the milk to culture for roughly 24 hours. The milk kefir has completed fermenting once the milk has slightly thickened and a slightly sour smell is released from the mixture.

Once the milk kefir has cultured, separate the grains from the finished product, storing the cultured milk in the refrigerator for up to 2 to 3 weeks or freezing for up to 2 months. Begin a new batch of kefir by repeating steps 1 to 4. This process is also used when waking up kefir grains that have been preserved for short-term and long-term storage.

When working with kefir grains, use nonreactive tools such as a fine-mesh plastic or stainless steel strainer and glass containers. Aluminum, brass, iron, copper, and zinc can contaminate the cultured milk. Plastic can easily harbor bacteria harmful to kefir grains.

Drying kefir grains for storage results in the grains having a yeasty smell with a hint of sour; there's no way around it. Washing the grains well in filtered water prior to drying may help reduce the scent, but not by much. Why is this important to know? Some people mistake the slightly sour smell as indicating the grains have gone bad and will throw them away.

You can easily purchase milk kefir grains through reputable sources online, or if you are lucky, a friend or family member will have some to share.

Milk grains should not be stored for longer than three weeks in the refrigerator or they can starve. To ensure they store well short-term, actively culture them for three to four weeks prior to resting them. Storing them is easy. Place the grains into a glass container along with 2 to 4 cups fresh milk, making sure the grains are fully covered. Screw the jar lid on tightly.

For long-term storage, you can dehydrate the milk grains and store them up to 6 months. Wash the grains thoroughly with filtered water. Lay them on unbleached parchment paper, and allow them to dry at room temperature for 3 to 5 days. Or use a dehydrator set between 78°F and 85°F for roughly 2 hours. Once completely dried, the grains will be brittle and will range between yellow to dark orange in color. Place the dried milk kefir grains into a Mason jar, and cover with powdered milk. Using the suggested storing method, vacuum sealing the jar or an air-tight bag will help to ensure no moisture reaches the grains. You can store the grains this way for up to 6 months in the refrigerator or for up to 12 months in the freezer.

HOW TO WAKE UP MILK KEFIR GRAINS

When you are ready to reactivate your milk kefir grains from short-term or long-term storage, the process is as simple as feeding the sleeping grains. They may take a few days to begin fermenting and up to a few weeks before they begin to multiply.

Short-Term Storage:
- Separate the grains from the milk and place into fresh milk.
- Allow the grains to culture (see page 183).
- It may take a couple of batches to fully wake up the grains.

Long-Term Storage:
- Separate the grains from the powdered milk by rinsing them in filtered water.
- Allow the grains to culture (see page 183).
- Frozen or dried grains can take up to 2 weeks to begin fermenting once again. Be patient and continue to culture the grains. Milk kefir grains can take up to 3 weeks before they begin multiplying, but do not be surprised if they begin multiplying sooner.

You will know the grains have awakened once the kefir has a pleasant sour smell and the kefir is slightly thicker than milk.

HOMEMADE CULTURED BUTTER

People love to consume cultured items such as sour cream, cottage cheese, and yogurt, though they tend to have no idea how amazingly delicious cultured butter is. I think we can all agree that homemade butter is out of this world. If you're making your own butter, step it up a bit and try making cultured butter. Cultured butter isn't something you use to cook, since the heat will destroy the live beneficial bacteria. Instead it should be used on freshly baked bread to reap the benefits of something extraordinarily healthy.

INGREDIENTS
1 quart unpasteurized heavy cream
Rosemary (optional)
Raw honey (optional)
Sea salt (optional)

METHOD
1. Pour the heavy cream into a glass vessel. A quart Mason jar works well.
2. Cover with a breathable cloth or coffee filter, and secure the cloth to the jar using a rubber band or twine.
3. Leave the jar on the counter for 6 to 12 hours. The temperature of your home will determine how long it takes for the unpasteurized cream to ripen. Once the cream has a slightly sour flavor, you'll know it's nice and cultured. (If the unpasteurized cream appears bubbly, smells off, or contains traces of mold, it has gone bad and should be immediately discarded.)
4. Pour the cultured cream into a mixer, blender, or food processor, and blend for 15 to 20 minutes, starting on low and increasing the speed as the cream thickens.
5. The butter is complete once the cream has thickened into a solid mass, much like butter, and the buttermilk has separated.
6. Strain the buttermilk using a fine strainer or cheesecloth. The buttermilk can be stored in the refrigerator and used for baking, cooking, or making bread.
7. Wash by pressing any remaining buttermilk from it. Once the liquid squeezed from the butter is clear, it is done being washed.
8. Feel free to add salt, herbs, and even raw honey to flavor, or leave it as is and enjoy. The butter can be kept in a dish or divided into silicone butter molds.

How to Use Water Kefir Grains, and How to Put Them to Rest

If you asked my children what water kefir is, they would tell you it is "healthy soda." And this momma is okay with allowing them to think that! This healthy cultured drink is packed full of probiotics, minor carbonation, and flavor. Do you need anything else? I think not.

Various flavors of water kefir and coconut water kefir drinks, much like kombucha, are available for purchase in the health food section of your local market, but the cost of one bottle is astronomical! Brewing at home is a fraction of the cost, *and* you get to customize the flavor.

This cultured drink is a dairy-free version of milk kefir and is a refreshing and sweet beverage. Water kefir, or coconut water kefir, is slightly fermented in flavor, almost tangy. Some people prefer it over kombucha when they first start consuming cultured drinks. Much like kombucha, water kefir can be flavored by using dried or fresh fruit, as well as juice (my kids like pineapple) and flavored extracts such as lemon, mint, or herbs. The grains for water kefir can be purchased online through reputable sources or from someone willing to share. We have had our grains for 2 years. Let me advise you that the moment your water kefir grains have doubled in quantity, preserve the excess amount. Do not wait! At some point, for one reason or another, you will lose kefir grains, making it important to always have extra grains on hand if this should occur.

Choosing the Water

Water kefir grains are living organisms, and they will need to be cared for to thrive. The type of water used should be selected with care to ensure that no damage will come to the grains. Water is just water, yes? No, it isn't when it comes to making cultured foods and drinks.

Well and spring water are high in mineral content, which benefits the water kefir grains and is the best option for brewing water kefir. Distilled water, city water or tap water, reverse osmosis, or filtered water from a water filtration system are not good choices. City water, also known as tap water, often contains fluoride, but this can vary county to county. Tap water is also treated with chlorine, making it harmful to the grains. Distilled, reverse osmosis, and

---

ADDING MINERALS TO YOUR WATER

If it is necessary to filter the water, you can easily add minerals back to it in order for it to be used for fermenting purposes. Without the proper minerals fermentation will not occur. It is best to try only one of the following mineral supplements at a time (from www.culturesforhealth.com) for each batch:

⅛ teaspoon unrefined sea salt

¼ teaspoon plain baking soda

½ teaspoon unsulfured blackstrap molasses

a few drops of liquid mineral supplement

Make sure to monitor this process closely. Taste each batch to see if it has cultured. Remember, you are looking for a slightly tangy flavor and whether the grains have multiplied. If both are happening, then you have successfully added enough minerals back into the filtered water.

water from a home filtration system tends to remove too many beneficial minerals, creating an environment that is not healthy to the grains. The poor options often cause the grains to stop growing, starve, or even die if they are exposed too long in water that lacks the necessary minerals.

If the drinking water in your home is from a filtration system, what can you do? If your main source is city water, or tap water, boil it for 20 minutes to remove the chlorine; however, this process does not remove the fluoride. If your city adds fluoride to the water, like most cities do, it will need to be removed with the assistance of an enhanced filtration system. This system can be a bit costly, but it is beneficial, especially if you will be fermenting regularly.

HOMEMADE WATER KEFIR

Homemade water kefir is easy to make and is something you will make regularly. This cultured drink only takes 24 to 72 hours to complete, and you can add flavor as desired. Never allow the grains to ferment longer than 48 hours, as it will starve the grains.

INGREDIENTS

¼ cup sugar

1 quart water

3 tablespoons seasoned water kefir grains

METHOD

1. Pour the sugar into a jar. Pour in 1 cup hot water, and mix until the sugar dissolves.

2. Add 3 cups of cool water.

3. Using a candy thermometer, check the temperature of the liquid. It should be between 68°F and 85°F.

4. Add the water kefir grains. Cover the jar with a cloth or coffee filter, and add a rubber band to keep the cover in place.

5. Allow the jar to culture (or ferment) for 24 to 48 hours.

6. Using a small plastic colander, separate the kefir grains from the finished water kefir.

The finished water kefir will have a slightly sour or tangy smell and taste, and I personally think it has a much milder scent and taste compared to kombucha. The finished water kefir can now be bottled in a swing-top bottle and stored in the refrigerator. At this point flavor can be added.

Once you decide that you and your family love water kefir, go ahead and make larger batches! This will allow you to have a continual brew going without missing a day of this healthy cultured drink, especially if you find your family consuming quite a bit of it.

REGULAR BREW

water kefir grains	sugar	volume of water
6 tablespoons	½ cup	8 cups
9 tablespoons	¾ cup	12 cups

LOW SUGAR BREW

water kefir grains	sugar	volume of water
6 tablespoons	¼ cups	4 cups
12 tablespoons	½ cup	8 cups
18 tablespoons	¾ cup	12 cups

As a family, we have never brewed more than 12 cups a day, which only happens when I know the kids are craving it. It also depends on how I will be flavoring it. You know kids. They tend to like one flavor more than another.

Also, if you are concerned about the amount of sugar per batch, less sugar can be used. However, this can starve the grains. Follow the recipe as indicated above, but instead of brewing up to 48 hours, brew for 72 hours. In truth, I would not increase the amount of water grains in a batch until you have some grains preserved. That way, if the grains are starved due to less sugar being used, there are backup grains on hand. Additional grains will consume the amount of sugar used; make sure not to brew longer than 48 hours.

A low-sugar brew will result in a batch with little flavor, almost watery versus a product with a slight sweetness to it. Don't worry, though, because it will still be cultured. In addition to a low sugar batch, a no sugar water kefir beverage can be made using coconut water. More information can be found on page 190.

Flavoring Water Kefir

Once the batch of water kefir has finished brewing, it can be consumed as is or you can experiment with flavor. Flavors can consist of fresh or dried fruits, fruit or vegetable juice, herbs, spices, and even extracts, or a combination of them all! A favorite second ferment for us is apple spice, whereas during the summer months we enjoy pineapple and mint.

There are a few processes by which flavor can be added to a batch of finished water kefir. You can add flavoring and drink immediately, create a water kefir "soda" through a second ferment, or allow the water kefir grains to ferment with juices or dried and fresh fruit and herbs.

Ready to drink. Fruit juice is the best choice when you want a ready-to-drink option. For something tart, such as lemonade, ¼ cup juice can be added to 1 quart water kefir, whereas fruit juice would be about ½ cup juice to 1 quart water kefir. If you're using extracts, 2 to 3 tablespoons will do the job. Keep in mind, this is roughly what we like to use. Feel free to add more or less, depending on how *you* would like it!

A natural "soda" through a second ferment. Once the brewing process has been completed, add the cultured water kefir to airtight swing-top bottles. Allow the bottles to second ferment on the countertop for 1 to 3 days. How long it takes to carbonate depends on the temperature of your home. If you would like to create a flavored ferment, simply use 4 parts water kefir to 1 part juice, and allow the mixture to second ferment for 1 to 3 days.

Brewing water kefir grains in juice. I only use this method when my kids have latched on to what I call "the flavor of the month." They'll go through phases of loving strawberry lemonade or orange-flavored water kefir. In this case, it's easier to create an "instant" drinkable brew. The process is to add the water kefir grains directly to juice instead of water, allowing the juice to culture for 24 to 72 hours as normal. The kefir grains are then strained, leaving you with a cultured juice. No additional sugar is needed when brewing in this method.

Using fresh and dried fruit. Fresh and dried fruit are not as convenient as juices when flavoring water kefir, but they still do a nice job. Once the batch is done brewing, remove the grains. Using a Mason jar, add fresh or dried fruit and allow the fruit to culture for 1 to 7 days until the desired flavor has been achieved. Fresh fruit will need to be removed every 24 hours, and new fruit will need to be added. Prior to bottling the batch in a swing-top bottle, remove the fruit, and store in the refrigerator. Dried fruit lasts longer and can keep up to 1 week prior to being changed out.

Herb and spice infusions. If you dabble in herbs and love flavoring with spices, this will be one method you will enjoy. The process begins with creating the herbal or spice infusion. For an herbal infusion, add a handful of fresh or dried herbs to a quart of water, and bring to a boil. Allow the infusion to sit for a minimum of 6 hours prior to straining the herbs. Creating the flavor will consist of 1 part water kefir to 1 part herbal infusion. Some herbs to consider for this would be hibiscus, nettle, raspberry leaf, pineapple sage, mints, and even ginger. A spice infusion using items such as clove and cinnamon would use the same process as an herbal infusion. If you are seeking to make an apple spice infusion, consider using apple juice instead of water. Again, creativity is the key!

Preserving, or Resting, Water Kefir Grains

Resting water kefir is very similar to resting milk kefir. The only exception is that you place water kefir grains into 1 quart fresh sugar water (¼ cup sugar dissolved in 1 quart water). Tightly cover the container. I like to use plastic lids that fit onto quart jars, and store it in the refrigerator. To keep the water grains healthy during this resting period, change the water every week. This will prevent them from starving.

For long-term storage, follow the same process as the one for milk kefir on pages 183–84.

When it is time to wake the water grains, feed them to get them culturing and growing once again. Depending on how long the grains rested, it may take time to get them going.

Water grains that were resting short term in the refrigerator can begin the culturing process as normal. Just rinse them well in water prior to beginning the process. Grains that were preserved for long-term storage must be hydrated prior to beginning the brewing process.

REHYDRATING PRESERVED WATER KEFIR GRAINS

It's time to get a batch of water kefir going again, but before you can begin the process, the grains will need to be rehydrated. Keep in mind that this may take up to three different batches before the grains are fully hydrated and active.

INGREDIENTS

¼ cup sugar

4 cups hot water

3 teaspoons dehydrated water kefir grains

METHOD

1. Dissolve the sugar in the hot water, and then transfer the sugar water to a large glass vessel.

2. Allow the sugar water to cool to between 68°F and 85°F.

3. Add the dehydrated water kefir grains, and cover with a clean cloth or coffee filter, securing it to the jar with twine or a rubber band.

4. Keep the jar in a warm spot between 68°F and 85°F for 3 to 4 days.

Note: The grains should be plump and translucent before they're ready to begin a batch. If they're not, begin the process of hydrating the grains again.

COCONUT WATER KEFIR WITHOUT SUGAR

I like coconut water. Actually, let me rephrase that. I *love* coconut water. For this very reason, coconut water kefir is a favorite of mine. It is much lower in sugar than water kefir and can be made with or without added sugar. This process is easier than making water kefir. All it takes is two ingredients and one simple step. Much like water kefir, it can be flavored with the fruit or fruit juice of your liking. Enjoy!

INGREDIENTS

3 tablespoons seasoned water kefir grains

1 quart coconut water

METHOD

1. Add the water kefir grains to the coconut water, and allow the batch to brew for 24 to 48 hours.

2. After 24 hours, run a taste test using a reuseable plastic straw. If the batch has a tangy, slightly fermented flavor, it is done.

3. Filter the grains from the cultured coconut water.

4. Add pureed fruit or juice for additional flavor or drink as is.

5. Bottle the fermented drink and store in the refrigerator.

Note: It is important when making coconut water kefir without sugar to feed the water kefir grains in between each batch. This is done by placing the grains into 1 quart water and ¼ cup sugar for 24 to 48 hours.

SHRUBS

A shrub is a sweetened vinegar drink flavored with fruit. Basically it's known as *drinking vinegar*. Before you skip this section, let me tell you it's good stuff and I would suggest you give it a try.

To make a shrub, three ingredients are required in equal parts: fruit, sugar, and vinegar. That's it. Do not hesitate to use spices and herbs to enhance the flavor to make it your own. You can use the cold or hot method to make a shrub, and both methods work exceptionally well. It all depends on how eager you are to have it on hand.

The Hot Method

The hot method is much quicker than the cold and is a variation on the traditional method. In a saucepan, add equal parts sugar and water to create a simple syrup. Once the sugar has fully dissolved, add sliced or crushed fruit and stir often to ensure the fruit is completely covered. Allow the fruit mixture to simmer until the fruit looks like it cannot release any more liquid. How long this takes will depend on the ripeness of the fruit. Strain the fruit from the syrup, and allow it to cool before adding the vinegar of choice.

Regardless of whether you are extracting the syrup using the hot or cold method, it is important to strain the syrup from the fruit, which you can do with a fine sieve. The fruit syrup can be reserved or used immediately.

To simplify the process, the vinegar can be added at the same time the fruit is simmering. Don't do this if you are adding raw apple cider vinegar and plan to keep the beneficial bacteria found in it alive, because the heat will kill the good bacteria.

The shrub can be stored in the refrigerator for up to 6 months.

The Cold Method

The cold method takes a little more time. I will say that the only downfall to this method is the possibility of drawing fruit flies, and I dislike fruit flies.

Using a nonreactive bowl, add equal parts sugar and fruit. For best results the fruit should be crushed or sliced. Make sure the sugar is thoroughly covering the fruit. Cover the bowl, and allow it to sit on the counter for 1 to 2 days, stirring often. How long this takes will depend on the ripeness of the fruit. Unripe fruits can take up to a few days to extract the juices. After the second full day, separate the fruit from the juices, and add an equal amount of vinegar of your choice. Bottle it up and store it in the refrigerator!

Three Components for Making a Shrub

Homesteaders generally make shrubs between summer and late fall as fruit becomes readily available. However, that does not have to be the case any longer. Markets will carry many fruit options throughout the year, allowing for those who love shrubs to enjoy them year-round. There really is no restriction on the type of fruit being used. It ranges from rhubarb and strawberries to peaches and apples. Much like with canning and dehydrating, using only the nonbruised parts of the fruit (including seconds) makes this an ideal way to enjoy ripe fruit.

To maintain the medicinal qualities of both raw honey and apple cider vinegar, do not heat these items. Instead create a shrub syrup by blending raw honey, ACV, and fruit in equal parts. Allow the mixture to sit in the refrigerator for 1 to 2 days prior to drinking as is or serving over ice with club soda.

"Fancy" raw sugars such as muscovado, demerara, and turbinado can be found in the health food section of your local market or online. These sugars are marked as raw, but they are in fact refined. One day I will attempt making a shrub using one of these sugars, but until then I will stick to my organic refined cane sugar.

Shrubs are designed to be mixed with something to subdue the vinegar flavor, though over time the vinegar does lessen, and you get a nice balance of tart and sweetness. What to mix with shrubs is up to you. We enjoy club soda or sparkling water for a nonalcoholic version. Shrubs mixed with gin, bourbon, whiskey, and even champagne create amazing cocktails. How much to add depends on how much flavor you like, ranging from 1 to 3 tablespoons of the shrub syrup.

Where do I even start in selecting a vinegar? How about with raw apple cider vinegar? This is the beginner's choice and the main vinegar choice found in many recipes because many people keep raw apple cider vinegar on hand.

If you are adventurous, live a little! Red, white wine, sherry, and even champagne vinegars can all be used to enhance the flavor of shrubs. Balsamic vinegar can also be used, but since it's quite heavy, I'd advise adding only a small amount mixed with another type of vinegar.

Herbs and spices can be added when creating the fruit syrup. Start by using 1 tablespoon at a time. If 1 tablespoon of herbs or spices is not enough, increase the amount the next time around. Just make sure to document your recipe.

GINGER BUG

A ginger bug is a culture of beneficial bacteria made up of freshly grated ginger, sugar, and water. It is allowed to naturally ferment by trapping wild yeast and beneficial microorganisms, which are found naturally in the environment. The ginger bug is the base ingredient for homemade fruit sodas, ginger ale, and root beer; and the process for making it is easy. Tedious but easy.

Feeding the Culture with Sugar

Much like other cultured items, the ginger bug will need to be fed daily to keep it strong and prevent it from starving. There are quite a few sugar options, but the most important thing to remember is that it must be real sugar, not stevia, anything containing aspartame (Nutrasweet or Equal), saccharin (Sweet 'N Low), or sucralose (Splenda). Real sugars such as organic refined cane sugar, honey, rapadura, sucanant, or jaggery will allow your culture to thrive and remain healthy.

Daily Maintenance

Remember what I said about the process being tedious? This culture will need to be fed daily, and only freshly grated or finely chopped ginger root will do. Missing a day can starve the culture, and that is not something you want to happen. If you starve the ferment, you'll have to start again. The decision to remove the skin is up to you, but if you are not using an organic ginger root, I would recommend you do so.

Cultured foods fermenting too close together can cross-contaminate, meaning the wild ferment can travel from one ferment to another. To avoid this from occurring, keep ferments such as fermenting foods, sourdough, kombucha crocks, kefir grains, and ginger bugs at least 4 feet apart from each other.

Water Options

The best water to use is well or spring water. It contains natural minerals needed to help keep the culture thriving. A full list of what types of water *not* to use can be found on page 176. These waters can not only hinder the culture from thriving, they may also kill it.

Resting the Ginger Bug

Much like a SCOBY, a ginger bug can be kept alive and placed into a "hotel" for storage when it is not in use. Unlike kefir grains, the ginger bug cannot be preserved, so you can only rest it short term. The ginger bug can rest in the refrigerator, much like hibernation, for an extended period. A Mason jar with a plastic lid placed on tightly will work well for this. Though it is resting, it will still need to be fed weekly with 1 tablespoon each grated ginger and sugar. Set a reminder on your calendar to do this.

Waking Up the Bug

When you are ready to begin using the ginger bug once again, it will need to be awakened. This can be done by first allowing it to warm up to between 72°F and 80°F and then feeding it daily. You will know the culture is active and awake once bubbles become present. How long this process takes depends on the temperature of your home. If you're waking the culture during the winter months, put it on top of the refrigerator or next to the stove to keep it warm and thriving.

HOW TO CREATE A GINGER BUG

Ginger bugs are required for making natural drinks such as ginger ale, root beer, and homemade flavored sodas. This concoction is packed with healthy probiotics and is an exceptionally healthy alternative to soda pop. An active culture produces bubbles around the top of the mixture and will fizz when stirred. It will also smell slightly sweet and yeasty. If the temperatures in your home are too cool or too hot, this can affect how long it will take the ginger bug to culture.

INGREDIENTS
1-2 fresh ginger roots
2 tablespoons grated ginger
2 tablespoons organic unrefined sugar
2 cups water

METHOD
1. Grate the ginger root, with or without the skin, into a wide-mouth, quart-size Mason jar.

2. Add equal amounts of ginger and organic unrefined sugar.

3. Add water to the Mason jar.

4. Stir with a nonreactive utensil, and secure a coffee filter, cheesecloth, or breathable towel over the mouth of the jar with a rubber band or twine. Leave on the counter to culture at 72°F to 80°F.

5. Each day for 5 days, stir the mixture and feed the culture by adding 1 tablespoon each of grated ginger root and sugar.

RAW APPLE CIDER VINEGAR

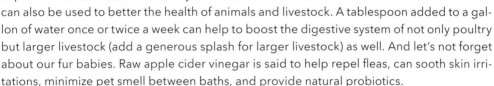

Raw apple cider vinegar is a staple on every homestead, whether it is store-bought or homemade. Once you see how easy it is to make at home, I am willing to bet you will make it quite regularly. The best time to make apple cider vinegar is during the fall, when you can use the scraps from canning apple products.

Research shows that unpasteurized ACV can help improve overall health. It not only benefits humans but can also be used to better the health of animals and livestock. A tablespoon added to a gallon of water once or twice a week can help to boost the digestive system of not only poultry but larger livestock (add a generous splash for larger livestock) as well. And let's not forget about our fur babies. Raw apple cider vinegar is said to help repel fleas, can sooth skin irritations, minimize pet smell between baths, and provide natural probiotics.

Quick Tips

It is important to understand that homemade ACV is not the same as what is store-bought. Though it contains the same beneficial healthy bacteria and is packed full of probiotics, it most likely will not have the same flavor or color.

Apple cider vinegar is the result of a wild ferment by which the yeast in the air has found its way to the apple scraps, allowing for the culturing process to begin. A "mother" can often form during the culturing process and consists of strands of proteins, enzymes, and friendly bacteria that have a murky appearance in a bottle of unfiltered apple cider vinegar. If the strands are allowed to continue forming, they often look like floating jellyfish in the bottle. A mother is not needed in order to start a batch, although having one speeds up the fermenting process.

Once a batch has cultured, the apple scraps need to be separated from the liquid and then bottled. Raw apple cider vinegar is an unpasturized item that may or may not contain remnants of the mother in each bottle.

Though ACV is a great ingredient to cook with, homemade apple cider vinegar should not be used for canning. To help minimize bacteria growth, a 5 percent acidity level is required when pickling fruit and vegetables. This makes home-brewed ACV questionable since the acidity level cannot be tested.

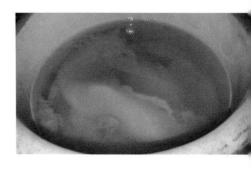

One final tip to remember: once heated, all of the good bacteria found in raw apple cider vinegar is killed, making it no longer a healthy beneficial vinegar but instead a pasteurized one.

HOMEMADE RAW APPLE CIDER VINEGAR

Making ACV is a special event that occurs each fall on our homestead. We save the peels, cores, and any scraps that remain after the apples have been preserved. Using the entire fruit to create zero-waste is incredible, and when I mean zero waste, that includes feeding the apple bits used to create the vinegar to our livestock or tilling them into our garden soil as compost! One final thing, if you plan to store your raw ACV in a Mason jar, use a plastic lid instead of a metal one. This will help to ensure the metal does not corrode while the ACV is being stored. One other thing: Using a cup from an existing batch of raw ACV will help jump start the new one, allowing for a quicker fermenting period.

INGREDIENTS
Apple peels, cores, and scraps
Sugar
Lukewarm water

METHOD
1. Place the apple scraps in a vessel or crock, filling it three-quarters of the way full.
2. Add 1 tablespoon sugar to every cup of lukewarm water. Stir until the sugar is almost fully dissolved.
3. Pour the sugar solution over the apples, making sure that the apples are fully submerged. A fermenting weight, heavy plate or bowl, or a resealable bag filled with the sugar water solution can help keep the apples submerged.
4. Cover the vessel with a tightly woven cloth or coffee filter, and secure it in place with a rubber band.
5. Store in an area where it can be watched for 2 to 3 weeks. How long it takes to ferment depends on the temperature of your home. Make sure the solution always covers the apples.

6. At this point, search for signs that the fermenting process has begun. Bubbles indicate that good bacteria are present. The liquid will change from clear to a yellowish color, it will have a slight vinegar odor, and it should taste like ACV. If it does not, allow it to ferment longer.

BOTTLING AND STORING
1. Strain the apple scraps from the liquid into a Mason jar or swing-top bottle. Use a plastic lid; metal lids and rings can corrode during a second ferment.
2. Signs of a mother may be present as you are bottling the completed ACV. There is no need to strain it prior to bottling.
3. The finished product should be stored in a cool, dark location. There is no exact temperature required since it is vinegar, although it is best to keep it away from the stove and refrigerator since they both release heat. A cold storage location, root cellar, or even under the kitchen sink are ideal locations.

FERMENTING VEGETABLES AND FRUIT

As I've mentioned, fermenting is a process that enhances the nutrient content of food. The good bacteria, through the act of lacto-fermentation, produces vitamins and enzymes that are beneficial for digestion while making the minerals found in cultured foods more readily available to the body. So, what does this all mean?

I think fermenting should be the number one method used to preserve foods, especially nutrient-rich vegetables and fruits. Freeze-drying is a close second due to retaining up to 97 percent of the nutrients. Nutrients, enzymes, minerals, *and* probiotics for the digestive system? Yes, please!

TOOLS NEEDED FOR FERMENTING

- fermenting lid
- glass vessels, crocks, or Mason jars
- stone or glass weights to keep food items submerged
- pounder to pack foods tightly into the vessel
- salt of choice

Does this mean everything you grow should be fermented? Absolutely not. As your garden starts producing, you can gather certain items to be fermented. Many fermented foods will keep for longer periods of time if stored properly, allowing you to reap the benefits of cultured foods throughout the winter months. Not to mention, if seasoned well, the cultured foods provide excellent flavor and make amazing sides to many dishes.

One last reminder, feeding the gut daily with cultured foods creates a solid healthy core, which is important to those who live, or seek to live, a holistic lifestyle.

WHAT TO FERMENT

Let's address the fruits and vegetables from the garden or local farmers' market that make good candidates for fermenting.

Leafy greens. Kale, spinach, chard, and collards are all excellent options for fermenting. Beet, carrot, and even horseradish greens can be also fermented. Pea and sweet potato greens are delicious options and are perfect as kimchi or seasoned as a side.

Root vegetables. Carrots and beets make the perfect pickled items as well as relish. But let's not forget about the vegetables that are not generally consumed raw, such as potatoes, sweet potatoes, and even taro. In his book, *The Art of Fermenting*,

Sandor Katz shares that precooking and allowing these items to completely cool is necessary prior to beginning the lacto-fermentation process.

Garlic scapes. One of my favorite items from the garden is garlic scapes, and fermenting is by far my favorite method of consuming these seasonal delights. Much like potatoes, garlic scapes are tough and should be precooked prior to being fermented.

FERMENTED GARLIC SCAPES

If you grow garlic, then you know the deliciousness of garlic scapes. Normally, scapes bring flavor to dishes such as pasta or pork tacos and can even be used to make pesto. If you are not growing garlic, the scapes can often be purchased at farmers' markets or at the Asian market in your area. Fermented garlic scapes have a slight garlic flavor while remaining crunchy and are packed with nutrients and vitamins. Fermented foods do not get much better than this.

INGREDIENTS
1 bunch garlic scapes
1½ tablespoons Himalayan sea salt
2 cups water

METHOD
1. Blanch garlic scapes for 30 seconds to soften the stems. Once blanched, immediately submerge scapes in ice water to stop the cooking process, and cool the scapes. (See page 27 for blanching instructions.)
2. Slice the scapes into 1-inch pieces, and pack them tightly into pint-size Mason jars.
3. Mix 2 tablespoons Himalayan sea salt with 2 cups water to create the brine. Pour the brine over the blanched garlic scapes, taking care to remove air bubbles.
4. Make sure the scapes are fully submerged under the brine with the help of a weight.
5. Add fermenting lid, and allow the scapes to ferment on the counter for 2 to 4 weeks, watching for signs of fermenting.

...nmend that ...d be canned ...er to prevent ... to follow this ...at doing so *will* ...cteria found in ...ereby defeating ...ating fermented ...alth reasons.

...the season. Tomatoes can also be fermented whole, sliced, and even crushed to be used in salads or for making salsa.

Fruits. Because fruits ferment much faster than vegetables due to their high sugar content, they can turn to alcohol quickly. This is not necessarily a bad thing unless it was unintentional. It is best to ferment fruit in small batches and consume them within a week. If you are looking to ferment fruit that will keep longer, consider a cultured chutney. The combination of fruits and vegetables helps to break down the amount of sugar present which in turn slows the process of creating alcohol ferment.

PREPARING THE GOODS

There is no real protocol regarding how foods should be prepared. In truth, it is about preference. Some fruits and vegetables can be done whole, while others will require being shredded or chopped. Most foods can be cultured by simply creating a pickling brine, whereas some are fermented using the water found within the vegetable and need to be salted first.

The Right Cut

Sauerkraut can be made with anything—leafy greens, turnips, cabbage—but you'll want it to be shredded. Can you imagine eating sauerkraut any other way? Pickled items like carrots, radishes, cucumbers, green beans, and okra are left whole, coined, or even cut into spears.

Salting and Brining

Salting refers to the process by which liquid is drawn from food. Sauerkraut and kimchi are examples of something being salted prior to the fermenting process and covers anything finely cut or shredded. The salt draws the liquid, which creates its own brine, and a little assistance can be offered by gently squeezing or pounding the vegetable, taking care to not crush it. The food and the extracted liquid are then added to the vessel to begin fermenting.

A 5 PERCENT WEAK BRINE FOR PICKLING

A 5 percent weak brine is ideal when it comes to pickled ferments. I am including the correct amounts for sea, pickling, and kosher salt below. All three are good to use for creating a salt brine for fermenting.

vessel size	sea salt	pickling or kosher salt	water
PINT JAR	1¼ tablespoons	1½ tablespoons	2 cups
QUART JAR	2½ tablespoons	3 tablespoons	4 cups
HALF-GALLON JAR	5 tablespoons	6 tablespoons	8 cups
1-GALLON CROCK	10 tablespoons	12 tablespoons	16 cups
2-GALLON CROCK	20 tablespoons	24 tablespoons	32 cups

A brine is used when pickling is desired and can be created with various herbs and spices. Typically, brines are made with a 5 percent weak brine. The brine can be made in advance and stored in the refrigerator for up to 1 month, which makes it quite convenient for busy schedules.

As I've mentioned, the best types of salt to use for fermenting are sea salt, pickling salt, kosher salt, or pink Himalayan salt. Table salt contains chemicals that prevent it from clumping and should not be used.

> For ferments intended to store longer, such as gallons of sauerkraut, use a heavier salting. Items using a brine, such as pickled items, increase from a 5 percent weak brine to a 20 to 25 percent strong brine. This is equivalent to 1 cup pickling salt to 1 quart water.

Well or fresh spring water is best for lacto-fermentation, though a few other options can be used. See page 176 for other acceptable forms of water and ones that should not be used.

Selecting a Starter

I don't want to confuse you, but did you know there are ways to ferment foods without the use of salt? Let me explain further. Well, for starters, you use a starter. Remember that a starter is a living, healthy bacteria that is found in either whey or from the brine of a previous ferment. If you are brand spankin' new to fermenting, this may not be available to you. The salt-free option is mostly for those who already have existing ferments to pull a pickling starter from. To avoid salt, fermenters use whey, the brine from a previous ferment, unflavored kefir water or kombucha, and a vegetable starter specific for lacto-fermentation. A vegetable starter can be purchased online through various sources with full instructions on the package.

> Whey, in its natural form, is the liquid gathered on the completion of making cheese, yogurt, and milk kefir. It can also be gathered from plain Greek yogurt purchased from the market. Yes, this is cheating, but it will get the job done until you begin creating your own whey.

Ideal Temperature for Foods to Culture

Fruits and vegetables ferment best between 60°F and 70°F but can still ferment as low as 50°F. The lower temperature of 50°F is ideal for those who tend to ferment during the winter months and may take up to 6 months to finish fermenting. Temperatures over 70°F cause the food to ferment faster, creating a stronger tangy flavor and causing the foods to break down more quickly.

It is best to do your fermenting in the spring and fall, though this should not stop you from culturing foods during the excruciating summer heat. It just means your fermenting foods will need to be watched more closely for signs of completion and moved to storage quicker.

Though your home will be cooler during the winter months, it is still possible to ferment during these cold months. LED lights wrapped around a glass vessel or crock help to keep the container warm enough to allow fermentation to take place. Fermenting vessels can also be placed close to a wood stove or on top of the refrigerator in order to keep warm.

Is It Fermented?

The only true way to test if a food item has completed fermenting is to taste it. Yep, it is as simple as that. It should have a tangy, slightly but not overbearing sour taste. Aside from taste, there are a few other ways to identify that a food item is complete: bubbles can be present as well as a slight sour smell.

Salsa and hot sauce are great examples of foods that bubble as they ferment. Bubbles from the gases being released during lacto-fermentation are a good sign that the process is working. Keep in mind, bubbles are not present in all foods being fermented.

As mentioned, cultured foods will have a sour smell that's not unpleasant. If something smells spoiled, shows signs of rotting, or contains mold, it should be tossed immediately.

Storing Finished Ferments

I would love to have a separate refrigerator or an entire space in a root cellar to store all of my amazing fermented foods. For now, I will continue making small batches and enjoying what we can consume when the garden is at its peak.

Much like any cultured drink, foods will continue to ferment quicker if they are stored in a cool and dark environment, making the refrigerator, root cellar, cold storage space, or anywhere it's 32°F to 50°F ideal locations. The live bacteria in cultured foods have a high chance of surviving freezing temperatures (fermented foods can be freeze-dried); however, foods that are allowed to freeze

As you begin consuming your fermented foods, keep the cultured items submerged in the brine. Also, as food is eaten, more air space occurs in the jar, leaving room for possible bacteria growth. To prevent this from happening, transfer fermented foods and brine into smaller jars. Continue the transfer until the jar is empty.

tend to be poor in texture, making them undesirable to consume.

Is It Mold?

We've been conditioned to think that mold is bad and should be tossed immediately. However, in the world of fermenting, many "things" are often mistaken as mold and more times than not are tossed without a second thought.

Here's what you should watch for: the surface of the brine should always be free of scum, which is a thin, clear or white translucent layer found on top of the brine. Don't panic if it has this layer; it can easily be removed and is in no way dangerous. Simply skim the surface every few days with a nonreactive utensil, and discard.

Kahm yeast is something that can also appear on the surface of a brine. Much like scum, it is not dangerous and can appear white, even pink, in color. Remove the kahm yeast by skimming the top of the brine and removing any food that may have the yeast on it.

The creamy-colored sediment at the bottom of a jar is also not dangerous. It's not pretty to look at, but it is okay to consume. This sediment generally occurs in a pickle brine and is more than likely caused by lactic acid within the jar with an excessive amount of yeast. What causes the sediment could be the heavy seasoning, which sinks to the bottom of the jar of pickled items.

Mold, on the other hand, is dangerous to consume. It can appear white, black, green, or even blue in color, is usually fuzzy in texture, and can be found floating on top of the brine or fermented drink. Once mold attacks a vessel of fermented foods and drink, it must be discarded immediately.

Kahm yeast can occur when not enough salt was added to the brine or when the foods are fermented in warmer than average temperatures. It is important to use only fresh, well-cleaned vegetables for fermenting. Jars, equipment, and hands should be washed thoroughly as well.

SPICY FERMENTED EGGS

Fermented eggs have a slight pickled taste, but it's not as strong as pickled eggs. Plus, they are healthy for you! So, don't knock 'em until you try 'em. The eggs partner well with salads, and they're great protein snacks. Trust me, when you finally make fermented farm-fresh eggs, you will love them. Truth.

INGREDIENTS

15 farm-fresh chicken eggs or
    30 quail eggs
½ teaspoon starter or ¼ cup whey (I like to
    use a brine starter from pickled items)
1 tablespoon sea salt
1 cup filtered water
⅛ teaspoon whole peppercorns
2 cloves fresh garlic
2 sprigs fresh dill
½ sliced jalapeño pepper (optional)

METHOD

1. Steam the fresh eggs for 21 minutes (11 minutes if using quail eggs).
2. Immediately submerge the eggs in ice water once done steaming.
3. Mix the starter culture (or whey) and salt into the water, stirring until everything dissolves. Generally, you don't need a starter to begin the fermenting process; however, since we are working with cooked eggs, to prevent spoilage, I favor using a starter instead of letting nature take its course.
4. Into a quart-size jar, add the peeled steamed eggs, peppercorns, garlic, dill, and jalapeño peppers.
5. Pour the brine over the eggs and other ingredients, making sure to completely cover the eggs. A weight will be needed to hold down the eggs.
6. Add a fermenting lid, and allow the eggs to ferment for 3 days on the counter. Fermented eggs will last up to 2 weeks in the refrigerator. If they begin to smell funky, you know they are not good to consume. Trust me, if they go bad, you will be able to tell!

SOURDOUGH

I use an amazing sourdough starter from dear friends of mine, and luckily so can you! Their starter produces some of the most amazing breads, waffles, and pizza dough you will ever consume. Where to purchase a starter can be found on page 240. I highly suggest you give them a try.

By now you should understand the benefits of consuming fermented foods. The options are unlimited when it comes to drinks, vegetables, and fruits. But it gets better as you begin to venture into making your own sourdough bread. I love fermented foods and drinks, but I love bread even more.

The process is extremely easy, and your family will still be able to benefit from consuming good bacteria through the enjoyment of homemade bread. The kids might not realize what this really means, and most likely they will not care, but you will and that is all that matters. So, go ahead, let them consume a slice or two of this delicious bread.

My dearest friend Amy of thefewellhomestead.com is allowing me to share her tips on how to create a starter and her amazing sourdough bread recipe, which has been happily approved and always quickly consumed by my family.

SOURDOUGH STARTER

INGREDIENTS
1 cup unbleached all-purpose flour
½–1 cup cold water

METHOD

Day 1: Combine flour and water into a quart-size Mason jar or large crock until the consistency is like thick pancake batter. Cover the top tightly with a cloth or paper towel secured with a rubber band. Set in a warm place on the counter out of direct sunlight. **Consistency is the key to this recipe, not the amount of flour and water.**

Days 2 and 3: Stir the mixture daily. Add ¾ cup all-purpose flour and ½ cup cold water **every 12 hours (or twice a day).** Make sure that your starter is less than halfway full in the jar. If it is more than half full, it could spill over during fermentation. Simply pour off excess. **In fact, I always take a cup of starter out before adding the flour and water.** Again, consistency (thick pancake batter) is more important than the amount of flour and water.

Days 4 and 5: Stir the mixture daily. Add ¾ cup all-purpose flour and ½ cup cold water once a day. Again, pour off any excess. You will continue doing this every single day from this point on. Transfer your starter to a permanent home such as a sourdough crock or larger jar. Do not use plastic or metal. Again, consistency (thick pancake batter) is more important than the amount of flour and water.

Your starter will begin smelling very fragrant after day 5. Before day 5 it might smell very sour and musty. Don't fret yet. As long as there's no mold and you're keeping up with feeding it properly, you'll be fine.

After it has successfully fermented, it will have a very lovely yeast smell to it, almost vinegary, and it will be full of bubbles. It can take up to 7 days of feeding your starter before it is ready to use. It will become very bubbly and active. Once it is ready to use, take out what you need (see following recipe), and add flour and water back into the mixture every single day. **If you are not going to make bread every week**, then you can refrigerate the mixture and feed it once a week. However, it does much better if you keep it on the counter and feed it daily.

HOMEMADE SOURDOUGH BREAD

I can vouch that sourdough bread purchased from the market is nothing compared to this. We devour it every time we make it. You will love it too.

INGREDIENTS
½–1 cup sourdough starter
¼ cup sugar
3 tablespoons oil
2 cups warm water
1 tablespoon salt
6 cups flour

METHOD
1. In a mixer or large bowl, combine all of the ingredients except 2 cups flour. Knead until smooth, adding enough of the remaining flour until the bread forms a soft ball.
2. Turn out onto a floured surface, and knead for 10 minutes (or do so in your stand mixer), until the dough is elastic and smooth.
3. Put the dough in a greased bowl, cover it with a towel, and leave it in a warm place to rise for 6 hours.
4. Punch down the dough, and knead it again for 3 minutes. Divide it into two buttered loaf pans, and let it rise again for 4 hours.
5. Bake at 375°F for 45 minutes or until the top is brown. The loaves will sound hollow when tapped.

There are quite a few fermenting lids on the market made from stainless steel, food-grade silicone, and even plastic. We prefer a stainless steel lid, with a built-in weight but we own, and use, many other styles of lids. Ultimately the choice is up to you.

Culturing foods and drinks often takes time and patience, but the final products will have you craving and loving all things tangy, slightly vinegary, and a wee bit sour. It is a wonderful way to preserve the harvest. Don't worry if your taste buds do not appreciate these flavors at first. Slowly incorporating fermented foods and drinks into your diet will help you transition into loving these items. This isn't a phase of preserving you should skip; it is truly vital to improving and maintaining your health.

Seven   ROOT CELLAR AND COLD STORAGE

Having a root cellar or an unfinished basement is not necessary for the storage of canned goods, cured meat and fish, or even vegetables or fruit, but it sure can help. Generally, older homes include root cellars or unfinished basements, and those of us without either have to become creative in how we keep our preserved foods stored in a cool setting.

Most items to be stored in a root cellar or cold storage will need to be cured prior to storing. The best places to cure or dry food items are a garage, a shed with the doors open, or under the cover of a tent or pop-up canopy. This allows the items to dry while protected from the weather.

All items being stored long term should never be washed; instead, they should be left as they were harvested, dirt and all! Additionally, they should be stored in a cool, dark environment. Don't fret if you do not have a root cellar. One can be constructed quite easily, and you can certainly set up a space for cold storage in your basement, garage, shed, or a crawl space under your house. Following a few guidelines and tips will allow you to consume food that you've grown or purchased from a local farmer deep into the winter months. Is sacrificing space in the garage or building a root cellar worth it? Most definitely.

ROOT CELLAR

Root cellars were built during a time when preserving was a means of survival. They were designed to keep food supplies cool and consistently humid year-round. Root cellars were built to prevent foods from freezing during the winter months or from overheating during the summer months, making them ideal places for storing crops that were harvested in the fall. Ferments, mead, wine, and beer stored well in cooler temperatures, and cured meat could be hung without worrying that it might spoil during the process. Produce such as root vegetables, cabbage, winter squash, apples, onions, and dried garlic store exceptionally well in root cellars (hence the name "root") and can easily keep for 2 to 4 months, with turnips and cured potatoes keeping as long as 6 months.

As sustainable homesteaders or small farmers, we find value in having a root cellar on our property. Thankfully, they can be quite easy to construct. Well, somewhat.

A root cellar should be at least partially underground. It could be as large as a small room under your house or as small as an extra-large cooler that's buried in the ground to store small amounts of produce. My in-laws, for example, buried a large freezer under their back deck, leaving access to the door so they could store root vegetables from the late summer and fall harvest.

A large root cellar can be built with cement walls or Masonry blocks into the side of a hill or underground, leaving access for the door. An actual roof can be added or grass can be grown over the structure, acting as insulation. Can't imagine what a grass house looks like? Remember the sod house from *On the Banks of Plum Creek* by Laura Ingalls Wilder? That's exactly what a root cellar with a grass roof resembles.

We have plans to add a small root cellar to our property; it will resemble a standalone structure with roughly 3 feet submerged into the ground. The location is ideal since we live in the woods. With mountains to the north of the structure, no sunlight will reach it, and underground springs running beneath it will leave the structure cool throughout the year. During the winter months in the Puget Sound, the structure will easily maintain temperatures of 30°F to 50°F. Only time will tell if we need to make any modifications to the mini standalone root cellar.

COLD STORAGE

Foods can easily be stored in a cool setting. How one does so takes a little creativity but is usually quite easy. Canned goods and ferments can be stored in closets throughout the house. Just make sure the closets remain cool, between 50°F and 70°F. Closets on the north side of the house tend to be cooler than those found in other parts of the home.

Older but still working refrigerators can be emptied of their shelves, and hang bars can be added in order to store foods while they're curing. Utilizing space in the garage for produce and canned goods is another option. Better yet, convert part of the garage into a cold storage room.

UNCONVENTIONAL STORAGE SPOTS

If you don't have a root cellar or a garage, and it is not in the budget to purchase a shed unit to store foods long term, what can you do? Actually, there are many other options on how produce can be stored long term. Unconventional? Yes. Does it work? Most definitely. We are homesteaders, and this is how we roll.

Any space within your home that stays below 60°F (but above freezing) is a candidate. Keep a thermometer in the room to monitor the temperature. A few good storage options to consider are:

• the basement steps
• an extra room with the heating vents closed
• a closet on an exterior wall, especially one with northern exposure
• an unheated attic
• an unheated porch
• a deck
• an unheated entryway or mudroom

THE RIGHT TEMPERATURE AND HUMIDITY

Luckily, many items can be stored in a root cellar or cold storage at roughly the same temperature and humidity, give or take a few degrees. Of course, this isn't true for everything (for example, sweet potatoes), but with the help of a thermostat and hygrometer, you will be able to monitor what is happening within the space.

PREPARING PRODUCE FOR STORAGE

Simply throwing food items into a root cellar or cold storage space doesn't mean they will keep. There is a bit of preparation involved. By following these steps, you will be consuming the bounty of your harvest for months to come!

NO WASHING NEEDED

It is important to not wash any vegetable after it's harvested. Washing shortens the lifespan of produce and adds moisture to it, which is not ideal for long-term storing. Feel free to brush off any loose dirt, but the best thing for produce is to keep it dirty.

CURING

Curing is the act of drying. Items such as onions, shallots, and garlic (even potatoes) will need to be cured prior to storing them long term. Again, no washing is needed before items are cured.

BRUISED OR DAMAGED PRODUCE

Because you are looking to store foods for an extended period, it is vital to not store foods that are bruised, damaged, or considered seconds. Potatoes or sweet potatoes, for example, that have been sliced by the shovel as they were dug up are considered damaged and should not be added to foods being stored for long term.

STORING CONTAINERS

Proper ventilation should be provided for all produce being stored. Wicker baskets, slatted wood stackable boxes, wire baskets, wire baker's racks, mesh bags, burlap bags, laundry baskets, and even cardboard boxes with holes are ideal containers to ensure proper ventilation. Airtight containers should not be used. Peat moss, sand, sawdust, and even straw can be used to store many root items.

THE MOST COMMON VEGETABLES AND FRUITS FOR COLD STORAGE

Here is a breakdown of fruits and vegetables from the fall harvest that are suitable for the root cellar and a cold storage. I also provide guidelines on how best to store them.

APPLES

Certain varieties of apples, much like root vegetables, will store well over the winter months. Honey Crisp, MacIntosh, Granny Smith, and Fuji are great for storing long term. That's not to say that varieties such as Gala, Delicious, and Golden will not keep; they just don't keep as long as the thicker-skin varieties.

Because apples give off ethylene gas, it's best to store them separately from other produce, and make sure they don't touch each other. Ideally, storing them on a drying screen roughly 1 inch apart is perfect for long-term storage. Another way to store them long term is to wrap each apple individually with newspaper prior to placing them into a crate, wire basket, or wicker basket. Make sure to check the apples often for spoilage, or better yet, store the larger apples on the bottom of the container and the smaller ones on top. Why? Smaller apples tend to go bad faster.

Apples store best in temperatures close to freezing, ideally between 30°F to 35°F.

GARLIC, ONIONS, SHALLOTS

You will know when garlic, shallots, and onions are ready to be harvested when their foliage begins to dry and brown. This generally occurs between August and September.

What does curing items like garlic, shallots, and onions entail? Air dry them until the skins have turned paperlike in texture. Do not dry these items in direct sunlight; they could become sunburned. It is very important to keep proper air circulation flowing around every bulb. If this is not done, the contact between the bulbs can cause rotting.

Ideally, garlic should be harvested when the foliage begins to die. Generally, a fall planting will allow for a July or August harvest. Garlic will need to dry (or cure) in a warm, dry, ventilated area. Elevating a drying rack or screen or placing the garlic on a baker's rack will allow it to dry properly. It can also be braided or tied in bunches

If garlic begins to show signs of new growth, it can be dehydrated to make a delicious garlic powder or garlic salt.

and hung to dry. The garlic head will have a paper-like layer around it once it is thoroughly dried; at that point any remaining dirt should be brushed off and the stems trimmed back.

After garlic bulbs are cured, there are a few options available on how to store them. Braided garlic is not only pretty on the eyes, but it is practical for those in smaller homes. Bunching a small amount together and tying the bunch with twine also works when it comes to small-space living. Storing them in a breathable container, such as a wire basket or a mesh bag, is another great option. When utilizing this method, cut the foliage 1 inch from the top of the bulb prior to storing.

Garlic is best stored between 32°F and 50°F with the relative humidity between 65 and 70 percent. It will keep up to 6 months.

The best time to harvest shallots is when the foliage turns yellow and dies back, generally around August to September. Shallots, much like garlic, will need to cure properly prior to being stored, taking up to 1 to 2 weeks to dry. Once completely dried, the foliage will brown, and the outer layer will have a paper consistency much like garlic.

Bending the onion leaves as the bulb reaches maturity forces the onion to stop growing and turn brown. The lack of water to the bulb will encourage the onion to ripen, preparing it to be stored for winter.

Remove the dried foliage by cutting roughly ½ inch above the bulb, making sure not to expose the inside of the bulb. Store cured shallots in a mesh bag or in a wired or wicker basket, between 32°F and 50°F with the relative humidity between 60 and 70 percent. They will keep up to about 6 months.

Onions should be harvested in late summer before the cold sets in. For those of us who live in the most western part of the Pacific Northwest, plan to harvest before the rainy season settles in.

Much like garlic and shallots, onions need to be cured prior to being stored for the winter months. The best way to do this is to place the bulbs between wooden slats that allow the foliage to hang below the slats. You will know when the onion has dried when the foliage has turned completely brown and there is a paper-like covering on the bulb.

There's no need to clip off the dried foliage if you will hang the onions. To hang onions, bunch them together and tie the dried foliage with twine, or braid it as you would garlic. If the onions will not be hung, snip the foliage off 1 inch from the bulb and store in a mesh bag or wire or wicker basket; even a plastic or metal crate will work fine. The best temperature to store onions is between 32°F and 50°F, with the relative humidity between 65 and 70 percent, storing up to 6 months.

CARROTS

If done right, carrots can be stored for up to 6 months in a root cellar or cold storage. The process is easy. All you need is a container and one of the following items: moist sand, straw, or sawdust. Sand works best for this type of storage, but the straw or sawdust will work well too.

Carrots store best in a dark, cold environment between 32°F and 38°F with the relative humidity at 95 percent. At no time during storing should they be exposed to light, and make sure to keep the carrot bottoms covered at all times.

Remove the carrot tops, as any bit of green left will cause the carrot to rot. Carrots should not be washed prior to storing. A plastic container with small breathable holes (you can drill them yourself) is perfect for storing. Begin by laying down about 4 inches of sand, straw, or sawdust, and then place the carrots on top, making sure they do not touch. Add another layer of sand, straw, and sawdust, and then another layer of carrots, and so on. The sand will need to stay moist during storage; once it begins to dry, gently hose it to keep the carrots fresh.

Keep in mind, carrots can be left in the ground and continually harvested throughout the winter. A thick layer of mulch, hay, or leaves should be used to cover any remaining carrots to protect them from the cold. The colder your environment, the thicker the protective layer should be.

Many root vegetables, such as those listed below, can be stored using the same method as for carrots. However, how long they will last in a root cellar or cold storage varies:

BEETS	4–5 months
PARSNIPS	1–2months
RADISHES	2–3 months
RUTABAGAS	3–4 months
TURNIPS	4–6 months

FALL CABBAGE

Fall cabbage can store for roughly 3 to 4 months in a root cellar or cold storage. Unbelievable, I know.

Cabbage stores best with its root and as many of the outer leaves intact as possible. The leaves act as a protective layer for what is to be consumed. The best temperature for storing cabbage is between 32°F and 40°F with the relative humidity at 90 percent.

The cabbage heads can be placed on shelves, leaving a gap to prevent the heads from touching. They can also be hung by the root or wrapped in several pieces of newspaper and placed on the floor or in a large container.

PEARS

Pears, especially Bartletts, are an excellent fruit to store long term and will store well for 2 to 3 months, making them a good option prior to using home canned pears.

Preparing them for storage is similar to preparing apples, however, pears should be stored between 30°F and 40°F with the relative humidity at 80 to 90 percent. Make sure to check the pears regularly, removing any that are softening quickly or that have spoiled.

POTATOES AND JERUSALEM ARTICHOKES

It is life changing when you can store potatoes throughout the winter months. Potatoes are a staple for us, and because we have successfully stored them in the wettest part of the continental United States, we have expanded our potato garden.

To keep potatoes for an extended period of time, you'll need to select spuds that are specific for long-term storage. Potatoes keep for an average of 3 to 4 months and even longer for specific varieties.

Remember, potatoes should not be washed prior to being stored, and they will need to be cured for roughly 2 weeks to allow the skin to harden prior to moving them to the root cellar or cold storage.

Ideally, potatoes should be stored without touching each other, but those of us with restricted room have been able to store them in crates, a laundry basket, or containers. Be sure that the container has proper ventilation throughout. All varieties of potatoes store best between 30°F and 50°F with the relative humidity at 90 percent.

Prepare Jerusalem artichokes for storage as you would potatoes; however, the temperature and humidity are slightly different: 32°F and 34°F with the relative humidity between 85 and 95 percent. These little tubers will last between 3 and 5 months in a cold storage or root cellar.

SWEET POTATOES

Much like the climate in which they are grown, sweet potatoes store best at temperatures between 50°F and 60°F with the relative humidity at 85 to 90 percent. When stored at the right temperature, sweet potatoes can last 4 to 6 months.

Like potatoes, sweet potatoes need to be cured prior to being stored, taking up to 2 weeks for the skin to become tough.

Sweet potatoes can be stored in a container such as a laundry basket, wire basket, or crate. They should be individually wrapped in newspaper when stored this way, or they can be shelved with space between each potato. However, there are many people who stack them in a laundry basket without individually wrapping them.

WINTER SQUASH

Winter squash is the easiest of all items to store long term hands down. The most important factor to remember is to leave a 2- to 3-inch stem to prevent possible rot from occurring. Also, make sure to harvest before the first frost. There are a few winter squashes that need to be cured for 10 to 14 days prior to placing them into cold storage: blue hubbard, buttercup, butternut, and spaghetti.

Winter squash stores best between 50°F and 55°F with the relative humidity level at 60 to 70 percent, except for acorn squash. Acorn squash does not need to be cured, storing best at 55°F or less.

White vinegar is excellent for preparing fruit and winter squash for storage. Simply wipe items with vinegar prior to storing them. Fresh berries soaked in a solution of 1 cup vinegar to 8 cups water will keep them fresher longer.

STORING WINTER SQUASH

There are quite a few varieties of winter squash, and their storage time varies. The times shared here are provided from Bonnie Plants, though I will argue that we have been able to store many of the winter squash listed here for a much longer time.

ACORN	1–3 months
BLUE HUBBARD	6–7 months
BUTTERCUP	3 months
BUTTERNUT	6 months
PUMPKIN, LARGE	3–4 months
PUMPKIN, SUGAR	1–3 months
SPAGHETTI	1–3 months

Squash can be stored in a large laundry basket or shelf but never directly on the floor. Moisture is a huge reason behind rotting squash.

Without the ability to store foods in a root cellar or cold storage, consuming foods might get boring. Yes, being able to pull foods that were canned, frozen, or dried will sustain you; but there is nothing better than eating something, *anything*, fresh throughout the winter months.

Essentially, a root cellar or cold storage is your family's food bank, and keeping track of what's stored in that space is important to ensure the food will not go to waste. The phrase "out of sight, out of mind" applies greatly to those who store fresh foods. Keeping track of what's there allows you to "shop" from them easily. Plan your garden according to what can be stored, and enjoy filling your storage space! More important, enjoy eating from it. Feel proud and accomplished that you've created your own private market. That's what this life is all about.

Eight FREEZING AND FREEZE-DRYING

I'm going to admit it, freezing vegetables and fruit is something that I need to do more often than I actually do. Our focus throughout the years has been to preserve foods using the other methods mentioned in this guide, but the larger the garden becomes, the more options we need on how our food is preserved.

Meat, whether we've raised it ourselves or purchased it from local farmers, has been our primary focus when it comes to freezing. Cooking from scratch is best when using fresh or frozen items, for example, a homemade pot pie using our own pasture-raised chickens and a garden blend of vegetables makes food taste better. When I'm asked why I don't spend more time freezing foods, the answer is simple: we do not have the freezer space and often lose power during the winter months. As it is, we currently run three freezers in a 1,050-square-foot home. Our two standalone freezers in the garage store pasture-raised chicken, pork, beef, rabbits, ducks, guinea hens, quails, and turkeys. In addition to freezing meat, we freeze foods that will later be processed into canned goods.

Ultimately, my goal is to freeze foods that cannot be canned, dried, or do not freeze-dry well. In addition to this, I'd like more options to what's being placed into the freezer, like vegetables and fruit, which can later be used for cooking. Additionally, I love knowing that freezing vegetables or fruit depletes very little of their nutritional content.

Foods that are frozen, if packaged correctly, can last between 6 months to a year. As with canned goods, it is important to label frozen items with the date they were packaged and to rotate them forward when new items are added to the freezer.

For those who rely heavily on a freezer to preserve foods, we strongly suggest having a generator on hand for times when the power may be out to prevent any loss of food items in the freezer. If you plan to live off grid, storing foods by freezing is not the best option. Let's talk about how to best prepare meat, vegetables, and fruit to maximize how long it will keep frozen.

HOW TO PACKAGE FOOD FOR THE FREEZER

Selecting the right items is the key to preserving foods through freezing. Luckily, there are amazing packaging products that will help you be successful. The proper packaging will prevent freezer burn and will maintain a higher quality in taste when the food is cooked and consumed. For these reasons, shrink-wrap poultry bags, a vacuum-sealer, and butcher's paper work exceptionally well when it comes to freezing meat.

Fruits and vegetables also need to be packaged with care to prevent freezer burn. These items may require two to three steps prior to freezing if they are to be stored for an extended period.

Over-the-counter plastic bags designed for freezing are not efficient for freezing foods long-term. Here are some supplies that are worth the additional expense.

ZIP TIES

Zip ties are an item you will want to have on hand when storing meat. They work great to tie the top of shrink bags, which are used for storing poultry and small game.

BUTCHER'S PAPER

Butcher's paper is amazing when it comes to protecting processed meat such as beef, pork, goat, and game. It was once made from pulp (same as paper) and coated with wax but is now coated with polyethylene. The polyethylene keeps out the moisture and allows for meat to be stored longer in the freezer. Butcher's paper can be purchased online.

ICE-CUBE TRAYS AND SILICONE MOLDS

Are you surprised that I list these items as necessary preserving tools? Don't be. These items hold the perfect portions when it comes to freezing pesto, farm-fresh eggs, and herbs or garlic in olive oil. Silicone molds work better to remove the content from the tray, though ice-cube trays work well in a pinch. Silicone molds can be purchased online. The size you select will be based on how large you'd like the portions to be.

MASON JARS

Half-pint and pint-size Mason jars are excellent for storing items such as home-rendered lard, saved bacon grease, peppers preserved in olive oil, and freezer jam. Quart-size Mason jars are excellent for freezing soups and broth. The best tip I can provide when storing food in Mason jars is to leave room for the food to expand. Generally, 1 to 2 inches is ideal.

TIPS TO FREEZING SOUP IN MASON JARS

The method of freezing homemade soup in jars works especially well when noodles or pasta have been added. Remember, these items should not be canned. Frozen soup makes for a convenient meal in a pinch.

- Allow the soup to cool prior to putting it into Mason jars.
- Wide-mouth jars work best for freezing. They're less likely to break once the food has expanded in the jar.
- Don't overfill jars. Make sure to leave 1 to 2 inches of headspace. The appropriate headspace allows the food to expand.
- Frozen jars of soup will last up to 3 to 4 months.

SHRINK-WRAP POULTRY BAGS

Poultry bags are available in various sizes, ranging from an average size for chickens that weigh between 3 to 6 pounds processed, to medium size for broiler chickens or ducks that weigh up to 7 pounds. Large bags can hold small turkeys weighing up to 20 pounds,

---

HOW TO USE POULTRY BAGS

Poultry bags generally come with basic instructions, but here are a few tricks that have worked well for us.

- Place the processed poultry into the bag neck first.
- Work as much of the air out of the bag as possible, and loosely apply the zip tie close to the chicken legs.
- Place a straw into the bag and the carcass of the body, and fully tighten the zip tie around the straw.
- Dunk the bag into the boiling water for the appropriate amount of time suggested by the poultry bag's manufacturer.
- Remove the straw immediately, and zip-tie the bag tightly.

The use of a straw helps to remove any air in the carcass and ensures the bag is shrunk tightly around the processed poultry. Any straw will do, though we find that thick reusable straws hold their shape better.

and extra-large poultry bags can be used for turkeys weighing between 20 and 30 pounds when processed. These bags should come with zip ties. If not, zip ties from your local hardware store will work in a pinch to seal the bags.

VACUUM SEALER

A vacuum sealer is perfect for packaging small game such as rabbit or quail, for storing various cuts of meat, and for foods that have been cured and will be frozen. Because this is an item you'll use often, I would suggest spending the money on a good-quality vacuum sealer. I would also strongly suggest purchasing one with a jar sealer attachment.

With these few products on hand, you'll experience a sense of relief knowing that your frozen items will keep for an extended period without getting freezer burn.

FREEZING MEAT, FRUIT, AND VEGETABLES

To guarantee the quality of what's being frozen, care must be spent when preparing the food. Some items will require blanching or being prefrozen as individual pieces to maintain the quality of the food.

The following tips will help to ensure that foods being frozen will store for their maximum time to prevent waste.

MEAT

If fresh meat is packaged and frozen properly, it will maintain its true flavor for an extended period of time. If it's packaged incorrectly, freezer burn or moisture can set in and affect the overall flavor of the meat. Any cut and type of meat can be frozen, but various types of meat tend to freeze longer than others. Poultry tends to keep longer, between 9 and 12 months. Various cuts and types of red meat generally keep between 4 and 12 months.

Tips on freezing meat:
- Freezing meat in meal-size portions or by desired cuts will allow for minimal waste and proper planning for cooking.
- Meat and poultry should not be stuffed prior to freezing.
- Storing meat in temperatures of 0°F or colder will allow it to keep better.
- Package meat using vacuum-sealed bags, poultry shrink-wrap bags, or butcher's paper.
- It is best to repackage meat purchased from the market prior to freezing, as the market's packaging often allows air to pass through, which can lead to freezer burn.

CAN FREEZER-BURNED MEAT AND FISH BE CONSUMED?

Foods with freezer burn or ice crystals can still be consumed, though the quality of the meat is not at its prime. With that said, there are ways to mask the taste and still be able to enjoy the meat.

- Remove any section of the meat that is freezer-burned, including the skin on poultry and fish.
- Brine the meat using a salt and water brine with herbs and spices for 24 hours. Changing the brine every few hours will help to infuse the meat and mask the unpleasant flavor.
- Marinating the meat in an acidic liquid such as vinegar, citrus juice, or wine will also help mask the unpleasant flavor.
- Slow cooking the meat in a liquid solution (such as a soup) will help return the lost moisture to meat or fish.
- Slicing the meat into smaller bite-size pieces for stew or soup will often mask the freezer burn flavor.

FRUITS, BERRIES, AND GRAPES

Freezing fruits is a great way to preserve them until you are ready to use them for cooking, in smoothies, or for making jams and jelly. The flavor of frozen berries is as good as the day they were picked and more times than not will be sweeter.

Tips on freezing fruits, berries, and grapes:
- It is best to freeze fruits when they are at their peak of freshness.
- Wash fruit well, removing any sections that are damaged or bruised.
- Fruit and berries should be prefrozen prior to being packaged to prevent the fruit from sticking together. Arrange berries and grapes in a single layer on a baking sheet. If more than one layer is needed, place parchment paper between the items prior to adding a second layer. Other fruits such as apples, stone fruits, mangos, and bananas should be sliced prior to freezing.
- To prevent browning, submerge sliced fruit in a citric solution of 1 quart water to 1 tablespoon lemon juice prior to freezing.
- Once the individual berries or sliced fruit have frozen, store by vacuum-sealing the fruit into weighed servings, making sure to write the serving amount on each bag.
- Fruits freeze best at 0°F or colder.
- Store frozen fruits for roughly 1 year. Any longer will cause the quality of the fruit to decline.

VEGETABLES

The National Center for Home Foods Preservation states that vegetables require blanching or steaming prior to freezing, though many will argue that it is not necessary. Blanching and steaming stop the enzyme action that causes loss of flavor, color, and texture and help to slow the loss of nutrients while destroying any bad microorganisms lingering on the surface of the vegetable. The argument against blanching states that many vitamins and minerals are lost once an item has been blanched, defeating the purpose of storing vegetables in their raw

HOW TO WATER BLANCH FRUIT AND VEGETABLES

I've referred to blanching throughout this book, and it's extremely easy to do. There is also steam blanching, quick blanching, and microwave blanching, but I prefer water blanching.

Why? Steam blanching takes almost two times longer than water blanching. Quick blanching is only good for a handful of items (broccoli being one of them), and microwave blanching, well, nothing good comes from microwaving. Here's the basic water blanching method:

1. Fill a pot with water and bring it to a boil.
2. Prepare vegetables to be blanched based on how they will be preserved (peeled, sliced, cubed, etc.).
3. Put prepared vegetables in a blanching basket, and submerge the basket in boiling water for the appropriate time indicated by the National Center for Home Foods Preservation.
4. Remove the blanching basket, and immediately submerge into ice water to stop the cooking process.

form. Once the vegetable has been blanched, it should immediately be submerged in ice water to stop the cooking process. Frozen vegetables do not need to be thawed prior to cooking them.

Tips on freezing vegetables:

- Vegetables freeze best when they are at their peak of freshness.
- Prepare vegetables based on how they will be served. Root vegetables can be sliced or cubed, leafy greens should be sliced, green beans should be snapped, and snap peas can be frozen as is.
- Prior to freezing, vegetables should be blanched then immediately submerged in ice water to stop the cooking process. The National Center for Home Food Preservation provides specific blanching and steaming times based on what is being preserved.
- Vegetables should be prefrozen prior to being packaged to prevent the items from sticking together. Arrange the blanched vegetables in a single layer on a baking sheet. If more than one layer is needed, place parchment paper between the items prior to adding a second layer.
- Vegetables freeze best at 0°F or colder.
- Store frozen vegetables for roughly 18 months. The quality of the vegetables may decline if stored longer than that.

FREEZING FRESH EGGS

Freezing eggs is one of the better methods for preserving them long term (up to a year). Ice cube trays and silicone molds can be used for this. We prefer to freeze them gently scrambled, though there are other methods for freezing farm fresh eggs: by separating the yolks and whites or cracking the egg and freezing the yolk and whites together.

If you're freezing them to use later as an ingredient in a dish, one to two eggs is a usual serving. For a dish that calls for more eggs, such as a quiche or frittata, freezing three to four scrambled eggs in a section of the tray is more practical.

Once the eggs have frozen, pop them from the silicone mold or ice cube tray and place into resealable bags for easy access. If you are freezing a few dozen for long-term storage, vacuum-seal the bags to help prevent freezer burn or ice crystals.

When ready to use, remove as many eggs as you need, and thaw them in a bowl in the refrigerator overnight or place the eggs in a plastic bag and allow them to thaw in cold water. Once thawed, they should be used right away.

LIQUIDS, PESTO, AND FREEZER JAM

Other foods that freeze well are liquid-based items such as broth, pesto, and freezer jams. Mason jars and plastic food-grade containers are excellent options for storing these items, though ice cube trays or silicone molds prevent waste and come in handy when single servings are needed.

Once frozen, simply remove the pre-frozen cubes from the ice trays or silicone molds, and place them in resealable bags for easy access or vacuum-seal for long-term storage.

It is said that freezer jam has much more flavor than canned jam, and those with freezer space will often put up quite a few jars of various types of jam each year. Because we would rather reserve our freezer space to store meat, fish, cured items, foods waiting to be processed, and ice cream, freezer jam is not something we preserve.

HOMEMADE GARDEN PESTO

A flavorful way to preserve basil is to make a delicious homemade pesto. If you happen to run short on basil, feel free to use spinach, or try dandelion leaves, cilantro, or even beet greens as a filler! Trust me, each type of green used will create a delicious variety of pesto! For long-term storage, freeze pesto in ice cube trays or single-serving silicone molds. Once they are frozen, transfer the cubes to resealable bags, or vacuum-seal them for long-term storage.

INGREDIENTS
2 cups packed fresh basil leaves

⅓ cup pine nuts or walnuts

Salt and freshly ground peppercorn, to taste

3 garlic cloves, minced

½ cup freshly grated Parmesan cheese

½ cup extra-virgin olive oil

METHOD
1. Place the basil leaves and pine nuts into the bowl of a food processor and pulse several times. Stir in the salt and pepper.

2. Add the garlic and Parmesan cheese; pulse several more times. Scrape down the sides of the food processor.

3. While the food processor is running, slowly add the olive oil.

Foods high in oil do not freeze-dry well and can turn rancid as they sit. Pesto is an excellent example of this. It is best to store prepared items high in oil in the freezer rather than freeze-drying them.

HERBS AND VEGETABLES IN OIL

Storing herbs in oil and then freezing them is ideal when the garden is abundant. Why is this method ideal over drying? It's really about convenience. The process is to freeze 2 parts herbs to 1 part oil. These items store for months in the freezer and cook nicely when added to dishes.

Sweet peppers, including hatch chili peppers, can be prepared and then frozen in half-pint Mason jars. This size jar is an ideal serving size and easily thaws in the refrigerator.

PRESERVING PEPPERS IN OLIVE OIL

This is our favorite method to preserve sweet and hatch peppers, and the final product is beyond delicious. The peppers can be used in sauces, casseroles, as a topping for pizza, or for that perfect omelet, quiche, or frittata. Heck, they're good with anything and everything!

INGREDIENTS
peppers
olive oil

METHOD
1. Roast the peppers over a gas flame, on the grill, or under the broiler until they are fully roasted on all sides.
2. Place the peppers in a bowl, and cover for 10 minutes. The skins will slip off easily.
3. Remove the stems, seeds, and cores. Thinly slice the peppers into strips.
4. In a half-pint Mason jar, layer olive oil and roasted peppers, making sure the top layer is olive oil. Leave a 1-inch headspace.
5. Remove all air bubbles, and make sure the peppers are fully submerged in the oil.
6. Freeze the jars for long-term storage.
7. Once the air has been removed from the jar, the olive oil prevents any further air from entering the jar. Depending on who

you ask, peppers in oil will keep between a week to a few months. That's why it's best to preserve them in small batches.

CURED FOODS

Cured foods that do not contain nitrites will keep for a short period time once the curing process has been completed. To preserve these items for a longer period, store them in the freezer. Items like bacon, ham, and sausage fall into this category and freeze well in a vacuum-sealed bag from 2 months to 1 year.

FREEZE-DRYING

Freeze-drying is one of the more advanced methods for preserving the harvest and also one of the most incredible. I often wonder if I had started out with a freeze-dryer, would I have bothered learning about canning and dehydrating.

Though it is an expensive appliance, a freeze-dryer is beneficial if you wish to preserve foods for long-term storage, ranging from 10 to 25 years. You may not feel the need to store foods for this long, though individuals with dietary restrictions benefit greatly by consuming foods that have been freeze-dried.

Unlike any other method, freeze-drying allows foods to retain up to 97 percent of their nutrients and retain their aroma, flavor, color, and shape throughout the freeze-drying process and when the food is reconstituted. Foods that are freeze-dried at home are quite different from commercial brands. Dried milk is a great example of this. Commercial dried milk is powdery in texture and tends not to taste like milk, whereas home freeze-dried milk is flaky in texture and tastes as milk should.

For those who are looking to build an emergency food supply, this appliance will get you there. Purchasing freeze-dried foods can cost thousands of dollars. With the use of a home dryer, you can do it for a lot less and produce foods your family enjoys. Over the span of a year, a family can store enough food to last them for years to come. Freeze-dried foods are also great to take hiking, camping, hunting, and on road trips. The world of freeze-drying has truly revolutionized how to preserve foods for daily consumption as well as for long-term storage.

WHAT CAN BE FREEZE-DRIED?

A freeze-dryer is capable of preserving a plethora of items such as vegetables, herbs, fruit, desserts, prepared meals, smoked meat and fish, pasta, grains, and dairy. In addition to this, meat and seafood can be freeze-dried cooked or raw, clearing up room in the freezer for other items.

Cooked meat, seafood, and prepared meals are excellent convenience foods for when preparing a homemade meal seems like a daunting task. Freeze-drying also helps to minimize waste when it comes to leftovers.

Items that do not freeze-dry well are foods high in fat and sugar, such as jams, jellies, and marmalades.

RECONSTITUTING FREEZE-DRIED FOODS

Fruits, vegetables, and ice cream can be consumed in their freeze-dried form, while cooked meats, fish, and prepared meals can be reconstituted with a little water or broth. Freeze-dried salsa can be reconstituted with a mixture of fresh lime juice and water. Vegetables can be reconstituted directly in the dish being prepared such as a soup or stew, whereas fruit can be reconstituted in pies or cooked in a simple syrup. Both items can also be reconstituted by misting with water.

Not everything will need to be rehydrated to be consumed. Fruit, for example, can be consumed as is, as can

vegetables. These items can also be seasoned prior to freeze-drying to create healthy snack options. For example, cinnamon can be added to apple slices or herbs can be added to vegetables to make flavorful chips.

THE APPEARANCE AND TEXTURE OF FREEZE-DRIED FOODS

Freeze-dried foods exit the freeze-dryer looking similar to how they went in, with the texture being crispy, brittle, and crunchy, unlike dehydrated foods. People who rely on dehydrating as a form of preserving foods are often shocked by how enjoyable freeze-dried foods taste.

Aside from retaining their whole form and 97 percent of their nutrients, many of these items, such as vegetables and fruit, can be ground to create a powder. Powdered fruit and vegetables can be used in protein shakes, milkshakes, or to flavor foods.

FREEZE-DRYING LIVE CULTURES

Live cultures such as sourdough starter, kefir grains, SCOBY for kombucha, the mother for raw apple cider vinegar, and those used to make cheese, sour cream, yogurt, and buttermilk can be freeze-dried to be used at a later date.

Freeze-drying is a much more effective method than dehydrating live cultures since there is no damage to them during the process. Both the starter and the liquid containing the live culture can be dried without any issues.

The freeze-dried cultures generally take a few days to awaken. Don't lose patience, and just continue to feed the starter until you see signs that it is awakening from its sleep state. How long this will take can vary based on the type of live culture.

FREEZE-DRYING EGGS

Freeze-drying eggs for long-term storage is an important option, especially for homesteaders and small family-owned farms. Freeze-dried eggs give us the option of having egg powder on hand for years to come.

To prepare the eggs for freeze-drying, mix the eggs using a mixer or an immersion blender. Do not overmix the eggs. Prefreezing the eggs will help to shorten the freezing time while still producing an excellent-quality powdered egg.

1 tablespoon egg powder = a small- to medium-size egg
2 tablespoons egg powder = a medium- to large-size egg

Note: The freeze-dried eggs do not need to be reconstituted and can be added directly to what is being prepared. As with anything being reconstituted, the outcome may to be too watery or too thick. Play with the amount suggested to achieve the consistency you are seeking.

FREEZE-DRYING DAIRY

A freeze-dryer is an incredible tool that allows homesteaders and home preservers to easily preserve dairy items such as eggs, milk, yogurt, sour cream, cream cheese, heavy whipping cream, ice cream, pudding, cheeses, and raw milk with the cream on top. These items tend to have a long drying cycle due to the oils found within them. Prefreezing will often help to shorten the freeze-drying time.

HOW DOES FREEZE DRYING WORK?

The process of freeze-drying works by placing fresh or cooked foods into the dryer, where they are frozen to -30°F or cooler. The food chamber then becomes a vacuum, drawing the liquid from the food. The process time is automatically set, although customized times can be programmed based on how long an item may take to dry. For example, dairy will take much longer to dry than fruit or vegetables because of the natural fat found within it.

Our family relies on herbs for medicinal purposes. Freeze-drying can remove up to 99 percent of their water content, which produces a more potent product than what dehydrating or air drying can provide.

Some people may be concerned about the cost of running a freeze-dryer, but I have yet to see a change in my electric bill, and we use our freeze-dryer about twice a week. The average cost of running a freeze-dryer can fluctuate from $1.25 to $2.50 per day, which is not unreasonable considering how much food can be preserved and stored in a month. Keep in mind, this cost factor is determined by the electric utility company in the area in which you live.

The freeze-dryer should be placed in a spot that maintains an average temperature of 30°F to 90°F. Storing it in the pantry, a spare room, or even garage is ideal. Higher ambient temperatures will affect how long it takes a batch to complete.

HOW LONG IS THE FREEZE-DRYING PROCESS?

This depends on the type and quality of food you are drying. Items like herbs, meat, peas, corn, and apples generally dry quickly (about 12 hours), while sliced squash, watermelon, complete meals, eggs, broth, and dairy items may take between 20 and 40 hours. As I have mentioned, pre-freezing foods will allow for a quicker drying time.

HOW TO STORE FREEZE-DRIED GOODS

There are specific containers and packaging that work best to store freeze-dried foods, and many of them can be purchased online. For short-term storage, foods can be stored in Mason jars with an oxygen absorber and vacuum-sealed using a jar sealer. This will prevent any moisture from entering the jar.

OXYGEN ABSORBERS

Regardless of how long freeze-dried items are being stored, oxygen absorbers are required to absorb any moisture in the container. Oxygen absorbers can be purchased online or at many locations which sell canning goods, and are from 20cc up to 3,000cc, depending on the distributor.

Since most home freeze-dried foods are stored in Mason jars and mylar bags, here is a cheat sheet on how many oxygen absorbers to use per bag size. Think about it like this: for every gallon of food one 300cc to 500cc oxygen absorber should be used.

mylar bag size	oxygen absorber per bag size
1 quart	100cc
1 gallon	one to two 300cc
2 gallons	two 500cc or one 1,000cc
5 gallons	one to two 2,000cc or two to three 1,000cc

mason jar	
Pint or quart size	one 50cc

Foods being stored long term require mylar bags, 10-pound metal food containers, and food-grade plastic buckets to store them properly. A 10-pound metal food container is a can that can hold up to 10 pounds of dried goods and is the standard size for long-term storing.

There are two types of mylar bags available on the market. The first is an open bag that must be sealed using a device known as an impulse sealer or hot iron. The second contains a built-in zipper that can be opened and closed.

MAINTAINING A FREEZE-DRYER

The freeze-dryer is an appliance that will require some regular maintenance. The oil will need to be filtered after every use to run efficiently (although some people filter the oil after every three runs). This is an extremely simple process and generally takes only 15 minutes to complete. If the freeze-dryer is not to be used for an extended period of time, the oil will need to be drained from the machine. Newer freeze-dryers are available with an oil-less pump, eliminating the need to change the oil. In addition to filtering the oil, the inside chamber should be wiped down after each use to ensure there is no standing water.

I cannot imagine preserving food without our freeze-dryer. This appliance has allowed us to prepare foods for long-term storage. With Justin working construction, it was important that we had food stored, and freeze-drying (along with other methods) has allowed us to do just that. If you have not considered freeze-drying, I would encourage you to think about it. Having rations of freeze-dried foods available for emergency purposes or for travel is a valuable thing.

AFTERWORD

Here is a bit of honesty for you. I am sitting here in front of the wood stove, a cup of coffee in hand, which, by the way, may or may not contain a splash of our homemade Irish cream liquor, holding back a few tears. I am desperately searching for how to end this beast of a book, but I can't stop thinking about the journey that allowed me to write such a detailed guide. In our day-to-day life, we do not realize how far we have come, but this book has put everything into perspective. I am thankful that I've been given the opportunity to gather the plethora of information needed and put it in one central place. Homesteading is an ongoing process of learning, and I am hoping that I've made part of your journey a bit easier.

Looking back to when I first began preserving foods, I realize I was overthinking the process. I was terrified that I could make my family sick, possibly even kill someone, so I spent hours researching how to make jam or pickled green beans. I am still shocked that I didn't give up or get discouraged, but as you can tell, I persevered and ended up preserving a *lot* of jam. I also turned everything I could into pickles. I often think back to the days when Justin was my official taste tester. He encouraged me to continue canning and to learn more methods for preserving foods. Bless his heart. He was so proud of the homesteading woman I was becoming.

I wrote *The Farm Girl's Guide to Preserving the Harvest* to encourage you to learn how foods are preserved and become comfortable with doing it your own way. Ultimately, the decision is yours on how you want to proceed, and I hope I have given you enough information to do so. Knowledge is power, my friend. Always question what you read and make sure to research everything twice before moving forward. This will help you be successful on your journey.

Thank you for taking ownership of the foods you consume and the life you live. Enjoy your journey, my friend. You can now say that you own your food source.

My gift to you, my famous Irish cream liquor recipe. Consider it a parting gift and a thank you for entrusting me to get you where you need to be.

HOMEMADE IRISH CREAM LIQUOR

For those cold nights by the wood stove or with coffee ice cubes during the summer months, this recipe, with its full flavor, reminds you why homemade is better.

INGREDIENTS

1⅔ cups good ol' Irish whiskey or Kentucky bourbon

1 cup heavy cream

1 (14-ounce) can sweetened condensed milk

2 tablespoons chocolate syrup, or melted dark chocolate

2 teaspoons vanilla extract

2 tablespoons cold coffee

METHOD:

1. Start with the whiskey or bourbon, and add heavy cream. (We're a whiskey kind of family.)

2. Add the condensed milk, and then add the chocolate syrup or melted dark chocolate.

3. Next, add the vanilla extract.

4. Finally, add the *cold* coffee. Please note, the coffee will need to be cold to keep the proof of the whiskey.

5. Use an immersion blender to mix all ingredients together. Do not blend it too long. You don't want any foam; you simply want to mix the ingredients together. This will keep in the refrigerator for up to 2 weeks. Shake well prior to serving.

ACKNOWLEDGMENTS

Justin, my incredible husband, without you this book and the life we live would not have existed. I am the architect and you are the builder, and together we have learned what it really means to live. Thank you for freeing and empowering us to live a simpler life. Also, thank you for supporting my crazy ideas, as difficult as they may sometimes be. Summer lovin', happen so fast . . .

To our parents, every day you encourage us, never once stating that the life we have chosen is crazy or unnecessary. Justin and I hope we've done you proud and cannot thank you enough for the support and love you have given us our entire lives. You're pretty proud of us, aren't you?

"Train a child up in the way he should go, and when he is old he should not depart from it." To our children, granddaughter, and future grandchildren, may we always be the parents you are proud of, and may our life encourage you to seek a simpler life with a clean food source. We love each one of you and could not be prouder of the individuals you are.

Mrs. Amy Fewell, you have encouraged me like no other, and when I struggled to jump, you pushed me. We are two peas in a pod and sisters in life and faith. This book would not have been possible without you, and for that I thank you.

A special thanks to Shailendra Bhat for assisting us with portrait photos!

RESOURCES

Being first-generation homesteaders, we have spent years researching, reading, and testing various tools to help us succeed on this journey. With that said, we would like to help you minimize your search for the right tools, appliances, and books by listing what we use on our homestead. We've also included websites that might answer additional questions you come across.

HOME PRESERVATION WEBSITES

If you have a question about a recipe, something you read online, or whether a method will work, these sites can help you. I would suggest bookmarking them.

National Center for Home Food Preservation (nchfp.uga.edu)
Penn State Extension (extension.psu.edu)
Clemson Cooperative Extension (clemson.edu/extension)
Oregon State University Extension (extension.oregonstate.edu)
WSU Extension/Washington State University (extension.wsu.edu)

WHERE TO PURCHASE TOOLS AND APPLIANCES

For your convenience, we have added a one-stop shop on our website, afarmgirlinthe making.com. There you'll find a more complete list of our favorite tools, appliances, and books for canning, dehydrating, fermenting, curing, storing, as well as an herbal shop for brining needs.

HOME FOODS PRESERVATION EDUCATION

If you are interested in the most current information about preserving foods at home, consider taking a course offered through your local extension office or online. These courses will enable you to participate with your community in guiding others into the world of preserving foods at home. We've taken the online course through Michigan State University (canr.msu.edu/foodpreservation). The cost was minimal, but the information was great.

OUR CHOICE OF TOOLS AND PRESERVING NEEDS

FREEZER STORAGE SUPPLIES

FoodSaver
Mylar bags by Top Mylar
Shrink-wrap poultry bags
Butcher's paper

CANNING SUPPLIES

Pressure canner: dial, weighted, or dual-purpose
Hot water bath canner
Steam canner
Steam Juicer
Mason jars
Tattler lids
Mini slow cooker
Mandoline
Canning tools (jar lifter, magnetic lid holder, bubble removing stick, digital timer)
Slow cooker
Propane camp stove
Butane burner
Immersion blender
Electric roaster oven
Crockpot
Blanching colander
Weck Jars

DEHYDRATING SUPPLIES

FoodSaver Vacuum Sealer
Mason jar vacuum sealing lid
Oxygen absorbers

FERMENTING SUPPLIES

Fermenting lids
Fermenting weights
SCOBY
Kefir: milk and water grains

Yogurt starter
Sauerkraut starter
Swing-top bottles
Glass crock
Ceramic crock
Stone crock
Cheese cloth
Breathable cloth
Weights: glass or stone

BOOKS

Ball Blue Book Guide to Preserving by Ball Corporation
The All New Ball Blue Book of Canning and Preserving by Jarden Home Brands
The Prepper's Canning Guide by Daisy Luther
Food in Jars by Marisa McClellan
Fermentation for Beginners by Drakes Press
DIY Fermentation by Rockridge Press
The Big Book of Kombucha by Hannah Crum and Alex LaGory
Fermented Vegetables by Kristen K. Shockey and Christopher Shockey
Homemade Sausage by James Peisker and Chris Carter
Dehydrating Foods: A Beginner's Guide by Jay Bills and Shirley Bills
The Joy of Smoking and Salt Curing by Monte Burch
WECK Small Batch Preserving by Stephanie Thurow and WECK

OUR FAVORITE PRESERVING SITES

CANNING

Camp Chef Stoves (campchef.com)
Presto (gopresto.com)
All American Canners (allamericancanner.com)
Ball and Kerr Canning (freshpreserving.com)

APPAREL

Lady Farmer (lady-farmer.com)
Fluffy Layers (fluffylayers.com)

FREEZE-DRYING

Harvest Right (harvestright.com)
Top Mylar (topmylar.com)

DEHYDRATING

Excalibur (excaliburdehydrator.com)
FoodSaver (foodsaver.com)

FERMENTING

Sourdough Starter (aldermanfarms.net)
Kraut Source (krautsource.com)
Farm Curious (farmcurious.com)
Kombucha Kamp (kombuchakamp.com)
Cultures for Health (culturesforhealth.com)
Britt's Pickles (brittsliveculturefoods.com)

FOOD STORAGE CONTAINERS

Garden Supply (gardeners.com)

WEBSITES YOU MIGHT ENJOY

The Fewell Homestead (thefewellhomestead.com)
Timber Creek Farm (timbercreekfarmer.com)
Urban Overalls (urbanoveralls.net)
Pasture Deficit Disorder (pasturedeficitdisorder.com)
Homesteading Honey (homestead-honey.com)
Joybilee Farm (joybileefarm.com)
Bunny's Best (facebook.com/Bunnys-Best)
The Northwest Cherry Growers (https://www.nwcherries.com/)
Washington State Fruit Commission (https://wastatefruit.com/)

INDEX

curing methods for, 152, 153, 154, 155, 156, 169
dry-curing, 156
dry rubs for, 155
freeze-drying, 227
freezing, 220, 221
marinating, 154
preservation methods not advised, 39
pressure canning, 32, 87, 91, 109
salmon recipes, candied, 109
salt-curing, 158
smoking, 160, 161
sources for, 149
floating, 28, 29, 67
flour, 29, 59–60, 103, 104
flowers, 113, 125
foam, 28, 67
Food and Drug Administration (FDA), 28, 48, 89, 199
food mills, 21
food preservation, overview
benefits of, 5, 16, 43, 78, 81
fear of, 5–6, 15
overview, 4
purpose, 3–4, 43
terminology for, 26–31
tools for, 16–26
food timers, digital, 20
freeze-dryers, 23, 226, 227, 230, 231
freeze-drying, 16, 23, 135, 202, 226–31
freezer burn, 220, 221
freezing and frozen foods
benefits of, 16, 217
challenges of, 217, 218
eggs, 223
food restrictions, 123, 148
fruits, 221–22
herbs and vegetables in oil, 225
jams, 219, 224
liquids, 224

meats, 14, 220, 221
for oils and grease storage, 103
pesto, 224
preparation and packaging for, 218–20
storage expiration dates, 218
tools and supplies for, 23, 24, 218–20
vegetables, 222–23
fruit butters, 32, 53, 68
fruit flies, 191
fruit juices, 19, 50–52, 188–89. *See also* citrus juices
fruit leathers, 123, 145
fruits
acid levels of, 47, 48
blanching instructions, 27
brandied recipes, 71
canning, 11, 32, 47, 48, 53, 54, 71
cold storage of, 211, 213–14
dehydrating, 113, 117, 118, 122, 123, 124, 129, 145
discoloration of, 20, 28, 57, 58, 122, 127, 145, 222
fermented drinks with, 180, 186, 189, 191–92
fermenting, 197–202, 199
freeze-drying, 227
freezing, 221–22
overripe uses, 124
pectin in, 55
peelings of, 131, 137
as raw dehydrated food, 117
steam juicing, 50–52
funnels
bottle, 25, 180, 181
jar, 20

gardening, 4, 8–14, 127
garlic
cold storage of, 210, 211–12
dehydrating/drying, 119, 130, 132